The Daily Evening and Morning Offering

(AGNIHOTRA)

ACCORDING TO THE BRĀHMAṆAS

The Daily Evening and Morning Offering

(Agnihotra)

ACCORDING TO THE BRĀHMAṆAS

H.W. Bodewitz

MOTILAL BANARSIDASS PUBLISHERS
PRIVATE LIMITED • DELHI

First Indian Edition: Delhi, 2003

(First published in 1976 by E. J. Brill, Leiden, The Netherlands)

ISBN: 81-208-1924-1 (Cloth)
ISBN: 81-208-1951-9 (Paper)

Also available at:

MOTILAL BANARSIDASS
41 U.A. Bungalow Road, Jawahar Nagar, Delhi 110 007
8 Mahalaxmi Chamber, 22 Bhulabhai Desai Road, Mumbai 400 026
236, 9th Main III Block, Jayanagar, Bangalore 560 011
120 Royapettah High Road, Mylapore, Chennai 600 004
Sanas Plaza, 1302 Baji Rao Road, Pune 411 002
8 Camac Street, Kolkata 700 017
Ashok Rajpath, Patna 800 004
Chowk, Varanasi 221 001

Printed in India
BY JAINENDRA PRAKASH JAIN AT SHRI JAINENDRA PRESS,
A-45 NARAINA, PHASE-I, NEW DELHI 110 028
AND PUBLISHED BY NARENDRA PRAKASH JAIN FOR
MOTILAL BANARSIDASS PUBLISHERS PRIVATE LIMITED,
BUNGALOW ROAD, DELHI 110 007

CONTENTS

PREFACE

Originally, the present publication was planned for the series *Nisaba* (published by Brill, Leiden). It was to have consisted of a translation (with some notes) of all the relevant passages in the brāhmaṇas dealing with the agnihotra arranged in a systematical way. On account of the copiousness of the notes it had to be published in a different series. Some traces of the original plan in the form of too general information meant for the non-specialist may have escaped my attention in revising the work. On the other hand it is to be hoped that the elaborate commentary, for the greater part consisting of philological notes, will not dishearten the reader who is mainly interested in the information provided by the brāhmaṇas on this important rite. A discussion of the previous translations could not be left out of account.

The result, presented here, is a more or less complete translation (dispersed through the various Sections) of the agnihotra passages of KS. and MS. (previously untranslated), TB. (tr. Dumont), AB. and ŚāṅkhB. (tr. Keith), ŚB. (tr. Eggeling), JB. (tr. Bodewitz, referred to as *JB. I, 1–65*), ṢaḍvB. (tr. Bollée), GB. (tr. Patyal; typewritten thesis; not consulted) and VādhS. (tr. Caland). The latter, although a sūtra, has been included as far as its brāhmaṇalike *anvākhyāna* portions are concerned. The expiations are omitted as well as passages referring to other incidental aspects of the rite such as the temporary absence of the sacrificer (*pravāsa*). No attention is paid to the worship of the fires (*agnyupasthāna*) which may be performed in combination with the agnihotra. Incidental references to this rite outside the agnihotra sections of the texts have been included. In the translation and the notes, as well as in the appendix (on traces of the agnihotra in the *gṛhya* and *dharma* texts), the *prāṇāgnihotra* is left out of account, since it has been extensively treated elsewhere (in the study added to my translation of JB. I, 1–65, referred to as *Agn. and Prāṇāgn.*). The short introduction aims at giving some general conclusions which may be drawn from the material translated in this publication. They refer to the meaning of the rite as well as to the relation between passages.

Three aims underly the undertaking of this work:

a) Dumont's important contribution on the agnihotra only covers the sūtras. At the end of his introduction Dumont draws attention to the importance for Vedic rites of the "interprétation qu'en ont donnée les prêtres". Insight into the meaning of the agnihotra may be increased by making a counterpart of Dumont's book which deals with the interpretation of the agnihotra as found in the brāhmaṇas.

b) The arrangement of the material which is made in the present publication presents some interesting parallels. In connection with his edition of "Specimens of verbal correspondence of the Jaiminīya Brāhmaṇa with other Brāhmaṇas" Oertel (*JAOS* 23, p. 325) observes that "such comparisons also throw light on the manner in which our present *corpus Brāhmaṇicum* was composed". See also Oertel's review of Caland's edition of ŚB. Kāṇva rec., *ZII* 5, p. 101. It is true that this book does not offer much support for the hypothetical existence of "pre-brāhmaṇic itihāsa-collections" assumed by Oertel (*JAOS* 18, p. 16) and others. More important, however, may be the procedure of transmission, elaboration, adaptation, etc. of certain motifs as shown by the arrangement of the texts followed here. It is difficult to ascertain whether the oldest agnihotra sections (KS.; MS.) drew their ritualistic matter from existing collections. At least the later sections do not seem to hark back to pre-brāhmaṇic material, but apparently represent a development of the oldest versions and seem to be the product of discussions on these ritualistic topics held in course of time.

c) In my study of the *prāṇāgnihotra*, a substitution of the agnihotra on which some exaggerated statements had been made in the past, I came across some traces of the agnihotra in the *gṛhya* sūtras and later texts other than the obvious correspondence of the *gṛhya* agnihotra performed with one fire. The appendix i.a. will indicate some agreements between the interpretations of the brāhmaṇas and traces of these concepts in the daily Hinduistic rites. The importance of the agnihotra will be established not only by showing its continuations outside the *śrauta* sphere, but also by collecting references to this rite outside the sūtras and brāhmaṇas (see introduction).

For the publication of this work thanks are due to the Netherlands Organization for the Advancement of Pure Research (Z.W.O.), which also paid the correction of the English diction.

ABBREVIATIONS

Texts

AB.	Aitareyabrāhmaṇa [ed. Th. Aufrecht, Bonn 1879]
ĀgnGS.	Āgniveśyagṛhyasūtra
ĀpDhS.	Āpastambadharmasūtra
ĀpGS.	Āpastambagṛhyasūtra
ĀpŚS.	Āpastambaśrautasūtra
ĀśvGPariś.	Āśvalāyanagṛhyapariśiṣṭa (ed. Aithal)
ĀśvGS.	Āśvalāyanagṛhyasūtra
ĀśvŚS.	Āśvalāyanaśrautasūtra
AV.	Atharvavedasaṃhitā
BĀU.	Bṛhadāraṇyakopaniṣad
BaudhŚS.	Baudhāyanaśrautasūtra
BGS.	Baudhāyanagṛhyasūtra
BhārGS.	Bhāradvājagṛhyasūtra
ChU.	Chāndogyopaniṣad
GB.	Gopathabrāhmaṇa [ed. D. Gaastra, Leiden 1919]
GGS.	Gobhilagṛhyasūtra
HirGS.	Hiraṇyakeśigṛhyasūtra
HirŚS.	Hiraṇyakeśiśrautasūtra
JB.	Jaiminīyabrāhmaṇa [ed. Raghu Vira and Lokesh Chandra, Nagpur 1954]
JGS.	Jaiminīyagṛhyasūtra
JUB.	Jaiminīyopaniṣadbrāhmaṇa
KapS.	Kapiṣṭhalakaṭhasaṃhitā
KāṭhGS.	Kāṭhakagṛhyasūtra
KauśS.	Kauśikasūtra
KhādGS.	Khādiragṛhyasūtra
KS.	Kāṭhakasaṃhitā [ed. L. v. Schroeder, Leipzig 1900–1910]
KŚS.	Kātyāyanaśrautasūtra
MBh.	Mahābhārata
MGS.	Mānavagṛhyasūtra
MNU.	Mahānārāyaṇopaniṣad (ed. Varenne)
MS.	Maitrāyaṇīsaṃhitā [ed. L. v. Schroeder, Leipzig 1881–86]
MŚS.	Mānavaśrautasūtra
PārGS.	Pāraskaragṛhyasūtra
PB.	Pañcaviṃśabrāhmaṇa
PrāṇāgnU.	Prāṇāgnihotropaniṣad
ṚV.	Ṛgvedasaṃhitā
ṢaḍvB.	Ṣaḍviṃśabrāhmaṇa [ed. H. F. Eelsingh, Leiden 1908]
ŚāṅkhB.	Śāṅkhāyanabrāhmaṇa [ed. B. Lindner, Jena 1887; the numbering of this ed. has been followed (= Kauṣītakibrāhmaṇa); see also ed. Sreekrishna Sarma, Wiesbaden 1968]
ŚB.	Śatapathabrāhmaṇa [ed. A. Weber, London 1855]
ŚGS.	Śāṅkhāyanagṛhyasūtra
ŚŚS.	Śāṅkhāyanaśrautasūtra
TĀ.	Taittirīyāraṇyaka
TB.	Taittirīyabrāhmaṇa [ed. Rajendralal Mitra, *Bibl. Ind.* 1872]

TS.	Taittirīyasaṃhitā
TU.	Taittirīyopaniṣad
VādhS.	Vādhūlasūtra [ed. W. Caland, *AO* 2; 4; 6 (*agnihotra*: *AO* 4)]
VaiGS.	Vaikhānasagṛhyasūtra
VaiSmS.	Vaikhānasasmārtasūtra
VārGS.	Vārāhagṛhyasūtra
VāsDhŚ.	Vāsiṣṭhadharmaśāstra

Journals, Series, etc.

AJPh	*American Journal of Philology*
AO	*Acta Orientalia*
Bibl. Ind.	*Bibliotheca Indica*
BSOS	*Bulletin of the School of Oriental Studies*, London
Bull. Madras Govt. Mus.	*Bulletin of the Madras Government Museum*
Fs.	*Festschrift*
HOS	*Harvard Oriental Series*
IIJ	*Indo-Iranian Journal*
Ind. Stud.	*Indische Studien*, Leipzig
JAOS	*Journal of the American Oriental Society*
JAs	*Journal Asiatique*
KZ	*Zeitschrift für vergleichende Sprachforschung begründet von A. Kuhn*
MO	*Le Monde Oriental*
Nachr. Akad. Gött.	*Nachrichten von der Gesellschaft der Wissenschaften zu Göttingen*
OR-T	*Orientalia Rheno-Traiectina*, Leiden
Proc. Am. Philos. Soc.	*Proceedings of the American Philosophical Society*
SbBAdW	*Sitzungsberichte der bayerischen Akademie der Wissenschaften*
SBE	*Sacred Books of the East*
TAPA	*Transactions of the American Philological Association*
Ved. Stud.	*Vedische Studien* (Geldner/Pischel)
WZKM	*Wiener Zeitschrift für die Kunde des Morgenlandes*
WZKSO	*Wiener Zeitschrift für die Kunde Süd- und Ostasiens*
ZDMG	*Zeitschrift der Deutschen Morgenländischen Gesellschaft*
ZII	*Zeitschrift für Indologie und Iranistik*

INTRODUCTION

I. *Interpretation(s) of the agnihotra*

Dumont's (deplorably) concise introduction still forms the starting-point for most statements on the meaning of the agnihotra found in the secondary literature. Further, Oldenberg's remark (*Religion des Veda*, p. 437 f.) that originally the agnihotra was the regular maintenance of the fire rather than a real sacrifice, may be noted. Oldenberg is correct in maintaining that the evening and morning agnihotra do not represent sacrifices to Agni, resp. Sūrya (as ultimately they seem to have become in the *gṛhya* sūtras, where the formulas *agnaye svāhā* and *sūryāya svāhā* are used). However, this does not imply that the daily care of the fire ("freilich ... kultisch ausstaffiert") originally formed the only concern of the Vedic Indians. His misconception of the original agnihotra seems to be due to the fact that he regarded this sacrifice primarily as an offering to Agni, i.e. as an homage paid to the sacred fire. The cooking of the milk (which was definitely the original oblation) and its possible connection with the Pravargya were left out of account by Oldenberg.

Several interpretations of the agnihotra are furnished by the brāhmaṇas. It is obvious that not all of them should be taken at face value. Indeed, several were made ad hoc. Even the transmission of one particular interpretation throughout a number of texts does not cogently prove that we have to do with a primary, essential, original aspect of the rite. It may only prove that some motifs were so interesting to the authors of the brāhmaṇas, or provoked so much discussion, that they found their way into the majority of the texts.

Van Buitenen, *The Pravargya* (Poona 1968), p. 23 may be right in stating: "It is probably futile even to attempt a holistic explanation of any Vedic ritual. While single rites originally might have had single purposes and their meaning thus might at one time have been explicable from this purpose, it is clear that in the course of the centuries a tremendous conflation of ritual has taken place so that no ritual, *agnihotra*, *iṣṭi*, etc., can be presumed to be in any sense unitary". Still I think it might be worth-while to try to make a distinction between primary and secondary elements in the exegetical totality of the brāhmaṇas. It is not to be assumed that the basic meaning of the rite is not to be found at all in the various interpretations of the brāhmaṇas.

Among the aims of the agnihotra mentioned by Dumont in his introduction the following ones seem to me secondary: "un des principaux objets de l'agnihotra est de perpétuer à la fois la continuité du sacrifice et la continuité de la race du sacrifiant" (..) "L'agnihotra est un sacrifice qui a pour objet de procurer au sacrifiant la prospérité, la santé, la longévité, la richesse en bétail et, surtout, une nombreuse descendance mâle, c'est-à-dire la continuité de la race". "L'agnihotra est un charme de fécondité" (*L'Agnihotra*, p. VII). These aspects may definitely play a role (though "continuité de la race du sacrifiant" seems to be assumed on account of a reference to the *agnyupasthāna* rather than to the agnihotra itself), yet they do not make the impression of being exclusively connected with the agnihotra. Fertility and procreation turn up in other contexts as well. Some aspects may be explained as secondary interpretations based on the fact that this rite is performed daily and during one's entire life rather than the other way round: i.e. the agnihotra is not performed daily and during one's entire life in order to achieve the mentioned aims, but these aims came to be associated with this ritual because of its daily and lifelong performance. This may play a role in the case of the continuity of the sacrifice (mentioned by Dumont). On the other hand, in some texts the fires are related to the *āhitāgni* himself, the hearth is connected with the head of the family, and the fires are identified with the *prāṇāḥ* of the sacrificer. As a result the daily agnihotra offered in these fires may be explained as a daily confirmation of this relationship, and as producing several benefits for the performer. However, this need not be the primary aim of the rite.

The central meaning of the agnihotra (in my view) was also noticed by Dumont: "Mais l'agnihotra était aussi, primitivement, un charme solaire" (p. VIII; see also Caland's note on ĀpŚS. 6, 5, 6 referring to a "'Survival' eines ursprünglichen 'Suncharm'"). Often in this connection attention has been too exclusively concentrated on the morning agnihotra where the sun is produced by this suncharm (see e.g. Oldenberg, o.c., p. 109 f.). Dumont is undoubtedly correct in observing "Ce charme solaire a vraisemblablement pour but non seulement d'aider le soleil à se lever, mais aussi de l'aider dans son éternelle course quotidienne, de l'est à l'ouest pendant le jour, et de l'ouest à l'est (alors qu'il est invisible) pendant la nuit". Rather, the evening agnihotra should be stressed as being of importance. The daily and nightly course of the sun have no demonstrable connection with the ritual except for the course taken by the walking sacrificer in the morning and evening performance, to which Dumont refers. The moments of sunset and sunrise are essential.

Accompanying and magically maintaining the cosmic process of sunset and sunrise rather than producing the sun from an unknown nowhere by a solar charm are the central functions of the agnihotra. The formulas recited during the offering of the libation do not contain a dedication to a deity, but imply a statement of truth: the cosmic-ritualistic truth that the light (of the sun) is the fire, that the sun has entered into the fire. The Agni-hotra is not a daily homage to Agni or the daily care of the sacred fire, but a transference of the sun (the heated milk) into Agni.

Just as the Pravargya urges a strengthening of the sun before the monsoon rains (see van Buitenen, o.c., p. 29 ff.), the agnihotra must transport the sun, already weakened at the end of the day, through the dangerous darkness and coolness of the night. It is reinforced and heated (as milk on the gārhapatya) and thereupon transmitted to Agni (present in the āhavanīya fire).

Therefore the evening agnihotra is primary. It is the real offering into Agni. It has the formula "Agni is the light, the light is Agni". The morning performance merely seems to be a duplication (with some necessary adaptations). The mystery of the sun's disappearance has been brought under control. Its reappearance is produced by kindling the fire. The offering of hot milk strengthens the new sun which now rises. The misleading emphasis on the morning performance in the secondary literature may be due to the fact that this performance takes in a central position in the discussion on the right time for the offering.

This assumption of a primary meaning does not imply that the so-called secondary aspects are without importance. Several secondary interpretations are based on the alternation present in the primary aspect of the agnihotra, viz. sun-into-fire: sun-out-of-fire (or: fire-into-sun). It may be true that fertility and procreation form the obsession of the brāhmaṇa authors and that their association with the agnihotra is not essential (especially with regard to far-fetched concepts of *mithuna*). However, in the Yajurvedic texts at least this aspect plays an important role. Moreover, the birth of the sun at daybreak corresponds to actual birth from the darkness of the womb. Another important secondary function of this rite belongs to the sphere of eschatology, especially in the later texts.

Next to the basic cosmic aspect (sunset, sunrise) the rite also has several (secondary) microcosmic (or: *adhyātmam*) implications. Sunrise and sunset have a counterpart in inhalation and exhalation; the birth of the sun corresponds to delivery, the escape of the sun from darkness to the deliverance from evil and sin. The *prāṇāgnihotra* is based on the identification of fires and *prāṇāḥ*. On the ritualistic level the simple daily rite is equated with several impressive great sacrifices.

As a result of all this the position of the agnihotra in Vedic literature is not insignificant. In the agnihotra sections of the brāhmaṇas it is called the beginning or starting-point of all sacrifices. Outside these texts the agnihotra is also very favourably mentioned. Already AV. 11, 7, 9 refers to this rite in connection with the extolling of the *ucchiṣṭa* of the offering together with *śraddhā*, *vrata*, *dakṣiṇā*, *iṣṭa* and *pūrta*. AV. 10, 3, 22 mentions it in a statement of truth ("As truly as glory is in the agnihotra . . ."). The verse of ChU. 5, 24, 5 on all beings sitting round (or: worshipping, expecting much from) the agnihotra as hungry children round a mother is found in a rather late text, but may be old and thus betrays the important position of this rite. TU. 1, 9, 1 mentions the agnihotra as one of the highest aims beside *ṛta*, *satya*, *tapas*, *dama*, *śama*, fires, hospitality, *mānuṣa* ("humanity"?), offspring, begetting, procreation. A similar enumeration including the agnihotra is found in another Taittirīya text, viz. MNU. (= TĀ. 10) 505 ff. (with *satya*, *tapas*, *dama*, *śama*, *dāna*, *dharma*, *prajanana*, fires, *yajña*, *mānasa* (cf. TU. *mānuṣa*) and *nyāsa*. See also MNU. 519 ff. MNU. 527 states that every night and morning the agnihotra forms the expiation for the (faults committed in the) houses. It is well-sacrificed, well-offered. It is the introduction of the sacrificial sessions. It is the light of the world. Therefore they say the agnihotra is the highest. Hārīta, quoted by *Gṛhastharatnākara*, p. 99 ff., says that there is no *dharma* higher than the agnihotra, no *tapas* higher than the agnihotra, etc. (mentioning *dāna*, *dama*, *pūjā*, *yaśas*, *siddhi*, *gati*, *sthāna*, *vrata*). See also the *agnihotramahimā* of *Smṛticandrikā* II (*Āhnikakāṇḍa*), p. 409–411 (quoting Hārīta and other *smṛtis*). The Pali texts also refer to the importance of the agnihotra. Hillebrandt, *Ritual-Litteratur*, p. 18 mentions Mahāvagga 6, 35, 8 (Vinaya P. I, 246, 33): *aggihuttamukhā yaññā* ... The commentary explains that *mukha* means "foremost" (*aggihottaseṭṭha; aggihottapadhāna*). For the verse see also MBh. 2, 1395 (see crit. app. of the crit. ed.) with the reading *agnihotramukhā vedā* ..., which is apparently a wrong version of this verse (Sutta Nipāta 568). Sutta Nipāta 249 mentions the agnihotra along with other high aims (*tapas, yajña,* etc.) On the lofty position of the agnihotra among the brahmins see also Dhammapada 392.

Because in course of time the agnihotra came to mean the daily worship of the sacred fire, the term agnihotra became identical with the sacred fire. The worship of the agnihotra (mentioned in Epic and Pali texts) was the maintaining of, and offering in, the fire(s). As such, the agnihotra was considered as the fire-ritual in general, and as one of the means (beside Soma ritual, good works, asceticism, etc.) for obtaining the highest aim. At that moment it had already become outdated for the saṃnyāsins (MNU.) and the Buddhists. Only in the form of the *prāṇāgnihotra* does the rite retain its importance for the unorthodox; soon, however, this *prāṇāgnihotra* developed into a rather generally accepted *bhojanavidhi*.

II. *The agnihotrabrāhmaṇas and their relationships*

The arrangement of the translated passages chosen for this publication gives optimal information on the main points and central elements of the exegetical work done by the Vedic prose texts on the agnihotra. For the interpretation of the rite the division into Sections was preferred, since the situation of the brāhmaṇas cannot be compared with that of the sūtras, which mainly deal with the systematical treatment of the ritual. Therefore Dumont's procedure applied in his work on the agnihotra could not be followed. Moreover the Sections throw light on detailed agreements and differences among the texts. A perusal of the whole book will confirm the more or less accepted views on the relations between the translated texts, at least as far as the agnihotra sections are concerned. The chronology mentioned in *Jaiminīya Brāhmaṇa I, 1–65*, p. 13 still holds good.

The KS. has the oldest passage. The identical KapS. has been left out of account here. Next comes the MS., which is almost identical on some points. Arguments for this view are to be found in the remarks made between the translated passages and in some of the notes. As a rule, elaboration, rearrangement, (wrong) adaptation, etc. form the criteria for the relationships. The Taittirīyas do not deal with the agnihotra in their Saṃhitā. Their treatment of the rite in the TB. has several parallels in the mentioned Saṃhitās, but is definitely later. Some development is to be seen in various Sections. The brāhmaṇa of the White Yajurveda, ŚB., obviously belongs to a continuum ranging from the KS. up to this comparatively late brāhmaṇa. Correspondences are to be found especially with the TB. In the ŚB. knowledge of some of the non-Yajurvedic texts may be supposed. This has undoubtedly influenced its point of view. Direct influences in the form of borrowings, adaptations and similar arrangements of the text are, however, scarce. Among the non-Yajurvedic texts the GB. is definitely later; in all probability the same applies to the JB. and the ṢaḍvB.

In this connection the position of the *anvākhyānas* of the VādhS., which represent some second thoughts and reactions to other texts made by the Taittirīyas, is interesting. Some parallelisms with the ŚB. and the JB. may imply that these *anvākhyānas* were made in order to uphold the position of the Taittirīyas, whose brāhmaṇa was rather old, and to remain involved in the later discussions. As such, they are a reaction to the ŚB. and to other texts and are consequently later. Moreover, the occurrence of Janaka, Yājñavalkya and Uddālaka Āruṇi, typical representatives of the White Yajurveda, is an indication of lateness in this Taittirīya text. The famous brahmins Yājñavalkya and Kauṣītaki are significantly called *pūrvye śrotriyāḥ*.

This tendency of the Taittirīyas to adapt their texts to new circumstances seems to be found even in the TB. itself in its agnihotra section. There are a few later additions. In two relevant cases the relation to the Ṛgvedic brāhmaṇas plays a role. The agnihotra passages of these brāhmaṇas (of which the AB. is the older) seem to be later than those of the TB. However, in the *vaiśvadeva* of the milk (see Section 16) a later addition in the TB seems to be based on (or borrowed from) the AB. Similarly the discussion on the right time for the performance of the agnihotra has been adapted in the TB. Its own point of view is rejected under influence of the ŚāṅkhB.

The AB. is older than the ŚB., probably also in its agnihotra sections. AB. 7, 12, however, seems to be based on the ŚB. The existence of several layers in a brāhmaṇa and of several addenda and insertions within these layers cannot be denied.

Chronological developments are especially evident in the discussion on the right time for the performance and in the *vaiśvadeva* of the milk. In the *vaiśvadeva* of the actions performed at the end of the rite conciseness is found in the oldest versions, whereas elaboration prevails in the later texts. The *brahmodyas* mainly occur in the late brāhmaṇas.

In one respect the arrangement into Sections forms a drawback. The relationships between the complete *agnihotrabrāhmaṇas* do not become evident enough. Detailed correspondences are to be found in the translated and annotated Sections. In this introduction the composition of the agnihotra passages will be sketched. In some cases the development and relationships of the texts become clearer in this way. The most important line of development runs through the Yajurvedic texts.

A. *Kāṭhaka Saṃhitā* 6, 1–8; 35, 19

a) Aetiological myths: 6, 1–3
b) Systematical treatment of the ritual: 6, 3–5
c) Views of the Praiyamedhas on the offering: 6, 6
d) Expiations: 6, 6
e) Symbolism: 6, 6
f) Agnihotra of the kṣatriya: 6, 6
g) Symbolism: 6, 7
h) Addenda on A-b: 6, 7
i) Expiatory agnihotra for Rudra: 6, 7
j) Symbolism of the fire and stages of inflammation: 6, 7
k) Symbolism: 6, 8
l) Expiations: 6, 8
m) Alternative formulas: 6, 8
n) Concluding actions of the ritual: 6, 8
o) Expiations: 35, 19

It is evident that the composition of this *agnihotrabrāhmaṇa* is rather loose. Several additions have been made, which were not inserted in the systematical treatment of the ritual. The composition of MS. looks superior. In some respects the material has been rearranged.

B. *Maitrāyaṇīya Saṃhitā* 1, 8, 1–10

a) Aetiological myths: 1, 8, 1–2 [= A-a]
b) Systematical treatment of the ritual: 1, 8, 3–5 [= A–b–h–n]
c) Milking of two cows: 1, 8, 6
d) Expiatory agnihotra for Rudra: 1, 8, 6 [= A–i]
e) Symbolism of the fire and its stages of inflammation: 1, 8, 6 [= A–j]
f) Symbolism: 1, 8, 6
g) Views of the Praiyamedhas: 1, 8, 7 [= A–c]
h) Right time for the performance and relevant expiations: 1, 8, 7 [= A–l and A–d; for the right time see A–b]
i) Symbolism: 1, 8, 7 [= A–e]
j) Why the agnihotra has no *upavāsa*: 1, 8, 7
k) Why no *anupraharaṇa* should be made: 1, 8, 7 [rejection of A–n]
l) Symbolism: 1, 8, 7 [= A–e]
m) Agnihotra of the kṣatriya: 1, 8, 7 [= A–f]
n) Expiations: 1, 8, 8–9
o) *vaiśvadeva* of the milk: 1, 8, 10

The MS. has not only rearranged and systematized the *agnihotra-brāhmaṇa* of the KS., but also has added several new subjects. A new section of expiations (followed only by the *vaiśvadeva* passage) forms an appendix to the agnihotra section. In later texts the expiations either form such an appendix or are placed elsewhere in the text.

C. *Taittirīya Brāhmaṇa* 2, 1, 1–11 [translated by Dumont, *Proc. Am. Philos. Soc.* 108/4 (1964), p. 337 ff.]
Taittirīya Brāhmaṇa 1, 4, 3–4 [expiations, not included in the present publication; for a translation see Dumont, *Mélanges* .. *Renou* (1968), p. 337 ff.]
Taittirīya Brāhmaṇa 3, 7, 2–3

a) Aetiological myths on details of the rite: 2, 1, 1
b) Aetiological myths: 2, 1, 2, 1–6 [= A–a; B–a]
c) Right time for the performance (and some interpretations): 2, 1, 7–12 [cf. B–h; for the procreative aspect attributed to the rite in connection with the right time and with the offering in general see A–b (KS. 6, 5)]

d) Systematical treatment of the ritual: 2, 1, 3–4 [cf. B–b–k]
e) Symbolism: 2, 1, 5, 1–3 [cf. A–e; B–l]
f) Symbolism: 2, 1, 5, 3–4
g) Milking of two cows: 2, 1, 5, 4–5 [cf. B–c]
h) Material of the oblation: 2, 1, 5, 5–6
i) Symbolism: 2, 1, 5, 6–11
j) Aetiological myth (cf. C–b) ending with symbolism: 2, 1, 6
k) *vaiśvadeva* of the milk: 2, 1, 7 [cf. B–o]
l) Milking of the cow and another *vaiśvadeva*: 2, 1, 8 [cf. B–o]
m) Views of the Praiyamedhas: 2, 1, 9 [cf. B–g]
n) Procreative aspect of the agnihotra and an expiation for sacrificing too late: 2, 1, 9 [cf. C–c; B–h]
o) *vaiśvadeva* of the fire: 2, 1, 10 [cf. A–j; B–e]
p) Pouring of water around the fires: 2, 1, 11
q) Expiations: 1, 4, 3–4
r) Expiations: 3, 7, 2 [cf. A–o]

The relationship with the MS. is evident. There are some additions. The expiations have been completely detached from the *agnihotra-brāhmaṇa*.

D. *Śatapatha Brāhmaṇa* 2, 2, 4 – 2, 3, 3 [translated by Eggeling, *SBE* 12 (1882)]
Śatapatha Brāhmaṇa 11, 3, 1–2; 11, 5, 3; 11, 6, 1–2; 12, 4, 1–4 [translated by Eggeling, *SBE* 44 (1900)]

a) Aetiological myths: 2, 2, 4 [cf. A–a; B–a; C–b; C–j]
b) Right time for the performance (and some interpretations): 2, 3, 1, 1–9 [cf. C–c]
c) Interpretations of the agnihotra: 2, 3, 1, 10–13
d) Systematical treatment of the ritual: 2, 3, 1, 14–20 [cf. A–b; B–b; C–d]
e) Interpretation of the agnihotra: 2, 3, 1, 21
f) Interpretations of the offering: 2, 3, 1, 22–39 [cf. also A–b; B–b and A–m]
g) Symbolism: 2, 3, 2, 1–8
h) *vaiśvadeva* of the fire: 2, 3, 2, 9–14 [cf. A–j; B–e; C–o]
i) Interpretation of the agnihotra: 2, 3, 2, 15
j) Addenda to D–d: 2, 3, 2, 16–18
k) On the *agnyādhāna*: 2, 3, 3, 1–6

l) Interpretations and symbolism of the agnihotra: 2, 3, 3, 7–20
m) Symbolism: 11, 3, 1–2
n) *vaiśvadeva* of the milk and of the actions after the offering: 11, 5, 3, 1–7 [cf. B–o; C–k, but also A–b, B–b and C–d; ŚB. combines both *vaiśvadevas* in this *brahmodya*]
o) Expiations (esoteric): 11, 5, 3, 8–13
p) The story of Bhṛgu: 11, 6, 1
q) Interpretations of the agnihotra in a *brahmodya*: 11, 6, 2
r) Expiations: 12, 4, 1–4

There are several parallels with the earlier Yajurvedic texts, especially with the TB., but many new subjects are introduced. The innovations especially refer to interpretations of the agnihotra. Some of them have been included in the mystic addenda of the 11th book, and do not belong to the *agnihotrabrāhmaṇa* itself.

Completely different is the composition of the agnihotra section of the AB. This Ṛgvedic brāhmaṇa only deals with some aspects of the rite which seem to have formed a matter for debate and to have drawn the attention of those texts for which the agnihotra was not a primary concern.

E. *Aitareya Brāhmaṇa* 5, 26–31; 7, 3; 7, 5–8; 7, 9 (end); 7, 10; 7, 12 [translated by Keith, *Rigveda Brahmanas* (1920)]
a) Interpretation of (a detail of) the rite: 5, 26
b) *vaiśvadeva* of the milk: 5, 26 [cf. B–o; C–k]
c) Expiation: 5, 27
d) Symbolism: 5, 28 [cf. A–e; B–l; C–e]
e) Interpretation: 5, 28
f) The right time for the performance: 5, 29–31
g) Expiations: 7, 3; 7, 5–8; 7, 12
h) The agnihotra of a sacrificer without a wife: 7, 9–10

The later Ṛgvedic brāhmaṇa, ŚāṅkhB., shows an increasing involvement in this rite which is to be performed by the adhvaryu, or by every sacrificer himself, i.e. also by the Ṛgvedins.

F. *Śāṅkhāyana Brāhmaṇa* 2, 1–9 [translated by Keith, *Rigveda Brahmanas* (1920)]

a) Interpretation of the agnihotra: 2, 1
b) Systematical treatment of the ritual: 2, 1–2

c) Offering in the other fires (and *virāj* symbolism): 2, 3
d) *upasthāna*: 2, 4
e) *pravāsa*: 2, 5–6
f) Aetiological myth and interpretation of the agnihotra: 2, 7–8
g) The right time for the performance: 2, 9 [cf. E–f]

Compared to the AB. the text of the ŚāṅkhB. offers much more information on the rite. It is a real *agnihotrabrāhmaṇa* (as found in the Yajurvedic texts). However, it does not reach the richness of interpretations found in the later brahmaṇas ŚB. and JB.

G. *Jaiminīya Brāhmaṇa* 1, 1–65 [translated by the author (Leiden 1973)]

a) *agnyādhāna*, agnihotra and cremation: 1, 1–2 [cf. D–k]
b) Aetiological myth: 1, 3–4 [no parallels in the Yajurvedic texts]
c) Symbolism: 1, 4
d) The right time for the performance: 1, 5–6 [cf. F–g]
e) Interpretations of the agnihotra: 1, 7–18 [cf. D–b–l]
f) Symbolism (in a *brahmodya*): 1, 19–20 [cf. D–m]
g) *vaiśvadeva* of the milk: 1, 21 [cf. B–o; C–k; E–b; see also D–n]
h) A detail of the ritual: 1, 21
i) Interpretations of the agnihotra (in a *brahmodya*): 1, 22–25 [cf. D–q?]
j) Agnihotra of twelve days performed after the *ādhāna*: 1, 26–38
k) Systematical treatment of the ritual: 1, 39–41
l) The story of Bhṛgu: 1, 42–44 [cf. D–p]
m) Symbolism, eschatology and an insertion on the funeral rites: 1, 45–50 [cf. D–q?]
n) Expiations: 1, 51–65 [cf. D–r]

The *agnihotrabrāhmaṇa* of the JB., which probably is later than the ŚB., has brought together some agnihotra sections which were spread throughout the ŚB. In its composition the initial position of a passage referring to the *agnyādhāna* (even before the aetiological myth) is quite systematical. The arrangement of this *agnihotra-brāhmaṇa* has no clear parallels.

H. *Ṣaḍviṃśa Brāhmaṇa* 4, 1–2 [translated by Bollée (thesis Utrecht, 1956)]

a) Aetiological myth: 4, 1, 1–5 [cf. G–b]
b) Symbolism: 4, 1, 6–11 (except the interpolation of 4, 1, 7–8)
c) Expiation (substitution of the fire): 4, 1, 12 [cf. C–r]
d) On the performer of the rite: 4, 1, 13–14
e) Symbolism: 4, 1, 14–15
f) Aetiological myth: 4, 2 [cf. G–b]

The composition of this section in the brāhmaṇa which is appended to the Pañcaviṃśa Brāhmaṇa is corrupt. It is not a complete *agnihotrabrāhmaṇa*. A systematic treatment of the rite is lacking. The only other brāhmaṇas in which such a fragmentary agnihotra section is found are AB. (the first non-Yajurvedic text dealing with the agnihotra) and the most recent brāhmaṇa, the GB. There is no reason to suppose that the ṢaḍvB. is old.

I. *Gopatha Brāhmaṇa* 1, 3, 11–15 [translated by Hukam Chand Patyal, type written thesis, Poona 1969]

a) *vaiśvadeva* of the milk and of the actions after the offering: 1, 3, 11–12 [= D–n]
b) Expiations (esoteric): 1, 3, 13 [= D–o]
c) *prāṇāgnihotra*: 1, 3, 14
d) Views of the Priyamedhas: 1, 3, 15 [cf. B–g; C–m]

There is not much originality in this agnihotra section of the GB. (nor in the GB. in general). The *prāṇāgnihotra* passage has parallels in the ŚāṅkhĀ. and the ChU.

The last text surveyed here is the VādhS., which does not imply that it is chronologically the latest. Probably it has to be placed directly after the ŚB. and the JB. The character of this text is rather different from that of the real brāhmaṇas. It represents some addenda on subjects mentioned before by the Taittirīyas. Moreover Caland's edition does not give the complete text. A well-balanced composition is not to be expected. However, it begins (like the other Yajurvedic texts) with an aetiological myth.

J. *Vādhūla Sūtra* 3, 19–40 [translated by Caland, *Acta Orientalia* 4 (1926), p. 19 ff.]

a) Aetiological myth: 3, 19 [cf. C–b]

b) Expiation (esoteric): 3, 20 [cf. C–q; D–r (ŚB. 12, 4, 1, 11)]
c) Aetiological myth (primeval agnihotra transferred from Prajāpati and the gods to man); heaven obtained by the agnihotra: 3, 21 [cf. G–j (JB. 1, 37)?]
d) Aetiological myth (Prajāpati's fourfold ladling out); heaven obtained by the agnihotra: 3, 22
e) Detail of the ritual: 3, 23
f) Interpretation of the agnihotra: 3, 24 [cf. G–e]
g) On the formula of the offering: 3, 25
h) Symbolism: 3, 25
i) The right time for the performance: 3, 26–27
j) Detail of the ritual: 3, 28
k) Aetiological myth (in which the *samidh* plays a role?): 3, 29
l) Symbolism of the *samidh*: 3, 30
m) The offering on the flaming *samidh*: 3, 31–32
n) A detail of the ritual: 3, 33 [cf. i.a. G–h]
o) Symbolism: 3, 34–36
p) *vaiśvadeva* of the milk: 3, 37 [cf. i.a. G–g]
q) Interpretation of the rite: 3, 39
r) Discussion on the offering on the *samidh*: 3, 39
s) Symbolism in a *brahmodya*: 3, 40 [cf. D–m; G–f]

Summarizing this survey of the agnihotra sections we may state that the original *agnihotrabrāhmaṇas* are found in the Yajurvedic texts KS., MS., TB. and ŚB., which show a clear development. In the sūtras the non-Yajurvedic texts play an important role, whereas on the level of the brāhmaṇas an old text like the AB. only deals with some controversial points; it is the later ŚāṅkhB. which provides the *agnihotrabrāhmaṇa*. Among the Sāmavedins (who hardly deal with the agnihotra in their sūtras) the Kauthumas have a concise and fragmentary treatment in the appendage of the PB., viz. the ṢaḍvB., whereas the Jaiminīyas give an extensive, but rather late (and perhaps later added) *agnihotrabrāhmaṇa*. GB.'s contribution is limited and hardly original. The old TB. was supplemented in the *anvākhyānas* of the VādhS.

1 *Myths on the origin of the rite*

1.1 *The creation of Agni; the origin of the exclamation* svāhā; *Prajāpati rubs his forehead and produces an oblation to Agni.*

KS. 6, 1: (In the beginning) Prajāpati existed here.[1] From him Agni (Fire) was emitted. He rushed upwards from his head.[2] He (P.) wiped off the blood (*lohita*) left on it. He smeared it on the earth. From that the Udumbara tree was produced. That is why it ripens (with) reddish (*lohita*) (fruits).[3] He (A.) rushed forward (i.e. fled away). His (P.'s) own (*svā*) voice requested him (P.): "Offer an oblation". He wiped off (the blood?) from here (i.e. from his forehead).[4] Saying *svāhā*[5] he offered this. Therefore this offering (which is made in the agnihotra ritual here) is performed thus (i.e. with the exclamation *svāhā*). For his own (*svā*) voice requested[6] him. Therefore there is no hair on the forehead, nor on the inside of both hands. Therefore the sacrificial ladle (*sruc*) has the length of one ell. He offered his own eye then (or: thereby),[7] i.e. yonder sun (thinking or saying:) "In Agni is the light, the light is in Agni".[8] He offered light into light. He offered *brahman*, he offered truth,[9] he offered yonder sun. For that is the (symbolical meaning of the) agnihotra oblation. He by whom the agnihotra is thus offered (i.e. with the knowledge of these implications) becomes more illustrious day by day. Before that time night and day did not exist. They were both created together with that oblation.[10] In that he (the priest or the sacrificer who performs the rite himself)[11] offers in the evening, he thereby makes (the light of the sun) shine away from here for his adversary. In that (he offers) at daybreak, (he makes it shine) in this direction (or: to the west) for his own benefit. The agnihotra is offered for the sake of preserving Agni (or: the sacrificial fire). By offering in the evening he keeps[12] him for the night, (by offering) at daybreak for the day. The offering to Agni (Fire)[13] was the first oblation offered in the fire. And this offering (with which the present text deals) is called the Offering in (or: to) the Fire (Agni). Its name is *agnihotra*. There is not anyone more excellent among his equals than the one for whom the agnihotra is offered thus.

— The later version of this myth in the MS.[14] has the following significant differences and innovations. Having described the smearing of the blood on the earth (the Udumbara motif), this version directly introduces the offering of Prajāpati's eye (the sun).

MS. 1, 8, 1: 115.1–5: He (Agni) having been emitted from him (Prajāpati) went away in search of his own share. Prajāpati found nothing that he could sacrifice (to the searching Agni). He took his own eye and offered it as an oblation (thinking or saying:) "Agni is the light, the light is Agni, *svāhā*".[15] They consider yonder sun to be that eye. They consider that they offer yonder (sun) in this (fire) here (i.e. in this agnihotra ritual). Now the eye is truth. He who knowing thus offers, performs the agnihotra with truth[16] (as oblation). He who knows thus is becoming[17] truthful.

— The passage continues with an explanation of the name agnihotra[18] and of its function which is similar to the (simpler) version of the KS. and then starts anew with:

MS. 1, 8, 1: 115.12–13: After having been emitted from him (P.) he (Agni) went away in search of his own share. Prajāpati found nothing that he could sacrifice. His own voice spoke to him: "Offer an oblation".

— The text continues with the motif of the origin of *svāhā* and the rubbing of the forehead. As the other evidence is contrary to the assumption that the KS. would contain a secondary combination of two myths borrowed from the MS., a different analysis has to be made. First, it may be noted that the rubbing of the forehead is not quite functional in the context of the MS. Later versions explicitly state why Prajāpati rubbed his forehead. It can only be connected with the beginning of the passage, in which the blood on the forehead (as well as its first rubbing off) had been mentioned. In fact, the opposition is not between two different kinds of oblations (eye and blood), but between two motifs: the explanation of the formula *agnir (agnau) jyotir jyotir agniḥ* (eye = sun) and of the exclamation *svāhā*. The *svāhā* motif and the eye-sun motif could have been combined easily in one smooth passage, but the fact that this has not been done proves that the passage of the KS. represents two different myths. Occurring together in one passage, the two motifs produce a duplication of the oblation to Agni. Originally, offering the eye may have formed an independent myth, as appears from TB. 2, 1, 6, 4 ff., where P. for fear of A. offers the sun which has been shaped from himself.[19] The MS., probably realizing the twofoldness of the myth in the KS., its source, explicitly represents the two parts separately. In doing so it changed the order of the two motifs as found in the KS. (perhaps because *svāhā* comes after *agnir jyotir jyotir agniḥ* in the recitation), and therefore severed the rubbing of the forehead from the beginning of the passage. The MS. adds a new element to P.'s rubbing his forehead:

MS. 1, 8, 1: 115.16–19: Therefore they say of someone whose hair is brushed upwards (i.e. grows by nature) from the right to the left (i.e. whose crown is at the right side?):[20] "It is a good (excellent) sign". For Prajāpati, the excellent one, brushed it in that way in the beginning. The ladle (*sruc*) should be of the same measure as this (arm).[21] With this (arm) the oblation in the fire (or: to Agni) was offered in the beginning.

— A later version is found TB. 2, 1, 2, 1 ff., where is explained why Prajāpati wants to regain Agni (who had taken all the creatures with him). P.'s efforts stop A. Moreover, this produces a new interpretation of the rubbing of the forehead.

TB. 2, 1, 2, 1–2: Prajāpati emitted Agni. The creatures were emitted after him. He (A.) stayed with him without obtaining a share. (Thereupon) he ran away from him together with the creatures. Wishing to stop him he went after him. He was not able to stop him. He was troubled with heat.[22] Agni stopped, thinking: "Prajāpati forsooth is suffering from heat".[23] He (P.) wiped off (the sweat)[24] upwards from his forehead. That became ghee (sacrificial butter). Therefore, if someone's hair has a right crown[25], they call this[26] an excellent sign connected with Prajāpati. Because he rubbed from his forehead, there is no hair on the forehead.

— Before giving the usual explanation of the origin of *svāhā* the TB. adds a new motif, the origin of reflection or hesitation:

TB. 2, 1, 2, 2–3: He was ready to present it (the sweat/ghee) to Agni (or: he held it over the fire). Then he became uncertain: "Shall I offer? Shall I not offer it?" This was the origin of reflection (hesitation). He who reflects, knowing thus, certainly takes the better decision. To him his voice said: "Offer!" . . . etc.

— A still more elaborate, and later, version is found in the Śatapatha Brāhmaṇa:

ŚB. 2, 2, 4, 1–7: Prajāpati existed alone here in the beginning. He thought: "How could I procreate?" He exerted himself, practised austerity and produced Agni from his mouth. Because he produced him from his mouth, Agni is an eater of food. He who thus knows Agni to be an eater of food becomes an eater of food[27] himself. Thus he brought him forth then before (*agre*) the (other) gods. Therefore he is (called) Agni. For Agni is the name of what in reality is Agri.[28] He came first by birth. If someone comes first, they say:

"He comes in front (*agre*)". This is the reason why Agni is called Agni.[28] Prajāpati thought: "An eater of food is this Agni whom I have generated from myself. There is nothing else but me as food here, whom (I hope) he may not eat".[29] At that time the earth indeed was barren. There were neither plants nor trees. This passed through his mind. Then Agni turned towards him with open mouth. When he (P.) became afraid, his own greatness departed from him. Now his own greatness was his speech. His speech departed from him. He (P.) sought an oblation in himself. He rubbed (his forehead). Because he rubbed (his forehead), therefore here (inside the hands)[30] and here (on the forehead)[30] there is no hair. On that occasion he either obtained a ghee-oblation[31] or a milk-oblation. Both, however, are (products of) milk. This (oblation) did not meet with his[32] approval. It was mixed with hairs. He poured it out (on the earth)[33] saying "Suck it quickly".[34] From this the plants came into existence. Therefore they are called *oṣadhayaḥ*. He rubbed (his forehead) a second[35] time and then obtained another oblation, either a ghee-oblation or a milk-oblation. Both, however, are (products of) milk. This (oblation) met with his [32] approval. He reflected (upon it): "Should I offer? Should I not offer?" His own greatness said to him:[36] "Offer!" Then Prajāpati realized: "My own (*svā*) greatness has spoken (*āha*)[37] it to me". So he offered it saying "*svāhā*". Therefore there is offered with *svāhā* (in the agnihotra). Thereupon the one that gives out heat (i.e. the sun) rose.[38] Thereafter the one that ventilates (i.e. the wind)[39] came forth. It was then that Agni turned away. And by offering Prajāpati reproduced himself and saved himself from Death, Agni, who was about to consume him. He who offers the agnihotra, knowing thus, reproduces himself and saves himself from Death, Agni, who is about to consume him.

— After a small paragraph (2, 2, 4, 8) which appears to be an insertion, the ŚB. by way of an afterthought adds a statement on the origin of reflection (*vicikitsā*)[40] based on TB. 2, 1, 2, 2. Moreover, there are more influences from the TB. Prajāpati offers to Agni out of fear, whereas in the versions of the KS. and the MS. the aim of the offering was to get back or retain Agni. The TB. has both motifs. For the one followed by the ŚB. see below. ŚB. 2, 2, 4, 10 further mentions the origin of the Vikaṅkata tree (Prajāpati rubbed his hands) comparable to the Udumbara motif (see above).

TB. 2, 1, 6, 4–5: When Prajāpati created (emitted) the gods, he created Agni as the first of them. Failing to find something else to seize he returned to Prajāpati. He (P.) became afraid of death. He shaped yonder sun out of himself. Having offered this he fled. Then he overcame death. He who knows thus overcomes death. Therefore if they do not offer for one who knows thus during one or two days, there has been offered (all the same). For the agnihotra is yonder sun.

— The motif of Prajāpati's fear for Agni is found also outside the context of the agnihotra. See e.g. VādhS. 4, 65 *a*. A combination of both myths from the TB. is found in the VādhS. where the following Taittirīya *anvākhyāna*[41] is found:

VādhS. 3, 19: Prajāpati alone was here[42] (in the beginning). He ....[43] Then Prajāpati created the creatures among whom Agni was the first.[44] Now Agni is Death. He pursued Prajāpati in the form of someone who would eat him.[45] He (A.) made a rush[46] at him. (Out of fear) for him he wiped off (the sweat of his forehead).[47] Therefore there is no hair on the forehead. Therefore, if someone's hair has a crown on the right side, they say: "(That is) an excellent sign connected with Prajāpati".[48] He (A.) made a second rush at him. He pursued him. For him he (P.) threw it down (i.e. the hair rubbed off from the forehead). That became Ulapa grass.[49] While running on (toward him) he took it. Therefore, when in hot sunshine (the fire) burns the fields of dried Ulapa grass, consuming them it runs on.[50] He made a third rush at him. He pursued him. For him he threw it (i.e. the hair) down. That became trees. With those he was detained longer. It is also therefore that in the trees now this deity is detained longer.[51] Therefore a piece of wood should be put on the fire by someone who knows thus (thinking:) "Death should stay away from me, be it only for a moment".[52] Death stays away from him who, knowing thus, puts a piece of wood on the fire.

— For a different Prajāpati-Agni myth see ŚB. 2, 3, 3, 1 f. and TB. 2, 3, 7, 1:

ŚB. 2, 3, 3, 1–2: When, emitting the creatures, Prajāpati emitted Agni, the latter, as soon as he was born, started burning all here. And similarly the creatures who existed then started (or: sought) to crush him in great confusion.[53] Being unable to stand this, he went to man. He said: "I cannot endure this. Come, let me enter into you. After having reproduced me maintain me. Just as you reproduce and maintain me in this world, even so I will reproduce and maintain you in yonder world". He (man) answered: "So be it". He reproduced and maintained him.

— In this myth Prajāpati has hardly any function beyond creating Agni. The aetiology refers to the establishing of the fires (*agnyādhāna*) and their maintenance by man (through the agnihotra ritual), rather than to the agnihotra and its primeval example set by Prajāpati. In the context *puruṣa* denotes man and has no cosmic implications (the Puruṣa, the Universe as Prajāpati's body). See also the Kāṇva recension of the ŚB. quoted by Minard, *Trois Énigmes I*, 543. In the following passage from the TB. the situation seems to be different:

TB. 2, 3, 7, 1: Prajāpati emitted the (cosmic) Person. Agni said: "This should be my food". He (Prajāpati) feared: "He will burn me completely". He saw this *caturhotṛ* litany which saves the body (or: self). With this he offered. With this he saved himself.

— In this myth (in a passage which glorifies the agnihotra as having i.a. four instead of one *hotṛ* on account of the identification with the fourfold ladling out), the *puruṣa* is not just man (the *prajās* of the other passages), but the Person, the Universe, Prajāpati's body (as Sāyaṇa's commentary rightly observes). If this interpretation is correct, Prajāpati is again threatened by the burning Agni. The offering made to avert the danger, however, is not the primeval agnihotra, but a ritual which is identified with the agnihotra.

NOTES

[1] See Minard, *Trois Énigmes* I, 91 *a* on the "ouverture classique des cosmogonies". Here *idam* definitely should be interpreted as an adverb and the verb *as* not as a copula (as is done by some scholars in the parallel passages). Note that MS. 1, 8, 4 omits *idam* in this phrase (*prajāpatir vā eka āsīt*). For further parallels see Lévi, *Doctrine*, p. 13, n. 1.

[2] Cf. JB. 1, 73 (*Auswahl*, § 9) on Agni's eruption from the top of Prajāpati's head (instead of his mouth).

[3] The parallel version of MS. 1, 8, 1 has *tasmād lohitaṃ phalaṃ pacyate*. On this construction of *pacyate* with the accusative of the fruit see von Schroeder, *ZDMG* 33, p. 199.

[4] One of the indications that these texts were orally transmitted (and taught). A gesture was made by the person who recites (i.e. teaches) the text. See Caland, *Über das rituelle Sūtra des Baudhāyana* (Leipzig 1903), p. 5. For a similar rubbing with the hands expressed in the same inaccurate way compare BĀU. 1, 4, 6.

[5] The actual exclamation is *svāhā*. The etymology is based on *svā* + *āha* ("said") here. The sandhi form *svāheti* solves the discrepancy. For speculations on *svāhā* see GB. 1, 3, 16 and ṢaḍvB. 4, 7, 1–3.

[6] Are we to assume that a more original version of this myth had *āha* instead of *aiṭṭa* ("requested")? The present passage is the oldest transmitted text.

[7] The eye can be homologized with the sun (= Brahman) and be connected with truth (cf. the version of the MS.), the usual symbolic oblations of the agnihotra. Offering the sun into the fire is the central motif of this rite. In this context the themes of Prajāpati offering his eye and Prajāpati wiping off his forehead seem to have been combined.

[8] This formula accompanies the first libation of the agnihotra. The other texts have a nominative instead of the locative *agnau* ("in Agni").

[9] For the truth-sacrifice in connection with the agnihotra see *Agn. and Prāṇāgn.*, ch. V B. On the sun as cosmic truth see Heesterman, *Consecration*, p. 204 f.

[10] I.e. the primeval offering by Prajāpati, described in the preceding passage. On the origin of night and day as due to the agnihotra see JB. 3, 361 *atha ha tataḥ purāhorātre saṃśliṣṭe evāsatur avyākṛte. te u agnihotreṇaiva vyākṛte* "Before that time (i.e. before the first sunrise) night and day were together and not separated. It was only by the (primeval) agnihotra (of Prajāpati) that they became separated"). See my paper "Gab es damals auch *dyumnas*? Die Weltentstehung nach dem Jaiminīya Brāhmaṇa", *ZDMG, Supplement II (XVIII. Deutscher Orientalistentag, Lübeck 1972)* (1974), p. 292–298.

[11] As is usual in translations of Vedic ritualistic texts, I render the third person singular by "he". Mostly this refers to the priest, sometimes to the sacrificer who acts himself as the officiant. If some effects of the rite are mentioned, "he" means (at least indirectly) the sacrificer on whose behalf the sacrifice is performed. In case when it is important to know whether the priest or the sacrificer carry out an action, this will be stated in the notes.

[12] On the dative of the one "für den etwas zum Stillstehen gebracht wird" in connection with the causative of *ram* meaning "zum Stillstehen bringen" see Oertel, *SbBAdW* 1937/38, p. 75 f. On the other hand, as Oertel observes, *ram-* with locative often means "gern bei etwas (jemandem) bleiben". Cf. PB. 17, 7, 2 *tasmin paśavo ramante* and TB. 1, 4, 4, 9 *paśūn evāsmai ramayati*. The parallel version of MS. 1, 8, 1 uses the root *dhṛ-* (".. hält er Agni für die Nacht fest", tr. Delbrück, *Syntax*, p. 41).

[13] In this passage *agni* sometimes denotes the god of the myth, sometimes it refers to the sacrificial fire (one of the forms of Agni).

[14] See *Jaiminīya Brāhmaṇa I, 1–65*, p. 13 on the relative chronology of the agnihotra sections.

[15] See n. 8 and (about *svāhā*) n. 5.

[16] See n. 9.

[17] See Pāṇini 3, 2, 57 and von Schroeder, *ZDMG* 33, p. 198 on the construction *bhaviṣṇuḥ satyam* (= *satyaṃbhaviṣṇuḥ*, cf. *priyaṃbhaviṣṇuḥ*).

[18] For a different explanation of the term *agnihotra* see the ŚB. below. In the context of the *agnicayana* other explanations are found, see e.g. TS. 5, 7, 4, 2.

[19] "Prajāpati, while emitting the deities, emitted Agni first. Failing to find something else by which he could support himself he returned to Prajāpati. He (P.) became afraid of death. He shaped yonder sun out of himself. After he had offered it, he turned away ..".

[20] Or does it refer to baldness setting in on the right side of the (fore)head?

[21] See n. 4.

[22] Here *tap-* does not refer to austerities (the intentional production of heat or torment in or on the body), but to Prajāpati's becoming hot (as Dumont correctly translates) due to the exertion of the pursuit.

[23] The text as edited by the Bibl. Ind. ed. is corrupt. One might read *tāpī vai sa* (instead of *tāpi vai sya*), or with Böhtlingk (see Delbrück, *Syntax*, p. 266) and the Ānandāśrama ed., *'tāpi* (medio-passive aorist).

[24] Here "sweat" may be supplied as object, since Prajāpati exerts himself and becomes hot. The function of this wiping off is less clear in the versions of the KS. and the MS. (and completely different in the ŚB. and the VādhS.).

[25] Dumont: ".. is wiped upwards (i.e. erect) on the right side".

[26] Oertel, *Syntax of Cases*, p. 249 rejects the reading *tām* and prefers *tam* (as in MS.).

[27] The term "eater of food" (*annāda*; cf. *attṛ*) has economic as well as social implications and denotes the members of the prosperous, ruling establishment. See Rau, *Staat und Gesellschaft*, p. 34. See also Whitney, *AJPh* 3 (1882), p. 404 who interprets *attṛ* as "pillager" and *ādya* as "the person to be pillaged, or drained, or stripped of all that he has", as one who is "liable to contribution or taxation".

[28] For the same 'etymology' see ŚB. 6, 1, 1, 11. On the stereotyped phrases with the abstract forms in *-tā* and *-tvam* which usually conclude these 'etymologies' and which are often incorrectly rendered see Minard, *Trois Énigmes*, I, 382. ŚB. 2, 3, 1, 1 has a different 'etymology' of the name agnihotra.

[29] See Caland, *WZKM* 26 (1912), p. 112 ("*quem hic (vereor) ne devoret*"). See also Whitney, *AJPh* 3 (1882), p. 408 "whom, by all means, let him not eat".

[30] See Caland, *WZKM* 26, p. 112 (as well as the parallel versions) on the words to be supplied between brackets.

[31] Cf. the version of the TB. Sometimes ghee is offered instead of milk in the agnihotra ritual.

[32] According to Lévi, *Doctrine*, p. 26 Agni seems to disapprove of the oblation. I reject that interpretation.

[33] Eggeling translates "He poured it away (into the fire)", which makes no sense in the context. The oblation, which had been disapproved of, is not offered or poured out in the fire, but is poured away (*vy-ukṣ-*). Out of this being poured plants are produced. This means that he pours away over the earth. This interpretation is also important for the so-called etymology of *oṣadhayaḥ*, which can no longer refer to burning, but should be connected with the verb *dhayati* "to suck". The earth is requested to swallow as soon as possible the rejected oblation.

[34] On this 'etymology' see Minard, *Trois Énigmes*, II, 746. Eggeling translates "drink while burning". I follow Whitney's rendering (*TAPA* 23, 1892, p. 27) and take *oṣam* as an adverb. This suits the context; see n. 33.

[35] The second rubbing off in the ŚB. corresponds to the second one in the versions of the KS. and the MS. The first produces the Udumbara in the KS. and the MS. (out of blood) and plants in the ŚB. (out of his hair). Only in the TB. does Prajāpati offer directly (be it after some hesitation, the *vicikitsā* motif, also adopted by ŚB., but connected with the second rubbing off) to Agni (or: in the fire).

[36] Prajāpati's own voice (greatness) speaks to him (addresses him) from outside. It may be noted that the description of P.'s voice leaving him was rather forced. Indeed, terror makes someone speechless. The function of this motif in the context, however, is rather weak. Should it also prepare P.'s being addressed from outside by his own voice in the *svāhā* motif?

[37] This version in the late ŚB. is the first to have a clear 'etymology' of *svāhā* as *svā* + *āha*. In the other versions a synonym of *āha* is used. See also n. 6.

[38] The sun, offered into Agni according to the older versions, did not exist before the primeval agnihotra, which produced the distinction between night and day. It plays an important role in the speculations on the agnihotra.

[39] The wind or Vāyu has hardly any function in the agnihotra myths. Agni and Āditya (the sun) are important. Vāyu just completes the well-known tripartite division heaven, air, earth (sun, wind, fire).

[40] Eggeling's translation "And as to that same birth from out of doubt — when Prajāpati doubted he, while doubting, remained steadfast on the better (side), insomuch that he reproduced himself" contains some syntactical errors. First *vicikitsāyai janma* means "the origin of doubt". Secondly *tad vā etat eva vicikitsāyai janma* should be taken with *yat prajāpatir vyacikitsat*: "That (or: when) P. doubted (reflected), that was the very origin of doubt (reflection)".

[41] The *anvākhyāna* (often, as here, introduced by *idaṃ vā anvāhuḥ*) is a brāhmaṇa-like passage in the VādhS., which develops a subject treated in the TB. or the TS. (or parallel recensions of the mentioned Taittirīya texts). They are written in the style of the brāhmaṇas and do not seem to be much later than their parallels in the ŚB. (and the JB.). The present passage does not quote a sentence known from the TB. as its starting-point. Its treatment of the myth shows some resemblance to the versions of the TB. discussed and translated above.

[42] For my interpretation of *idam*, which differs from Caland's translation (*AO* 4, p. 20), see n. 1.

[43] Some words are lost in the text.

[44] Caland interprets *agnimukhāḥ .. prajāḥ* as "die Geschöpfe, die Agni zum Munde haben". The parallel versions prove that our translation should be adopted. See also ŚB. 2, 5, 1, 8; 3, 9, 1, 6; AB. 6, 14, 10; PB. 25, 14, 4 on Agni as the head (*mukha*) of the deities. In other contexts (e.g. ĀśvGS. 4, 7, 22) Caland's translation may be used.

[45] The versions of the ŚB. and TB. 2, 1, 6, 4 likewise depict Agni as Death who wants to devour Prajāpati. JB. 1, 28 mentions *atsyat* ("who will devour") as an epithet of Death (Yama). The sentence *sa prajāpatim atsyato rūpeṇābhipalāyata* verbally recurs at VādhS. 4, 109.

[46] The compounds of *palāy-* do not invariably denote a flight. Caland's rendering should be corrected, as was done by him in the translation of VādhS. 4, 109 (see preceding note).

[47] Cold perspiration seems to be required as object in this ellipsis. For a different ellipsis see n. 24.

[48] The text may be somewhat corrupt here.

[49] In the version of the ŚB. the hairs become plants and only the second rubbing produces an oblation. Here the situation is completely different. The adapted myth ultimately provides the aetiology for the *abhyādhāna* (laying a piece of wood on the fire before offering). The motif of offering an oblation has disappeared.

[50] Caland misinterprets this passage. Agni eats without making a stop. When fire burns a plain of dry grass, it rushes on and spreads with enormous speed.

[51] Caland: "diese Gottheit (nämlich Agni) ist ja auch heute in den Bäumen zur Ruhe gekommen (d.h. er ist latent im Holze anwesend)". The presence of Agni in wood (an idea not unusual in Vedic India) hardly explains why a piece of wood should be thrown into the fire in order to evade death. The point is that the wood (of the trees) detains (holds up) Agni/Death. A forest-fire does not have the speed of a fire which consumes a field of dry grass.

[52] Read perhaps *cin nu* for *cen nu*, as Caland proposes.

[53] Eggeling's interpretation of *ābilam* ("and so everybody tried to get out of his way"; "*ity ābilam āsa*, i.e. 'there was a (general rush) to a hole', (or

perhaps 'to the outlet')") seems to reflect a European music-hall panic. For *ābila* meaning "confused" see Mayrhofer's dictionary. Here *ābilam* is an adverb to be taken with the predicate *sampeṣṭuṃ dadhrire*. Perhaps *iti* denotes the parallelism with Agni's action (*dagdhuṃ dadhre*).

I.2 *The agnihotra is a reduced primeval sacrifice of thousand years performed by Prajāpati.*

JB. I, 3–4.[1] Prajāpati performed a sacrifice of thousand years. Having completed seven hundred years he gained that supremacy which he has now. Ascending to heaven[2] he spoke to the gods: "Bring ye to an end those (remaining) three hundred years". "So be it" (they said). Having completed the three hundred years they gained as much as Prajāpati. (I.e.) they all together, this (god) and that (god), were only equal in power to Prajāpati (alone). They said: "We have accomplished this (sacrifice) with our divine, immortal bodies. Human beings, forsooth, will not complete this. Come, let us abridge it". They abridged it to the year-sacrifice. They said: "This is something great. Let us abridge it". They abridged it to the twelve-day session. (...)[3] They abridged it to (...) the two (i.e. twice a day) agnihotra offerings. Further than this it was not (to be) subdued. Therefore the agnihotra is unsurpassed. Not overcome is he who knows thus.

— The brāhmaṇa continues (I, 4) with the equation of elements from the agnihotra with the Soma rituals. On the one hand this means a glorification of the agnihotra (as found in several other texts), on the other hand this is to show how the daily agnihotra is the ultimate abridgment of all sacrifices. Therefore JB. I, 4 concludes: "When he offers these two evening/morning oblations (of the agnihotra), he performs all those sacrifices through these two oblations. Therefore the agnihotra is unlimited". An interesting parallel of this myth is found in the ṢaḍvB. On the composition of that passage and its relation to the JB. (which seems to be more original) see author, *Jaiminīya Brāhmaṇa I, 1–65*, p. 24 f. The translation given below follows the reconstruction proposed there. The numbers refer to Eelsingh's edition:

ṢaḍvB. 4, I, I: Prajāpati practised austerities. When he was doing so, the idea was born: "I should like to create gods". These (i.e. the well-known) gods were emitted then (..) 4, I, 2: The gods, desirous of heaven, practised austerities. While they were doing so (their) essence[4] came forth (in the form of) earth, air and heaven. They irradiated[5] (these). While these were irradiated (heated), their essence came forth: from the earth the Ṛgveda, from the air the

Yajurveda, from heaven the Sāmaveda. They irradiated (these). While these were irradiated, their essence came forth: from the Ṛgveda the *gārhapatya* fire, from the Yajurveda the *dakṣiṇāgni*, from the Sāmaveda the *āhavanīya* fire. They irradiated (these). While these (fires) were irradiated, the Puruṣa (cosmic Person)[6] came forth with a thousand heads, a thousand eyes and a thousand feet. 4, 1, 3–4: They (the gods) said: "Who art thou?" He (the Puruṣa) said:[7] "(I am) Sacrifice by name". 4, 1, 3: The gods turned to Prajāpati (saying:) "With our divine bodies, with our immortal bodies we are able to accomplish this (Giant Sacrifice); forsooth, the human beings will not accomplish it".[8] 4, 1, 5: For them (i.e. the human beings or, rather, the gods pleading on their behalf) Prajāpati performed the essential form of the sacrifice in one day (*sadyo yajñasaṃsthām upaiti*). For this sacrifice (i.e. the agnihotra which forms the subject of this part of the text and which represents the one-day pattern of the cosmic sacrifice) comes to its conclusion within one day (or: daily) (*sadyo ha vā eṣa yajñaḥ saṃsthām upaiti*).[9]

— So far the agreement with the JB. is not significant. A creation myth (not without parallels), which partly serves for glorifying the position of the Sāmaveda to which this text belongs, forms the introduction. Just as in the JB. the gods ask Prajāpati for an abridgment of the superhuman sacrifice on behalf of the mortals. Prajāpati complies with their wish, but how he manages to reduce the cosmic Puruṣa-Sacrifice to the one-day or daily agnihotra is not described by the text as transmitted to us. Instead, the brāhmaṇa duplicates the motif of the agnihotra, as being an abridged form of an enormous primeval sacrifice, by including a parallel of the passage from the JB.:

ṢaḍvB. 4, 2: Prajāpati created here a sacrificial session of a thousand years. For them[10] he abridged the thousand-year sacrifice to the Gavāmayana, the Gavāmayana to ... (...)[11] .. to the agnihotra. He who, knowing thus, performs the agnihotra, has sacrificed with all (these mentioned) sacrifices.[12]

NOTES

[1] For a detailed commentary see author, *Jaiminīya Brāhmaṇa I, 1–65*.

[2] The gods, including Prajāpati in this passage, have to win heaven (by means of sacrifices) according to some passages in the brāhmaṇas. See especially JB. 1, 37 on the successive rise to heaven of Prajāpati, the gods and the primeval seers by means of the agnihotra.

[3] The other stages of the abridgment have been omitted here.

[4] The *rasa* may be essence, sap or just any liquid. The context shows that pure liquid is out of the question. Still it has to be borne in mind that the

translation "they practised austerities" may be rather flat. Heating is one of the central ideas in the root *tap-*. The gods accumulate heat in themselves (by concentration and austerities) and produce (as their essence) a secretion. In these contexts the *tapas* is mostly creative (see ṢaḍvB. 4, 1, 1) and may be connected with the process of emanation (by which Prajāpati accomplishes his creation).

[5] Bollée's translation "they practised austerities" does not express the correct meaning of *abhyatapan*, which has to be distinguished from *tapa 'tapyanta* at the beginning of this passage. After having accumulated heat in themselves, and having emitted the tripartite cosmos, they focus the creative (brooding) heat (produced by concentration and asceticism) outside themselves upon (*abhi*!) the successive essences which they extract by this process of heating. This implies that *teṣāṃ tapyamānānām* (except the first time) does not refer to the gods (Bollée: "from them, practising austerities"), but to the three parts of the cosmos and their respective *rasas*. AB. 5, 32, 1 (a parallel of the present passage in which Prajāpati himself performs the total creation) has *tebhyo 'bhitaptebhyaḥ*. On the construction with a genitive instead of an ablative see Oertel, *Syntax of Cases*, p. 131 f. (with a correct translation of this passage).

[6] The Puruṣa (cf. ṚV. 10, 90, 1), which here is secreted as *rasa* by the totality of the sacrificial fires, is identified with sacrifice (*yajña*) in this text.

[7] In my interpretation (and reconstruction of the composition) *ko nāmāsīti* can be retained and there is no reason to make the gods ask Prajāpati who this Puruṣa was (as is done by the commentary and Bollée).

[8] This translation is based on the reconstruction of the corrupt text with the help of the Jaiminīya parallel. In the context of the Jaiminīya version it could be reconstructed as follows: *devaśarīrair vā idam amṛtaśarīrais samāpāma na ha vā idaṃ martyās samāpsyanti*. See *JB. I, 1–65*, p. 24 f. However, in the ṢaḍvB. this sentence does not fit in the myth of the abridgment of the sacrifice of thousand years, since in the version of the ṢaḍvB. (4, 2) the gods have not performed a part of the thousand years (as in JB.). Here, it seems to be connected with the Puruṣa-Sacrifice (the 'Giant-Sacrifice'). In that case, instead of the perfect *samāpāma*, a future or present ("we are able to accomplish") is required.

[9] The term *saṃsthā* is used here with two different meanings. First as a technical term denoting the essential form of sacrifices (here the agnihotra as the elementary form of all sacrifices or of the cosmic sacrifice) and secondly only referring to the end of something. Similarly *upaiti* has a double meaning.

[10] One may compare "for them" (*teṣām*) with ṢaḍvB. 4, 1, 5. In both passages this may refer to the gods. It is, however, for the mortals, rather than for the gods, that Prajāpati reduces the primeval sacrifice to the daily agnihotra. Especially in the present passage *teṣām* is odd, because there is no antecedent in the immediate context. The arrangement of ṢaḍvB. 4, 1–2 is seriously confused.

[11] The intermediate stages, as in the Jaiminīya version, have been omitted here. They represent a gradual shortening of the sacrifices. In that connection Bollée's rendering of *ṣoḍaśin* ("sixteen-day rite") does not make sense. The "sixteenfold one" belongs together with the *ukthya* and the *agniṣṭoma* to the *ekāhas*, i.e. Soma sacrifices of one day (with several preparatory days). They form the pattern of the *jyotiṣṭoma*. See Hillebrandt, *Ritual-Litteratur*, p. 124 and 137.

[12] The equations of elements from the agnihotra with Soma rituals, which in the Jaiminīya parallel come after the abridgment of the thousand-year

sacrifice, are found in the ṢaḍvB. scattered throughout 4, 1 (4, 1, 6; 9–11; 15). The repetition of 4, 1, 16 ("He who knowing thus (i.e. knowing the abridgment) performs the agnihotra has sacrificed with all the sacrifices (mentioned in the abridgment)") at the end of ṢaḍvB. 4, 2, proves that those scattered equations with Soma sacrifices should come after the abridgment myth.

I.3 *Agnihotra instituted by the gods by way of exchange between heaven and earth.*

ŚāṅkhB. 2, 5–6: All the enjoyments concerning food, drinks, and sexual intercourse are continually and without interruption enjoyed with the night as their (ever repeated) starting-point.[1] The night is their filter. Whatever enjoyments there are, they are all produced from food. The gods said: "How could we receive those enjoyments from someone like ourselves?" They pressed out (lit.: upwards) the essence[2] of the waters. It became plants and trees. They pressed out the essence of plants and trees. It became fruit. They pressed out the essence of fruit. It became food. They pressed out the essence of food. It became seed. They pressed out the essence of seed. It became man.[3] Man here, when he breathes out or in, does not say with his exhalation or inhalation "I have breathed out" or "I have breathed in". With speech does he say this. Therefore exhalation and inhalation have a share in speech and are based on speech. (.....)[4] Therefore the whole self has a share in speech and is based on speech. This has been proclaimed in a verse: "Without Indra no form at all becomes pure".[5] Indra is speech.[6] For without speech no form at all becomes pure. One offers at night (reciting:) "The light is Agni, Agni is the light" He who is the light (at that moment) is called light. (So) one speaks the truth.[7] The self which is based on speech becomes based on truth. The gods are also based on truth.[8] Then one offers with *svāhā* (and) the gods receive this oblation from him whose offering is truth.[9] Moreover at the beginning of the night he speaks truth. Even if[10] thereafter he speaks falsely, truth is spoken by him, since he speaks truth at the beginning of the night. In the morning he offers (reciting:) "The light is Sūrya (the sun), Sūrya is the light" (....).[11]

— This myth of the ŚāṅkhB. has no parallels in the other texts. Moreover its structure and contents are completely different from the other passages which explain the origin of the agnihotra. Reasoning and argumentation rather than story-telling are its main features. In fact it explains the function of the agnihotra (as the outstanding example of the libation-sacrifice) in the context of exchange between heaven and earth. The *do ut des* (or *do ut dare possis*) concept, which is always present in ritualistic thought, here shows a reversal of the roles in the myth, where the gods are the starting-point and where they give in order that the human beings will be able to return the gift by way of sacrifice. It also explains the daily return of the agnihotra and connects it with other daily or recurring actions (eating food e.g., which later was developed into the symbolical agnihotra of the *prāṇāgnihotra*). The references to sexual intercourse, to eating food and to the waterdoctrine make this myth on the origin of the agnihotra a precursor of the *pañcāgnividyā* theory of the BĀU. and the ChU. Its position is much nearer to the Upaniṣads than to the Yajurvedic Saṃhitās.

NOTES

[1] Keith translates *rātryā eva te saṃtatā avyavachinnāḥ kriyante* by "verily these are made, together, without break, from the night". The combination of *saṃtata-* and *avyavachinna-*, however, invariably denotes something continuous and uninterrupted. Presumably this obscure statement at the beginning of a passage which describes the origin of the agnihotra should be connected with the fact that this rite continuously takes place every night and day. Compare the use of *saṃtata-* and *avyavachinna-* at ŚāṅkhB. 7, 4 ("In that in the evening and in the morning the fast drink is bestowed, the Agnihotra is offered continuously and without a break in this breath, Agni", — tr. Keith; note the connection between eating food and performing the agnihotra). See also ŚB. 1, 3, 5, 16 (".. thereby he makes the days and nights of the year continuous, and in a continuous and uninterrupted way revolve those days and nights of the year", — tr. Eggeling). The enjoyments are not produced from the night — the next sentence states that the night is just a filter —, but are made continuous due to the night. This does not form an interruption in this continuous flow, but only represents a filter which lets through this uninterrupted stream of enjoyments (i.e. this uninterrupted stream of agnihotra sacrifices). It may be observed that the daily agnihotra has evening and morning performances which are regarded as complementary. The evening performance forms the first sacrifice, the morning performance the second. In this way the continuity is maintained and night does not make a break between the daily agnihotras. One cannot say that the agnihotra is a one-day rite. It breaks through the boundaries of the night and thus is continuous. Moreover the night (ablative in the text) is the starting-point, since the first sacrifice is the night-performance.

[2] For this creation in stages through the *rasas* (essences) compare ṢaḍvB. 4, 1, 2 (see above), where the *rasa* is produced as secretion through heating. Here squeezing out seems to be the process.

[3] See *Agnihotra and Prāṇāgnihotra*, ch. VI on the water doctrine which explains the existence of all life on earth as based on (the heavenly) water.

[4] I have omitted some sentences which, in the typical style of the brāhmaṇas, form a repetition of what has been said before with some minor variations, i.e. the substitution of "exhalation and inhalation" (and the corresponding verb) by the other vital powers. Mostly breath (*prāṇa*) is superior in the well-known contests of the vital powers (*prāṇāḥ*). The dominant part played by speech (*vāc*) in this passage is rather far-fetched.

[5] ṚV. 9, 69, 6.

[6] This identification is not unusual. See e.g. AB. 2, 26, 1; ŚāṅkhB. 13, 5.

[7] See *Agn. and Prāṇāgn.*, ch. V B on the relation between truth and agnihotra. In connection with the discussion on the right time for the performance of the agnihotra, AB. 5, 31 also interprets the formulas of the offering as statements of truth. See further ŚB. 2, 3, 1, 30 "Thus offering is made with the truth; for, truly, when the sun goes down, then Agni (fire) is the light; and when the sun rises, then Sūrya is the light; and whatever is offered with the truth, that, indeed, goes to the gods" (tr. Eggeling). According to VādhS. 3, 36 the *gati* and the *pratiṣṭhā* of the agnihotra are truth (*satya*) and faith (*śraddhā*). See also Section 1.1 (n. 9).

[8] Cf. AB. 1, 6, 6 *satyasaṃhitā vai devāḥ* "the gods are composed of truth" (Keith's wrong translation "... are of truth compact" may have been influenced by the compound *satyasaṃdha-*); ŚB. 1, 1, 1, 4 *satyam eva devā* "the gods are truth". In both parallels there is an opposition between gods and men (who are connected with untruth).

[9] I.e. from someone like themselves. See the beginning of this passage.

[10] Read *sa yadi ha* (not *yad iha*) *vā api*.

[11] The rest forms a repetition in which day is replaced by night.

1.4 *Transference of the agnihotra by the gods to the human beings.*

— This section does not describe the primeval agnihotra as instituted by the gods or by Prajāpati, but its coming into existence among the mortals.

JB. 1, 37: Brahman once offered this same agnihotra[1] for twelve days. Having offered it for twelve days he extracted fame, glory, (the power of) procreation and immortality. After he had offered this agnihotra for twelve days and had transferred it to Prajāpati, Brahman rose to heaven. Prajāpati offered this agnihotra for twelve days. Havings offered it for twelve days he extracted knowledge, understanding, deliberation and austerity. After he had offered this agnihotra for twelve days and had transferred it to the gods and the (primeval) seers, Prajāpati rose to heaven. The gods and the seers offered this agnihotra for twelve days. After they had offered it for twelve days and had transferred it to the primeval mortals, they also rose to heaven. Brahman offered this agnihotra for twelve days. For twelve days Prajāpati, for twelve days the gods and the seers (also offered it). Having offered it for twelve days each time, they obtained what they wished and desired. How much more (will he obtain this) who offers thus (that)[2] during his whole life.

— The following passage from the VādhS. contains the same elements. The main difference is that in the VādhS. the period of twelve days does not play a role. Moreover Brahman (the neuter form, though referred to as "he" in my translation) does not stand above Prajāpati there.

VādhS. 3, 21: Prajāpati thus offered that agnihotra. By that he became successful; by that he satiated all beings, attained all what he has now attained, and won the world of heaven. Going to heaven he transferred it (the agnihotra) to his sons, the gods. The gods offered it, they satiated all beings by that, they attained all what they have now attained, and they won the world of heaven. <Going to heaven they transferred it to the seers. Thes eers ....>. Going to heaven the seers transferred it to their sons, the brahmins. The brahmins thus partake of this agnihotra. He who knowing thus offers the agnihotra, becomes successful, satiates[3] all beings, attains all he can attain, and wins the world of heaven.

NOTES

[1] I.e. the agnihotra of twelve days to be performed after the establishment of the fires (*agnyādhāna*) described in the preceding passage (J.B I, 26–36).

[2] Read *evaṃ* or *enad* instead of *enaṃ*.

[3] On the satiating (*tarpaṇa*) in the agnihotra see Section 17.

2 *The primeval agnihotra and creation*

— This section continues the myths of the preceding one as far as the Yajurvedic texts KS., MS. and TB. are concerned.

KS. 6, 2: He (i.e. Agni, who after the first offering by Prajāpati keeps fleeing from him) did not stop. He ran forth. He (P.) offered into (or: to) him. From that oblation man was born. He did not stop. He ran forth. He offered into him. From that oblation the horse was born. Therefore, when they are seen in front at night, man and horse are, so to say, hardly distinguishable from each other. He did not stop. He ran forth. He offered into him. From that oblation the cow was born, the sheep was born, the goat was born, barley was produced, rice was produced. From these seven oblations these seven domesticated (and cultivated) animals (and crops) came into existence. He did not stop. He ran forth. He offered into him. From that oblation spring came into existence, the rainy season came into existence, autumn came into existence, winter came into existence. When the thirteenth oblation was ready to be offered he (A.) became afraid. He returned to him (P.). He entered into his hands. Therefore there is no hair inside the hands.[1] For that is the receptacle of the fire. Therefore fire is produced after having been churned out by means of the hands. Therefore, when someone is struck, he stretches out his hands.[2] He looks for protection to Agni then. The presence of cattle depends on the presence of Agni. The presence of Agni depends on the presence of cattle. Cattle come to him and he comes to cattle who knows thus. He (P.) poured that oblation into the water. From this the cool season was produced. Therefore it is the most awful one, for it was neither produced from something offered, nor from something unoffered. That oblation started to burn the water. Thereupon the water became a thunderbolt (i.e. a cause of destruction) for Agni. Therefore, if one sprinkles water (in the ritual), one should not let the water come into contact with the fire. If one should do so, one would sacrifice with a (sacrifice/fire)[3] that has been struck. He (P.) placed the oblation in the plants. Therefore, even if the plants are not anointed (with ghee), they light up[4] (in the fire). From the plants the mammals (get their subsistence), from the mammals progeny (is born).[5] Therefore winter freezes the butter now (or: here). Therefore in winter dry wood has to be burnt. He (P.) gave to Agni his favourite speciality (*priyaṃ dhāma*).[6] To him who knows thus, he (Agni) gives food. He becomes an eater of food.

— Compare the version of the MS., which begins as follows:

MS. 1, 8, 1: 115.18 f.: From that oblation man was produced. He offered a second (oblation). From this the horse was produced. Therefore the horse has teeth in both jaws, for he was produced directly after man.

— The rest of the passage (including the nightly confusion of man and horse) agrees with the KS. About the thirteenth oblation the MS. states:

MS. 1, 8, 2: 116.8 f.: The thirteenth oblation was ready to be offered, when the cool season was produced. Therefore this one among the seasons is violent (or: unappeased) and rough. For it came into existence from something which had not been offered; it was produced from something unoffered.

— Obviously the version of the MS. is secondary. The cool season is produced from an oblation which is poured out nowhere. It is only much later (MS. 1, 8, 2: 117.5) that Prajāpati is said to have poured out the oblation into the water. The composition has become disturbed. The text first continues with an addition on the order of the creations:

MS. 1, 8, 2: 116.10 f.: As to this people in esoteric debates (i.e. the participants in *brahmodyas*) say: "Were the seasons produced first, or were the animals?" One should say: "The seasons as well as the animals". For both were created together.

— Agni's returning into Prajāpati's hands is mentioned in the MS. without any argumentation. The result of the myth of Prajāpati's pursuit of Agni is even flatter than in its source, the version of the KS. In fact the successive creations are essential; the story of the myth becomes more and more an expedient.

MS. 1, 8, 2: 116.12 ff.: He (A) again entered him (P..) here (i.e. in his hands). The hand is the part of the arm which forms a receptacle. Therefore the fire hardly burns (you) here. If someone who is beaten stretches out his hands, (he does so because) he seeks protection with Agni. Cattle obtain to Agni, Agni obtains to cattle. Cattle obtain to him and he obtains to cattle who knows thus. As to this Nārada used to say: "If one perceives a cow lying down on the earth, one may think she is dead, if one does not know better". For they enter the fire and the fire enters them. Therefore cows (are able to) come near to the fire during all seasons (*ṛtūn*). For they are not without (*ṛte*) Agni. Because he found (*avindata*) the cows right after his birth (*jātas*), therefore Jātavedas (Agni) is called Jātavedas. He (P.) poured that (oblation) into the water.

— The rest of the passage (MS. 1, 8, 2: 117. 5 ff.) agrees with the KS. A shorter version is found in the TB:

TB. 2, 1, 2, 4–6: From that oblation he created man. He offered a second one and created the horse. He offered a third one and created the cow. He offered a fourth one and created the sheep. He offered a fifth one and created the goat. Agni feared: "He obtains me by means of the oblations".[7] He again entered Prajāpati. To him Prajāpati said: "Be born (again)!" (He said:) "What will be my share, if I shall be born?" "To thee (in thee) there will be offered[8] here". It was the agnihotra which he got as his share in compensation for his birth. Therefore it (i.e. this ritual) is called agnihotra.

— This version condenses the passages of the KS. and the MS. The explanation of the name of the rite is quite different in the two mentioned texts, where, moreover, it occurs in a different context (see Section 1.1). Prajāpati's second libation (*uttarāhuti*), which forms the counterpart of the second libation poured out in the usual agnihotra ritual, is also mentioned in the myth of VādhS. 3, 19. Again an animal (i.c. the cow) is produced from that offering. However, no further creation is mentioned, and the passage takes a completely different turn. Since the text on the production of the cow from the second oblation is corrupt, I omit the translation here. So much is clear that Prajāpati (or Agni) asks where the oblation has disappeared. In the answer "she went" (*agād*) occurs, which occasions the "etymology" of the word cow (*gaus*).

NOTES

[1] For a different application of this motif see Section 1, 1 (KS. and ŚB.), where it occurs together with an explanation of the baldness of the forehead. Some versions, however, have omitted it there.

[2] Read *hanyamāno* for *hanyamānau* and *pragṛhṇāti* for *pratigṛhṇāti*. Compare the version of the MS.

[3] The version of the MS. is in favour of the ellipsis of "sacrifice".

[4] For my translation of *rebh-* (according to M.-W.'s dictionary "to crackle (as fire)") see Caland, *AO* 10 (1932), p. 320 who criticizes Keith's rendering ("snoring") of ŚāṅkhB. 17, 9 *ārephantaḥ* (to be read *ārebhantaḥ* according to Caland). He translates "lighted up" (by the flaming fires), "glistening". See also Mayrhofer's etymological dictionary on the twofold aspect of this root which on the one hand denotes sound and on the other hand glimmering.

[5] This passage represents a reflection of the current water doctrine (see

1.3, n. 3). I translate *paśavaḥ* by "mammals" in this passage where the term even includes human beings.

[6] See author, *JB. I, 1–65*, p. 46 f.

[7] The text of the Bibl. Ind. edition, reading *āhutībhir vai tam āpnotīti*, cannot be correct. The Ānandāśrama ed. correctly reads *māpnotīti*.

[8] The form *hūyātai* is a "third person sing. subjunctive passive of *hu*" (Dumont, p. 341, n. 9).

3 *The connection of Sūrya (and Vāyu) with the Agni-hotra. The origin of the milk oblation*

— In the preceding sections Prajāpati and Agni played the most important roles. Prajāpati, because he is indispensable in those myths which trace the origin of a rite (or something else) back to the primeval sphere; Agni, since the rite, as its name says, is primarily concerned with this god. Of the fundamental importance of the sun for this sacrifice we have had a glimpse in Section 1.1 (Prajāpati offers his eye=sun; see also n. 19). Moreover, in that section the ŚB. already referred to the other two members of the triad, Vāyu and Sūrya. All this is worked out in the following passages. One may also observe that the Agni-Prajāpati myths seem to be connected more closely with the evening performance of the actual agnihotra. For the morning performance the sun is more important. VādhS. 3, 29 refers to both aspects of the agnihotra in a passage in which Prajāpati takes night and day, which robbed his creatures (i.e. time making people die), as his food.

3.1. *The milk-oblation is the seed of the sun (or the sun itself).*

KS. 6, 3: 51.9–14: Sūrya (the sun) and Agni were in the same receptacle (*yoni*).[1] Thereupon Sūrya rose upwards. He lost his seed. Agni received it with an iron receptacle. He made it stick (burn) (to the iron pan). While it was burning (to the pan), he transferred it to the cow. It (became) this milk. Therefore fresh milk which is still warm, sticks to the untinned iron vessel. When[2] one performs the agnihotra with milk, then one offers yonder sun. For this is the agnihotra (oblation).[3] Rice is the milk of the bull. The bull is yonder sun. If one performs the agnihotra with rice-gruel, one offers yonder sun. For this is the agnihotra (oblation).

— This passage i.a. explains why the agnihotra is usually interpreted in its esoteric symbolism as the entering of the sun into the fire (at night) and its rising out of the fire (at dawn). The beginning of the parallel version of the MS. is quite identical. On the identity of milk and Sūrya's seed it has the following digression:

MS. 1, 8, 2: 117.16–19: It (i.e. the milk) should not be boiled too much. One would boil the seed dry.[4] If one should let it boil over, someone fond of drinking would be born in one's progeny. The seed of yonder sun is offered here. Uncooked it (would be) unfit for being offered. It should be offered at the moment when it is rising. For that is cooked, sacrificially pure, a mixture (i.e. a compromise of boiling well and boiling not too much) and (as such, i.e. as every mingling or biological couple) procreative.

— Above (Section 1.1, n. 19) a translation has been given of TB. 2, 1, 6, 4 ff. In the context that passage rather abruptly follows on another myth on the origin of the agnihotra in which besides Prajāpati and Agni, Vāyu and Āditya also play a role. In that preceding myth the function of the cow and her mythical origin are essential, as appears from the fact that the following passage (2, 1, 7 and 8) refers to milk and milking. As some sort of afterthought 2, 1, 6, 4 ff. was added. The starting-point was the participation of more gods than Agni (and Prajāpati). TB. 2, 1, 6, 5 concludes with: "For yonder sun is the agnihotra (milk)" (since Prajāpati had offered the sun into Agni out of fear for him). The identification of the oblation and the sun also forms the opening of the agnihotra passage in the ŚāṅkhB.

ŚāṅkhB. 2, 1: The agnihotra (milk) is the cauldron of hot milk which is put on the fire (in the Pravargya ritual).[5] Yonder one who gives out heat is that cauldron of hot milk. Him he gratifies thereby.

— In the context of the discussion on the right time for the performance of the agnihotra and esoteric speculations about the meaning of the rite, ŚB. also identifies the agnihotra (i.e. probably the oblation) with the sun:

ŚB. 2, 3, 1, 1: The agnihotra (oblation) is Sūrya (the sun). Because he rose in front (*agre*) of that offering the sun is the *agnihotra*.[6]

— The following context does not only refer to the time of the performance, but also to the sun's entrance into the fire as an embryo.

NOTES

[1] Often *yoni* means "lair, abode" or "receptacle" rather than "birth-place, womb". Here it may mean "abode", but below it is definitely "receptacle". In the version of the MS. the *yoni* in which Sūrya and Agni originally were living together is the same as the *yoni* with which Agni receives Sūrya's seed.

[2] I have adopted Caland's emendation (*WZKM* 26, p. 123) which replaces *ayaḥ pātram* by *ayaḥpātram* and *tat payasāgnihotraṃ juhoti* by *yat payasā* ... Caland, referring to KS. 6, 7: 56.20, translates *krūḍayati* by "gerinnen machen, dick machen".

[3] The identification of the sun and the agnihotra oblation was already made by KS. 6, 1: 50.1 and is quite current in the brāhmaṇas. See e.g. JB. 1, 7–8; VādhS. 3, 24. The falling of the sun or the seed of the sun into Agni, which here is regarded as the primeval agnihotra, represents a duplication of the other aetiological myth at the beginning of the agnihotra section (Prajāpati's offering). These inconsistencies are not unusual in the brāhmaṇas and need not point to interpolations or different layers of the text.

[4] Cf. KS. 6, 7: 56.19 f. and ŚB. 2, 3, 1, 14 f. (in the section on the heating of the milk: 6.3). See also ĀpŚS. 6, 6, 1. In the ŚB. the milk is Agni's seed.

[5] The homology of the agnihotra milk and the hot milk (*gharma*) of the Pravargya ritual (on which see van Buitenen, *The Pravargya*, Poona 1968) also occurs (in a different passage of the agnihotra section) at TB. 2, 1, 3, 2; KS. 6, 3: 52.9 and MS. 1, 8, 3: 118.12.

[6] Here *agre* is used in an 'etymology'. Probably this implied for the Vedic insiders a reference to the earlier 'etymology' of ŚB. 2, 2, 4, 2, where *agre* occurred with a different meaning and was connected with Agni (who should be called Agri). Shifting the attention from Agni to Sūrya, the ŚB. adapts its etymology of the agnihotra in favour of the sun. Even for a brāhmaṇa, this etymology would be too obscure without the knowledge of the other, more extensive passage. In my translation of the 'etymology' I have followed Eggeling. Or should *āhuter* be taken as an ablative and *agre* as meaning "in the beginning"? See also 4, n. 44.

3.2 *The agnihotra is offered to Sūrya.*

TB. 2, 1, 2, 6: About this (oblation)[1] which was about to be offered, Āditya (the sun) said: "Do not offer (it). This (should be) for both of us". Agni said: "How will they (i.e. the human beings) offer it to both of us?" He said: "In the evening they must offer it to thee, in the morning to me". Therefore there is offered to Agni at night and to Sūrya at daybreak.[2]

— The text continues (2, 1, 2, 7) by stating that the night is sacred to Agni, the day to Indra (here regarded as the sun) in connection with the view that there should not be offered before sunrise (otherwise both performances would be sacred to Agni). See also ŚāṅkhB. 2, 1 (continuing the passage of the preceding section):

ŚāṅkhB. 2, 1: He offers in the evening and in the morning. To Agni in the evening, to Sūrya in the morning. The day is sacred to Sūrya, the night to Agni. Thereby he gratifies day and night right from their beginnings.

NOTES

[1] This refers to the end of the preceding myth, which describes how Agni, after having re-entered his creator Prajāpati, is willing to be born again on the condition that he receives an (agnihotra) oblation. For the construction of the accusative see Oertel, *Syntax of Cases*, p. 85 f.

[2] This appears from the formulas recited on those occasions. The evening formula *agnir jyotir jyotir agniḥ* (or *agnau* instead of *agniḥ*) plays a role in Section 1.1. In the morning formula *agniḥ* is replaced by *sūryaḥ*. The present section is mainly concerned with the morning agnihotra, whereas 1.1 seems to focus attention primarily on the evening agnihotra.

3.3 *Participation of Āditya (sun) and Vāyu (wind) in Agni's oblation (agnihotra).*

TB. 2, 1, 6, 1–4: Prajāpati desired: "May an animated being (*ātmanvat*) be born to me". He offered (an oblation). To him an animated being was born (viz. the triad) Agni, Vāyu and Āditya. They said: "Prajāpati has offered (thinking:) 'May an animated being be born to me'. To him we have been born. To us an animated being should be born (as well)". They offered (oblations): Agni the breaths (or vital powers, *prāṇāḥ*), Vāyu the body, Āditya the faculty of seeing (or: eye).[1] Out of their offering a cow[2] came into existence. They contended about its milk (saying:) "It was produced out of my offering, (no) out of mine". They went to put their case before Prajāpati.[3] Āditya said to Agni: "If either of us should win, let it be in common for us". Prajāpati said: "Which offered what (oblation) and which what (other)?". "I have offered the *prāṇāḥ* (breaths, vital powers, lifebreaths, life)" (said) Agni, "I the body" (said) Vāyu, "I the sight (or eye)" (said) Āditya. "He who offered the *prāṇāḥ*, out of his offering she was produced. Since she was produced out of Agni's offering, therefore the agnihotra is called Agnihotra.[4] The agnihotra is the cow. He who knows thus, that the agnihotra is the cow, makes Agni amply furnished with outbreathing and inbreathing. He does not lose his breaths (or: life) who knows thus. To both of them (i.e. Agni and Āditya who has assured himself of a share before) Vāyu said: "Give me a share along with (you)". They said: "In that, after having put (the milk) on the gārhapatya fire, they run toward the āhavanīya fire, thereby they gratify you". Therefore, after having put (the milk) on the gārhapatya, he runs (with the oblation which has been ladled out) to the āhavanīya. Thereby he gratifies Vāyu.[5]

ŚB. 2, 2, 4, 10–18: Thereupon[6] those heroes among the gods, viz. Agni, the one who ventilates (Vāyu) and Sūrya, were born. He who thus knows these heroes among the gods, to him a hero is born. Now these (gods) said: "We depend on (*anu*)[7] our father Prajāpati. Well, let us therefore create what must depend on us". Having demarcated (a place) they praised with a *gāyatrī* stanza without the sound *hiṅ*. What they demarcated (i.e. the demarcation itself), was the ocean[8] and the (demarcated) place where the praise was sung (i.e. the *āstāva*), was the earth. Having sung the praises they went out (of the demarcation) toward the east, saying: "We (will) come back". (They came back, and) behold,[9] a cow (had) come into existence. She looked up at them and uttered the sound *hiṅ*. The gods knew: "This is the sound *hiṅ* of the ritual chant (*sāman*)". Before that time[10] their chant was without the sound *hiṅ*. This sound *hiṅ* of the chant was in the cow. Therefore the latter affords livelihood. He affords livelihood who thus knows that this sound *hiṅ* of the chant is in the cow. The gods said: "We have produced something auspicious here by producing the cow, because she is the sacrifice — for without the cow no sacrifice is performed —, and because she is food — for whatever food there is, that is (connected with) the cow. This very (word *go* "cow") is the name of these (cows); it (is the name) of the sacrifice. Therefore one should avoid[11] that (name) saying (instead) "the excellent, the auspicious". For him who, knowing thus, avoids that (name) saying (instead) "the excellent, the auspicious", these (cows) become manifold and the sacrifice inclines to him. Agni set his heart upon her (the cow) (thinking:) "May I become paired with her". He cohabited with her. He poured his seed in her. That became the milk.[12] Therefore it is cooked (i.e. warm) though being in a cow who is uncooked.[13] For it is Agni's seed. Therefore, whether it is in a black or in a red (cow), it is ever white[13] and resplendent like fire. For it is Agni's seed. Therefore it is warm when just milked.[14] For it is Agni's seed. They (the three gods)[15] said: "Come, let us offer this". "To whom of us shall they first offer this?" "To me" said Agni, "to me" said the one that ventilates, "to me" said Sūrya. They did not come to an agreement. Not having come to an agreement they said: "Let us resort[16] to our father Prajāpati. To whom of us he says it must be offered first, to him among us they shall offer it first". Having resorted to father Prajāpati they said: "To whom of us shall they offer this first?" He said: "To Agni. Agni will not fail to (or: will duly)[17] reproduce his own seed and thus you will reproduce yourselves". "Then to you" (he said) to Sūrya; "and whatever he (still) obtains of the (milk which is) being offered, that (belongs) to the one that ventilates (Vāyu)". This (is offered) to them even here (i.e. in this agnihotra ritual) nowadays in the same way. They offer to Agni in the evening, to Sūrya in the morning, and whatever he (still) obtains of the (milk which is) being offered, that (belongs) to the one that ventilates. By offering the gods engendered the same procreation which is theirs now,[18] they won the same supremacy which is theirs now. Agni won this world, Vāyu the intermediate space, Sūrya heaven. He who, knowing thus, offers the agnihotra, engenders the same procreation which they engendered then, wins the same supremacy which they won then. He shares the same world with them who, knowing thus, offers the agnihotra. Therefore the agnihotra should be offered.

NOTES

[1] The identification of eye and sun is quite current and obvious. It is doubtful whether the three gods offer their own eye, body and lifebreaths, as Dumont assumes in his translation. They offer something which becomes one of the constituents of the body of the cow. Vāyu, the god of the wind, is mostly connected with space between heaven and earth and consequently provides the cow with a body, i.e. with space on the microcosmic level. The homology of fire and *prāṇāḥ* is well-known from the prāṇāgnihotra and its startingpoints See *Agn. and Prāṇāgn.*, ch. III.

[2] For the creation of the cow out of a second (agnihotra) oblation see also VādhS. 3, 19. However, it is Prajāpati's own offering there.

[3] For this current expression, its syntactical variations and its interpretation see Oertel, *Zu den Kasusvariationen in der vedischen Prosa* [*SbBAW*, 1937/38], p. 32 f.

[4] For a different explanation of the name *agnihotra* see Section 1. 1 (KS. 6, 1).

[5] Midway between the gārhapatya and the āhavanīya fires the priest stops, lets the ladle sink and raises it again with the formula *vātāya tvā* (ĀpŚS. 6, 8, 10) or *vāyave tvā* (MŚS. 1, 6, 1, 32) "For the Wind thee". Vāyu (Wind) is connected with the space between heaven and earth, the *antarikṣa*. The gārhapatya represents earth, the āhavanīya heaven. Walking from earth to heaven and stopping in between, the priest honours Vāyu. Oertel, *Syntax of Cases*, p. 313 misunderstood the ritual and consequently the construction of this sentence, which does not contain a disjunct gerund.

[6] The preceding passage deals with Prajāpati's primeval sacrifice.

[7] Or: "we come after". Often, however, *anu* refers to agreement, conformity and dependance upon something or someone, rather than to succession. See also author, "Vedic *anuṣṭhu* and *anuṣṭh(u)yā*", *IIJ* 16 (1974), p. 1–17.

[8] In ancient India the ocean is often regarded as the border and limit of the earth. Here the ritual of the gods has a cosmic dimension. Cf. Prajāpati's cosmic agnihotra (Section 12).

[9] For this translation, which supplies something between brackets, see Delbrück, *Altind. Syntax*, p. 184. Eggeling's rendering does not correctly account for the exclamation *ed* (followed by an accusative and as a rule preceded by a verb of motion). For extensive literature on *ed* see Minard, *Trois Énigmes* II, 759–760.

[10] *purā tataḥ*. Eggeling's translation is untenable, as was demonstrated by Caland, *BSOS* 6, p. 299.

[11] Otherwise Eggeling, whose rendering ("repeat") of *pari-har-* does not seem to be correct in this context.

[12] Cf. Section 3.1 on the milk being Sūrya's seed (according to the version of the MS.).

[13] See Aufrecht's edition of the Ṛgveda Saṃhitā (1877)[2], p. XVII f. on the motif of white and warm milk in coloured and uncooked (raw) cows. More

parallels were collected by Geldner in a note on his translation of ṚS. 1, 62, 9. Oertel, *Syntax of Cases*, p. 148 refers to TS. 6, 5, 6, 4.

[14] On *prathamadugdha* not meaning "first milked" (Eggeling) see Minard, *Trois Énigmes* I, 551 *a*; II, 235 *a*. Wackernagel-Debrunner, *Altind. Gr.* III, p. 404 translates "sobald als gemolken", which does not fit here.

[15] According to Eggeling "the men" speak these words. The middle voice favours our interpretation. In the beginning the gods offer to each other and have to establish the order. The human beings later adopt this sacrifice together with the order of the deities.

[16] Or: return (to father Prajāpati who once had created them). However, the usual expression for having resort to Prajāpati is *prajāpatiṃ prati praśnam i* (see Caland, Introd. to ŚB. Kāṇva rec., p. 61).

[17] On *anuṣṭhyā* (which Eggeling translates by "forthwith") see author, "Vedic *anuṣṭhu* and *anuṣṭh(u)yā*", *IIJ* 16.(1974), p. 1–17 (for the present place see p. 14).

[18] Minard, *Trois Énigmes* II, 55 *a* is right in severely criticizing Eggeling's translation.

— The oldest texts (the KS. and the MS.) do not pay much attention to this point:

KS. 6, 5: 54.4 f.: He should offer the agnihotra in the evening when the sun has just[1] set, in the morning just before sunrise.

— The function of the evening and morning part of the performance, rather than the exact time of the performance, is most important in that context. Compare the version of MS. (in a slightly different passage):

MS. 1, 8, 7: 125.9: The agnihotra should be offered at nightfall and in the morning after it has become bright.

— These texts, though referring to the twofold character of the agnihotra (evening performance sacred to Agni, morning performance connected with the sun), do not contain an extensive discussion of the implications of offering before or after sunset and sunrise (MS. 1, 8, 7: 125. 10 only states: "They say: 'Whose agnihotra they do not offer at nightfall (*pradoṣam*), his agnihotra falls away (i.e. counts for nothing)'"; then follows an expiation). This situation changes in the later texts, in which a discussion of the exact time for the performance develops:

TB. 2, 1, 2, 7–12: The night belongs to Agni, the day to Indra.[2] If one should offer at daybreak before sunrise, both (i.e. the morning as well as the evening agnihotra) would be sacred to Agni. He offers at daybreak after sunrise. Thus, there is offered to Agni at night and to Sūrya at daybreak. During the night the creatures procreate. In the day-time they secure a good position. In that he offers at night, thereby he procreates. After sunrise he offers at daybreak. Thereby he secures a good position for himself. Prajāpati desired: "May I produce offspring". He discovered that this agnihotra formed a couple (*mithunam*).[3] He offered it after the sun had risen. The one (libation he offered) with the formula (*yajuṣā*) (recited aloud), the other silently (*tūṣṇīm*). Thereupon he reproduced himself. He for whom knowing thus they offer the agnihotra after sunrise, reproduces himself. And moreover this is like going by day and thereby discerning (where you go).[4] Now they also say: "If two virtuous men stay in the house of a man, and if he honours one of the two and not the other,[5] then he offends both people staying (there)". (...)[6] If he should offer at daybreak after sunrise, this would be like bringing food to a guest who has departed, to a guest-room which is empty.[7]

"What does become"[8] they say "of something which is not noticed by the one to whom they bring it?" If, therefore, he offers about the time of daybreak, it is right. And it is like offering food to someone at daybreak who is just wishing for it.[9]

— The original point of view of the TB. (which at the end of the passage is criticized and replaced by a compromise between the first view and its criticism)[10] is elaborated in the AB. The idea that the day- and the night-aspect of the agnihotra should be distinguished by offering after sunrise (and after sunset) is also found in the VādhS.:

AB. 5, 29–30: Vṛṣaśuṣma Vāṭāvata Jātukarṇya said: "We shall say the following to the gods: 'The agnihotra which used to be offered on both parts of the day,[11] is now offered on only one part of the day'."[11] A girl who was possessed by a Gandharva[12] said the same: "We shall say the following to the fathers: ...". — This agnihotra is offered on one part of the day, if he offers in the evening after sunset and in the morning before sunrise. It is, however, offered on both parts of the day, if he offers in the evening after sunset and in the morning after sunrise (.....)[13] Night and day are the two wheels of the year; (i.e.) by means of them one reaches here the distance of one year. If he offers before sunrise, this would be like going with a wheel on one side. But if he offers after sunrise, this would be like swiftly reaching the aim of a journey with a wheel on both sides (....)[14] The rising sun joins its rays with the āhavanīya fire (which then also is kindled and rises). Offering before sunrise would be like giving the breast to a child or a calf that is still unborn. Offering after sunrise, however, would be like giving the breast to a child or a calf that is (just) born. And corresponding to the fact that this (breast) is given (to the sun-child) the food of both worlds is given to him[15] both from this world and from yonder. If he offers before sunrise, this would be like presenting something to a man or to an elephant which have not stretched out their hand (trunk).[16] Offering after sunrise would be like presenting something to a man or to an elephant after the hand (trunk) has been stretched out. Having taken him up with this very trunk (arm) it (he)[17] places him in heaven who, knowing thus, offers after sunrise. Therefore he should offer after sunrise. The rising sun, forsooth, brings forth (*praṇayati*)[18] all beings. Therefore they call him the Prāṇa (cosmic Breath).[19] There is offered here in the (or: to the) breath[20] by him who, knowing thus, offers after sunrise. He offers in truth[21] by speaking truth who offers in the evening after sunset and in the morning after sunrise. He offers in the evening with *bhūḥ, bhuvaḥ, svar, Om.* The light is Agni, Agni is the light" and in the morning with "*bhūḥ, bhuvaḥ, svar, Om.* The light is Sūrya, Sūrya is the light". By him speaking truth there is offered in truth who, knowing thus, offers after sunrise. Therefore there should be offered after sunrise. About this there is recited the following ritualistic verse:[22] "Every morning they speak untruth who offer the agnihotra before sunrise, since they speak of something which should be mentioned by day (viz. the formula) "The light is Sūrya", while it is not (yet) daytime. For them there is no light then.

VādhS. 3, 26: The representation of night and day is formed by the agnihotra. Now some people here offer the evening oblation in the form of the day, and in the same form of the day the morning oblation.[23] Thus is done by some people here. But some (others) offer the evening oblation in the form of the night, and in the same form of the night the morning oblation.[23] Thus is done by some people here. But those who know it, say: "Darkness is evil. He should offer the evening oblation before the arrival of darkness. And in the morning .....[24] He who knows thus, becomes free from evil in this and yonder world".

— The VādhS. (just as the TB.) afterwards drops its own point of view and opines that neither clearly before nor clearly after sunrise there should be offered. Both the aspect of day and the aspect of night are wrong.

VādhS. 3, 27: Some declare afterwards:[25] "The world named Prajāpati's Shining,[26] in that I place thee together with the sacrificer". They say: "What is this world named Prajāpati's Shining?" They offer immediately after sunset in the evening, and before sunrise in the morning. That (moment) is the world named Prajāpati's Shining.[27] He who, knowing thus, offers the agnihotra, wins the world named Prajāpati's Shining. — The representation of all which is embraced is also formed by the agnihotra; the representation (i.e. characteristic) of offspring and cattle is that of embrace.[28] Now day and night also are death. These two do not reach that deity, the Sun. That deity rises over these two, while separating them; separating them he goes down afterwards. And death does not reach him who, knowing thus, offers.

— The treatment of this subject in the ŚāṅkhB. partly repeats the version of the AB., but it rejects offering after sunrise and ultimately agrees with the last view of the TB. and the VādhS. It also agrees with the JB. on some points.

ŚāṅkhB. 2, 9: "Should there be offered after sunrise or before sunrise?" they question. He who offers after sunrise, thus gives hospitality (in the form of presenting food) to the great god who has already departed. But he who offers before sunrise gives hospitality to the great god when he is (still) near. Therefore there should be offered before sunrise.[29] On the other hand Vṛṣaśuṣma Vātāvata, one of the men of old, (once) said about this, when he was lying down due to old age and had observed that both offerings were made in the night-time: "Do they perform both offerings in the night-time?" "Yes, indeed, in the night-time".[30] He said: "Having gone to yonder world we will tell this to the fathers, and they will not have confidence in it.[31] The same agnihotra which used to be offered here on both parts of the day, is now offered on only one part of the day". A girl who was possessed by a Gandharva said the same: "Do they perform both offerings in the night?" "Yes, indeed, in the night". She said:[32] "...". He should offer at the twilight. Night and day are an ocean (with low and high tide) which carries away everything. The two twilights are the fords where one may cross the water. Even as a stretch of water[33] may be crossed along two fordable places, so it is when one offers at twilight. Moreover night and day are a divine army[34] which is on the march in order to destroy. The two twilights are its wings. Even as it may quickly accomplish its march (campaign) with the two wings, so it is when one offers at twilight. Night and day are also the arms of death which form an enclosure. Even as someone (i.c. Death) who is about to grasp[35] with two enclosing arms, may be evaded along the opening (between the two arms), so it is when one offers at twilight.

With regard to this Kauṣītaki's own words[36] were: "After sunset, but before darkness, that is the time he should offer in the evening. That marks the path to the gods.[37] Having taken that (path) he safely reaches the world of heaven. Before sunrise, but after the darkness has been dispelled, that is the time he should offer at dawn. That marks the path to the gods. Having taken that (path) he safely reaches the world of heaven. But if he offers the agnihotra (at a time) different from that, the (dogs) Dark and Dappled[38] tear to pieces his agnihotra. Dappled is the day, Dark the night. If he offers about midnight, Dark tears to pieces his agnihotra. If he offers in the full daylight, Dappled tears into pieces his agnihotra. Therefore, forsooth, every time when he may offer, he should have in view the success of the offering".[39]

JB. 1, 5–6: ...[40] If one is desirous of heaven (one should offer the agnihotra bearing in mind the following verse:) "Two impassable, wide, large oceans come and withdraw in a revolving, alternating way like two footprints on a path". Night and day are the two impassable oceans. Those who offer by night enter the ocean of night and those who offer after sunrise the ocean of day. There is a crossing of these two just as if there were a ford (?) or a connecting causeway (viz. the moment) when the sun has set, but before darkness (and the moment) when the light appears, but before sunrise.

— The JB. continues with an identical description for evading the two dogs Dark and Dappled (cf. the ŚāṅkhB.). Then comes a passage which connects this very moment between night and day with Prajāpati (cf. VādhS. 3, 27 above):

Moreover the light[41] at these (moments) is Savitṛ. Savitṛ is Prajāpati and Prajāpati (is identical with) all the gods. Thus there is offered by him to Prajāpati, to all the gods. That is why this agnihotra is sacred to Prajāpati. When here at daybreak the light appears, in this very appearance of light[41] Prajāpati created the creatures (...) (JB. 1, 6:) Moreover night and day meet here[42] facing this point (*evaṃmukham*). The agnihotra (oblation) is food. Thus he places nourishment before the mouth (*mukhataḥ*) of night and day. In the same way they meet again at daybreak. The agnihotra (oblation) is food. Having thus placed nourishment before the mouth of night and day he escapes from those two dyings in yonder world (*punarmṛtyu*, lit. "repeated death") which are night and day.

— The ŚB., using the same argumentation as the TB. and the ŚāṅkhB., prescribes offering before sunrise. Strange enough, it does not mention the counter-argument put forward by the (definitely older) AB., and consequently does not contain the compromise at which the TB. and the ŚāṅkhB. (cf. the VādhS. and the JB.) arrive.

ŚB. 2, 3, 1. 1–9: Now the agnihotra is the sun. Because it came up from that offering[43] (*āhuter*) in the beginning (*agre*), [44] therefore the agnihotra is the sun. That there is offered in the evening after sunset (that is done by people wishing:) "that I may offer it[45] while this one (i.e. the sun) is (still) here on earth". That there is offered in the morning before sunrise (... etc.).

— The next paragraphs (2, 3, 1, 3–6) deal with interpretations of the agnihotra and will be included in an other section. The concept of the agnihotra as producing the (embryonic) sun indeed excludes offering after sunrise. The text continues with a discussion of the time for taking out the fire from the gārhapatya hearth to the āhavanīya hearth (a preparatory action to be distinguished from the actual offering):

(2, 3, 1, 7–9) If he takes (the fire for) the āhavanīya out (of the gārhapatya) before sunset — these rays of light are all the gods[46] and the light which is above[47] is Prajāpati or Indra — in that case[48] now all the gods come to his house, when he offers the agnihotra. If they come to someone's (fire) before it has been taken out, then they turn away from that (fire); and that becomes unsuccessful here for him from which the gods turn away.[49] And after this failure people, both he who really knows (what has taken place) and he who does not,[50] say of him: "The sun has set on his (fire) before it had been taken out". But[51] if he takes out the āhavanīya before sunset, then it is, as if he would honour a distinguished person who will come to pay a visit, by putting (his) room in order.[52] If they (i.e. all the gods) come to someone's (fire) which has been taken out, they enter his āhavanīya and they settle in his āhavanīya. When he offers in the evening after sunset, he thereby offers to them at the moment when they have entered the fire. And when he offers in the morning before sunrise, he thereby offers to them before they have left. Therefore Āsuri said: "We consider the agnihotra of those who offer after sunrise to be interrupted[53]. It is like taking food to an empty guest-chamber".[54]

— The next paragraphs (ŚB. 2, 3, 1, 10–12), though mentioning this offering before sunrise, do not seem to form part of a discussion on this subject. ŚB. 2, 3, 3, 9 mentions (in the context of an esoteric interpretation of the agnihotra) the time of the performance (after sunset; before sunrise). See Section 13.4.

NOTES

[1] Minard, *Trois Énigmes* II, 592 *a* prefers to interpret *amnas* as "à l'insu" and "en secret" and he translates: "C'est en secret, une fois le soleil évanoui, qu'on offrira le soir l'Agnihotra". Whatever the correct etymology of *amnas* may be, Minard's interpretation of this passage does not make sense. I follow Caland (note on his translation of ĀpŚS. 6, 4, 6).

[2] Here Indra represents the sun. On Indra as sun see *JB. I, 1–65*, p. 37, n. 12. Cf. also Sections 6, 15, n. 14; 16, n. 14.

[3] The couple does not only consist of the two libations (the one accompanied with a recited formula, *yajuṣā*, the other with a silent one, *tūṣṇīm*), but also of the twofold aspect of the agnihotra produced by offering after sunrise and after sunset (the day and the night agnihotra).

[4] Should a 'wordplay' be assumed on the two roots *pra-jan-* (*prajanayati* "to procreate"; *prajāyate* "to be born, reproduced") and *pra-jñā-* (*prajānāti* "to know")?

[5] This means that by offering before sunrise and after sunset only Agni is honoured. The image of the guest is quite current in these discussions on the right time for the performance of the agnihotra.

[6] A long passage which does not exclusively deal with the right time for the performance has been left out here and is translated in other sections.

[7] The own point of view is criticized and ultimately abandoned. A later addition may be assumed here. For the argumentation against offering after sunrise compare ŚāṅkhB. 2, 9 (offering to the great god who has gone away); ŚB. 2, 3, 1, 9 (taking food to an empty dwelling) and (in a slightly different context) VādhS. 2, 10 (offering hospitality to someone who has already passed by). See also *JB. I, 1–65*, p. 29 f. on the discussion of the right time for the performance.

[8] Or: "How is it then with that?" they say ... "since he to whom they bring that, does not know about it?" (tr. Dumont).

[9] Dumont translates *prārtha* by "who is ready to set out on a journey" (cf. also M.-W.'s dictionary). I doubt the correctness of this rendering. Perhaps we should translate "who is just ready for it (i.e. for the breakfast)". On emendations for *prārtha* in the (few) other passages where it occurs see Caland's note on PB. 11, 1, 6.

[10] This compromise, which is also found in the ŚāṅkhB. and the JB., means a return to the situation of the KS. and the MS., in which offering about sunrise is advocated. The passage of the AB. lies in between those of the KS. and the MS. on the one hand and the compromise of the mentioned Brāhmaṇas on the other hand. Dumont, p. 342, n. 14 is wrong in assuming that in the TB. *auṣasam* ("about daybreak") should mean "at dawn, before sunrise". He overlooks the compromise at the end of the passage.

[11] For this interpretation of *ubhayedyuḥ* and *anyedyuḥ* see Dumont, *JAOS* 59, p. 425 ff. The two parts of the day (= twenty-four hours) are night and day.

[12] The Gandharvas live inside the possessed (Gonda, *Religionen Indiens* I, p. 100) and have special relations with women, whom they possess before marriage (o.c., p. 101).

[13] A passage which elaborates the conclusion that offering before sunrise (and after sunset) means omitting the daytime is left out here.

[14] Some similar parables have been left out. For the verses which form their central element, see Horsch, *Die Vedische Gāthā- und Śloka-Literatur* (Bern 1966), p. 75 ff.

[15] In *tam asmai pratidhīyamānam* .. *annādyam anu pratidhīyate* I take *asmai* with *pratidhīyate* (as referring to the sacrificer) rather than with *pratidhīyamānam* (which would imply a reference to the datives *kumārāya* and *vatsāya* of the preceding sentence). For this position of the enclitic *asmai* see also Delbrück, *Altind. Syntax*, p. 22.

[16] The word *hasta* means hand as well as trunk.

[17] The image used here refers to the elephant rather than to man. In fact the sun is meant, as appears from the parallel passages.

[18] The verb *praṇayati* originally means "to bring forward, produce, display", which is the actual function of the sun. Here the 'wordplay' with *prāṇa* ("lifebreath"), which brings forth (*pra-*), seems to be essential.

[19] The cosmic Prāṇa as sun occurs already at AV. 11, 4, 12. See also *Agn. and Prāṇāgn.*, ch. IX (p. 271; 276; 278).

[20] This offering in the breath may vaguely refer to the prāṇāgnihotra. See *Agn. and Prāṇāgn.*, ch. III (especially p. 229, n. 27).

[21] The truth sacrifice is connected with the agnihotra. See *Agn. and Prāṇāgn.*, ch. V B. Cf. Section 1.1 (n. 9) and 1.3 (n. 7).

[22] See Horsch, *Gāthā- und Śloka-Literatur*, p. 77.

[23] I.e. they offer before sunset and after sunrise and thereby neglect the twofold (night and day) aspect. Those who offer after sunset and before sunrise are wrong as well.

[24] The meaning of *apāmṛkṣad iti prātar* is not clear. The text is corrupt and it is highly doubtful if *apāmṛkṣad* has any connection with *mṛj-* (Caland: "augenscheinlich Aorist zu *mṛj* oder *mṛś*"). In view of the fact that this text sharply distinguishes the aspects of the night and the day, it may be assumed that the morning performance should take place after sunrise or at least after the disappearance of darkness.

[25] These passages in the VādhS. mostly are *anvākhyānas*, later explanations or added expositions, which are based on the TB. (or related texts) and are introduced by *tad vā idam anvāhuḥ*. In the present case the basic brāhmaṇa on which they give this appended (*anu*) commentary is unknown.

[26] The name is Vibhāt and not Vibhān (Caland's translation), as appears from the accusative Vibhāntam and the parallels. In Keith's translation of TS. 1, 7, 5, 1 (where the same formula occurs in a passage which has no relation to the agnihotra) Vibhān is written; his translation of AB. 7, 26 (again no relation to the agnihotra) correctly has Vibhāt.

[27] I have followed Caland's interpretation (and have translated *vibhāt* by Shining), but one might translate as well "Prajāpati's world named Shining". For the connection between Prajāpati and this particular moment during which the agnihotra may be offered, compare JB. 1, 6.

[28] In the preceding passage of the VādhS. night and day were called the representation (*rūpa*) of the agnihotra, which had a night aspect (after sunset) and a day aspect (after sunrise). Here a different *rūpa* of the agnihotra is introduced. Besides the antithetic aspects of night and day, the agnihotra is also characterized by its two complementary performances. The meaning of *saṃśliṣṭa* is not quite certain in this context. Caland renders it by "zusammenhängend", but "die Gestaltung der Nachkommen und der Kühe ist die des Zusammenhängenden" hardly makes sense. As far as the agnihotra is concerned, the text seems to stress the fact that its performances do not belong to, or represent, night and day (as was put forward before), but, lying in between these two parts of the twenty-four hours, they are embraced (*saṃśliṣṭa*, literal meaning) by them. On the mortal embrace of the arms of death (i.e. night and day) from which one can escape by means of the twilight agnihotra see the ŚāṅkhB. (below). In the case of progeny and cattle being the *rūpa* of *saṃśliṣṭa*, the procreative aspect of the embrace seems to be meant.

[29] Before mentioning the AB.'s arguments against offering before sunrise (and after sunset) the ŚāṅkhB. first rejects offering after sunrise with the hospitality argument used by the TB. (after sunrise food cannot be given to a sun-guest who has departed; perhaps countering the AB.'s earlier argument that food cannot be given to a sun-man who has not stretched out his beam-hands before sunrise). The compromise, which leaves intact the AB.'s and the TB.'s negative arguments (against offering before, respectively after sunrise), comes at the end.

[30] See Caland, *AO* 10 (1932), p. 308 f. who criticizes Keith's interpretation.

[31] Caland, *AO* 10, p. 309 is right in rejecting Keith's "and they will believe us in it" and in reading *enan na śraddhātāro*, but I think that the fathers have no confidence in a sacrifice which is performed on one part of the day, rather than being incredulous of a statement pertaining to that matter.

[32] It may be assumed with Caland (o.c., p. 309) that after "she said" some-

thing (e.g. "Having gone to yonder world we shall tell this . ."; cf. the parallel of the AB.) has fallen out, and that the statement on offering at twillight is not to be attributed to the girl.

[33] The word *samudra*, though mostly translated by "ocean", in fact can hardly refer to such a large concept in this context. Perhaps a rather shallow estuary submitted to low and high tide is meant here. For the comparison cf. the lost Śailāli Brāhmaṇa quoted by ĀpŚS. 6, 4, 7.

[34] Keith renders *devasenā* by "missile of the god". The attribute *adhvaga* ("being on the march") does not favour this interpretation. Quickly accomplishing a march (*adhvan*) does not depend on the possession of wings (which might increase the speed), but on being complete and well-balanced, i.e. not missing one wing. An army with only one of the two wings does not make progress, just as the divine chariot to which ŚāṅkhB. 7, 7 refers in a similar parable. On *deva-* in this compound denoting the mythical, unearthly and metaphorical, rather than the purely divine, see author, "Gab es damals auch Dyumnas. Die Weltentstehung nach dem Jaiminīya Brāhmaṇa", *ZDMG, Supplement* II (*XVIII. Deutscher Orientalistentag*, Lübeck 1972) (1974), p. 293, n. 7.

[35] The metaphor is not wholly successful, since it does not account for two twilights where one may escape. For *parijigrahīṣyan*, which cannot be correct, there should not be read *parijigrahīṣan* (the usual desiderative being *jighṛkṣati*), but *parigrahīṣyan*.

[36] The own words of Kauṣītaki in this Śāṅkhāyana or Kauṣītaki Brāhmaṇa should stress the originality of this compromise at which the TB. also arrived and which agrees remarkably with the VādhS. At least the parallel of JB. 1, 6 is later.

[37] Afterwards the *devayāna* came to denote the path of the liberated in the upaniṣads (in contradistinction to the *pitṛyāna*).

[38] These two dogs are the watchdogs of the god of death. They are called Sārameyas after their mother Saramā.

[39] This means that the performer may never be careless about the exact time of the performance, but should pay attention to the success and possible mishap of his sacrifice whenever (*yadā kadācana*) he offers. I do not follow Caland's interpretation (*AO* 10, p. 309) "He, forsooth, may offer (it) at any time he likes", which does not make sense here. Moreover I do not understand why "by thus translating, the *iti* of the next sentence is better comprehensible ('thinking')". Probably *iti* concludes the quotation of Kauṣītaki's view.

[40] The preceding passage, which has been omitted, deals with the time prescribed for one who is desirous of cattle. For details see author's translation, p. 31 ff.

[41] For the interpretation of *dyumna* as "(appearance of) light" see my paper "Gab es damals auch Dyumnas?", *ZDMG, Supplement* II (1974), p. 292–298. Especially the second occurrence of *dyumna* in this passage seems to exclude the possibility of other translations.

[42] I.e. at the evening performance of the agnihotra, which is taken as a starting-point by the author/teacher of this text. The oral transmission (cf. 1.1, n. 4) is quite evident with *evaṃmukham*.

[43] The primordial offering to which the text refers here is described at ŚB. 2, 2, 4, 6 (. . *tata eṣa udiyāya ya eṣa tapati*).

[44] For this 'etymology' see 3.1, n. 6. Eggeling takes *agre* with a genitive *āhuter* and translates "in front". In my interpretation *āhuter* is an ablative and *agre* has its usual meaning.

[45] For this translation which differs from Eggeling's, see Caland, *WZKM*

26, p. 112 f. (*yaḥ .. juhavāni : qui sacrificem = ut ego sacrificem*). For the syntax of this sentence, which also contains an ellipsis, compare Delbrück, *Altind. Syntax*, p. 533 f. (dealing with the conjunction *yathā* instead of the relative pronoun *ya-* in similar circumstances). Minard, *Trois Énigmes* II, 524 *a* criticizes Caland's interpretation ("Construction en elle-même forcée, et syntaxe sans parallèle, car la relative finale a presqu'entièrement disparu de la prose"). However, his own rendering ("Quand il (= l'adhvaryu) fait l'oblation le soir après le coucher (du soleil), (il se dit): 'Celui qui est l'(Agnihotra), c'est pendant qu'il est ici que je veux faire l'oblation'") does not carry conviction.

[46] Not: "all those gods" (Eggeling). The pronoun *ete* has to be connected with *raśmayaḥ* ("these rays which we see before us"). See Whitney, *AJPh* 3, p. 408. On the identification of all the gods and the rays of light see also ŚB. 12, 4, 4, 6–7 and its parallel JB. 1, 62–63 (dealing with an expiation for the rising or setting of the sun over the āhavanīya, in the case when it has not been taken out in time). Probably *viśve devāḥ* denotes all the gods who come together as rays of light in the supreme god, the sun or Prajāpati, rather than the separate group of the so-called All-gods. My translation of JB. 1, 62–63 has to be corrected on that point. The agnihotra is sacred to all the gods (*vaiśvadeva*; see Sections 6, 15 and 16) and not to the All-gods.

[47] On *param* in this turn of phrase see Minard, *Trois Énigmes* II, 172 *a* and 889, where he observes that it may denote "highest, supreme" as well as "further, i.e. beyond the sun itself". The parallel expression of the Kāṇva recension *yat paraṃ bhāti* seems to me to favour the adopted translation. On the other hand the concept of Prajāpati as the supreme light (= sun) emitting the gods as his rays is attractive in this context.

[48] The syntax of this sentence is rather difficult. Eggeling, who starts a parenthesis after *ete vai viśve devāḥ* ("— the rays, doubtless, are ..") without marking its end, seems to assume a complete anacoluthon. It is, however, doubtful if his interpretation of the opening words *sa yaḥ .. uddharati* ("Then, as to his taking out ..") can be accepted. One would expect *tad yad* instead of *sa yaḥ*. Presumably, *etad* (which Eggeling does not render, if I am not mistaken) introduces the main clause. This may be confirmed by the following particle *u* (see Delbrück, *Altind. Syntax*, p. 508 on "*u* im Nachsatz einer zweigliedrigen Periode").

[49] This construction of the sentence was also proposed by Whitney, *AJPh* 3, p. 408.

[50] On *yaś ca veda yaś ca na* as "an adjunct of the subject of the following *āhuḥ*" see Whitney, o.c., p. 407 f.

[51] This sentence does not present another reason for taking out the fire before sunset (Eggeling's view), but deals with the same motif of the gods entering the house as guests. See also Minard, *Trois Énigmes* II, 442 *a*, who criticizes Eggeling's interpretation.

[52] For the simile compare ŚB. 3, 9, 2, 7; on honouring the guest see Minard, *Trois Énigmes* II, 442 *b*.

[53] *vichinna* means neither "useless" (in a free translation) nor "cut off (from its recipient)" (the literal meaning according to Eggeling). This term denotes the interruption of the sacrifice due to the carelessness of people who now and then omit an agnihotra performance. If one should offer after sunrise, every morning agnihotra would have to be annulled and consequently the agnihotra would in fact be interrupted once every twenty-four hours. See also 1.3, n. 1.

[54] Cf. n. 7 (referring to the close parallel of the TB.).

5 *The ingredient of the oblation (milk)*

— In Section 1.1 the oblation of the primeval agnihotra performed by Prajāpati is not always milk or ghee. The KS. and the MS. mention Prajāpati's eye or the sun (rubbed off from his forehead). According to the TB. that which was wiped off from the forehead was ghee. The ŚB. does not make a decision on this point. It may have been ghee or milk, which is after all a milkproduct. The other versions of Sections 1 and 2 are not explicit about the oblation. Section 3 deals with the milk-oblation and its relation to the sun. The sun or the seed of the sun are identical with the milk-oblation. KS. 6, 3 (see Section 3.1) even identifies the rice-gruel, which may replace the milk, with the sun. In the next section, which deals with the systematic description of the ritual, pouring water on the boiling milk is mentioned. In that passage substitutes for milk as an oblation play a role, such as clarified butter, which does not admit of this pouring on:

KS. 6, 3: 52.10 ff.: If he does not obtain milk, he may offer clarified butter. Of course that does not admit of an additional pouring of water. (..) If he does not obtain milk, he may offer a rice-gruel. Of course that admits of an additional pouring of water.

MS. 1, 8, 3: 118.14 f.: There should (or: may) be offered with melted butter by him who does not pour water on (the oblation). For there is not (or: cannot be) poured on it.

MS. 1, 8, 3: 119.6 f.: There should (or: may) be offered with cooked rice by him who pours on. For this admits of pouring on.

— Milk generally forms the material of the oblation. In the following passages, which have no reference to a primeval agnihotra with milk as its oblation, the reason why milk is offered is given:

ŚāṅkhB. 2, 1: He should offer milk. Milk is the essence of all plants. So he gratifies the fires with all fluids (or essences).[1] Regarding this point they say: "He should offer something of all food which he may eat.[2] All here is Agni's food. So he gratifies the fires with their own food".

ŚB. 2, 3, 1, 10: The life-giving food here is twofold: rooted and rootless. Although both belong to the gods, men subsist on them. Cattle are rootless and plants are rooted. The rootless cattle, having eaten the rooted plants and having drunk water, — then (or: therefrom)[3] this fluid (juice or essence, i.c. the milk) comes into existence.

— The text continues with stating that offering the agnihotra milk means giving to the gods the essence of the food which belongs to them. For this interpretation of the agnihotra see also Section 1.3. Instead of one cow two cows may be milked for the oblation.

TB. 2, 1, 5, 4–5: He should offer the milk of two (cows) for a man who is desirous of cattle. This agnihotra forms a pair.[4] He who knows thus is productive in offspring and cattle through couples. With the first (cow) he milks this earth, with the second yonder world (heaven). Having put (the milk of the first cow) on the fire he pours the other milk on it. By doing so he pours seed in a womb which is fertile.[5]

MS. 1, 8, 6: 122.17 ff.–123.1: They milk two (cows) for the agnihotra. When[6] they milk two (cows), the (heavenly) world[7] of the *agnihotrin* becomes better than (by) the milking of one (cow). The sacrificer wins this better world. Manu and (his wife) Manāyī procreated here (as the first people on earth) by (forming) a couple. When they milk with the cooking-vessel (*sthālī*) and with the milk-pail, he is procreated[8] through this couple.

— The milking of two cows is mentioned by MS. 1, 8, 9: 129. 5 in an expiation. See also ĀpŚS. 6, 14, 11. Perhaps the present passage refers to the expiation for diseases caused by Rudra, as may appear from its continuation. Instead of milk other material may be used (as has already been mentioned above):

TB. 2, 1, 5, 5: He should offer clarified butter for a man who is desirous of splendour (*tejas*).[9] Clarified butter is splendour. (Thus) he becomes splendid. (He should offer) milk for a man who is desirous of cattle. That is a representation of cattle. By means of their representation he (the priest) obtains cattle for him (the sacrificer). He becomes rich in cattle. (He should offer) sour milk for a man who is desirous of strength (*indriya*).[10] Sour milk is strength. He becomes strong. (He should offer) a gruel of rice for a man who is desirous of (possessing or ruling) a village. Men subsist on plants. He wins (over) his kinsmen for him by means of (giving them) a share. He becomes the headman of a village (or clan).[11]

— In the context of a discussion on the esoteric substitutes of oblation and fire, several kinds of oblations are mentioned:

ŚB. 11, 3, 1, 3–4: "If there should be no milk, what would you offer?". — "Rice and barley". "If there should be no rice and barley, what would you offer?" — "Whatever other herbs (crops) there are". "If there should be no other herbs, what would you offer?". — "Whatever wild herbs there are". "If there should be no wild herbs, what would you offer?". — "The fruit of trees". "If there should be no fruit of trees, what would you offer?". — "Water". "If there should be no water, what would you offer?". — He said: "Then there would be here nothing at all, and yet there would be offered, viz. truth in (the fire of) faith".

— The version of JB. 1, 19 does not mention other items. The parallel of VādhS. 3, 40 successively replaces milk by water, herbs, trees,[12] being and non-being (*sat* and *asat*), and ultimately refers to the offering of the sun in the fire and the fire in the sun. JB. 1, 14 containing formulas without parallels may deal with a *soma*-agnihotra.

NOTES

[1] That *rasa* here denotes essence rather than just any fluid, appears from Section 1.3 which describes the successive production of all kinds of *rasas* out of other products in the framework of the water doctrine. The same theory is also applied to the production of milk. See *Agn. and Prāṇāgn.*, ch. VI, n. 7. Keith's translation "with all kinds of sap" is not satisfactory. See author, *JB. I, 1–65*, p. 167 ff. on the "striving for totality or completeness in the brāhmaṇas", and especially p. 169 which criticizes Eggeling's rendering of ŚB. 6, 6, 3, 3 "by every kind of food" (correct: by all food).

[2] On *yadaśana* being one word see Caland, *AO* 10 (1930), p. 307.

[3] For the construction of this sentence see Oertel, *Syntax of Cases*, p. 40 f. It may be correct that *tatas* should have the force of a temporal adverb here. The option, however, is not between *tataḥ* "then" and *tataḥ* ("equivalent to the ablative of the demonstrative pronoun *tebhyaḥ*") referring to the cattle. The ablative in connection with *sambhavati* "to originate from" may refer to what has been eaten and drunk, rather than to the cattle. Milk is produced as the essence of all food which is eaten by the cattle. See n. 1 on *rasa*. See also Minard, *Trois Énigmes* II, 201 *a*, where an analysis of a temporal adverb is preferred.

[4] According to Dumont the agnihotra forms a pair on account of its evening and morning performances. I doubt if this pair is meant here. The couple of the first and second libation seems to be more suitable, since single (i.e. either evening or morning) performances are concerned with the milking of one or two cows. Or should we translate: "In this manner (*etad*) (i.e. by milking two cows) the agnihotra becomes a couple". The following passage from the MS. may support this interpretation.

[5] The milk which is poured on later comes from the second cow, i.e. from heaven. Thus it is like rain which fertilizes the milk of the first cow, i.e. the earth. See also Caland's note on his translation of ĀpŚS. 6, 14, 10.

[6] I have not followed von Schroeder's punctuation of this sentence.

[7] The *loka* (see Gonda, *Loka, World and Heaven in the Veda*, Amsterdam Academy 1966) here does not seem to refer to a particular position on earth, but to the future position in heaven. Offering the agnihotra with this pair or couple means procreating oneself in yonder world. For this heavenly rebirth by means of the agnihotra compare JB. 1, 17 (where the āhavanīya fire is the divine womb).

[8] See n. 7. If, however, this passage does not form a unity, and rebirth in heaven is not meant here, it may be assumed that obtaining many offspring and being successful in breeding cattle are expressed.

[9] On *tejas* (translated by Dumont with "fiery energy") see Vogel, "Het Sanskrit woord *tejas* (= gloed, vuur) in de beteekenis van magische kracht", *Meded. Akad.* 70, B 4, p. 83–125 (Amsterdam 1930), especially p. 123 on the identification of melted butter and *tejas*.

[10] See Caland's note on ĀpŚS. 6, 15, 1.

[11] The compound *grāmakāma* as such would seem to refer to the possession of a village, i.e. to being donated with the revenues of a whole village by the king. In the present context, however, this sort of situation apparently is not meant. The text refers to *sajātāḥ* (kinsmen) who are won over by a share to to accept the nomination for leadership. In this connection it may be observed that the *grāma* originally was a clan or group (cf. *saṃgrāma*, the clash of two armies, groups or clans) rather than a settlement. See Rau, *The meaning of* pur *in Vedic literature*, München 1976, p. 49 f. See also Caland's translation of ĀpŚS. 6, 10, 3 ".... der ein Dorf (d.h. die Oberherrschaft über seine Dorfstammesgenossen) wünscht". He wants to be a *grāmaṇī*.

[12] I.e. dry wood is burnt in the fire. Or a *samidh* may replace the libation (as in the *gṛhya vaiśvadeva* ritual).

6 *Systematic treatment of the ritual*

6.1 *The milking of the agnihotra cow.*

KS. 6, 3: 51.14 ff.: (Pottery) which is turned on the wheel and that which is not turned on the wheel are different things. That which is turned on the wheel, is sacred to the Asuras. That which is not turned on the wheel, is sacred only to the gods. Therefore one should not make the pot used for heating the milk by means of a wheel.[1] (..) Now there is spilled, if he turns over (the milk-pail and pours the milk into the agnihotra vessel). He should milk with the vessel used for heating the agnihotra milk. That is this earth.[2] Neither[2] here nor there does he spill. With this (earth) he sits near (the cow in order to milk her).[3] Thus there is not spilled by him. (..)[4]

MS. 1, 8, 3: 118.1 ff.: They milk[5] with the vessel used in the ritual (the *sthālī*). Thus they sit near (the cow)[3] with this earth — for neither on this side, nor on that side is there spilled over this earth — in order to avoid spilling. The vessel is made by an Aryan and has a raised border[6] in order to be suitable for the gods. For that (vessel) is suitable for the gods.[7] Sacred to the Asuras is the vessel which is made by a potter on the wheel.

— The TB. contains (at the beginning of the passage on the agnihotra) a myth on the origin of the cow in the agnihotra ritual. There it is also explained why for ten days one should not milk the mother of a newborn calf. This was the boon granted by the Aṅgirases to the calf in their primeval sacrifice:

TB. 2, 1, 1, 3: They (i.e. the Aṅgirases) led the calf to its mother. They said: "Do you cause (your mother) to give this oblation (i.e. the milk)". It said: "Let me choose a boon. When I am born, you shall not milk (the mother cow: *pṛśni*) during ten days.[8] Let me stay with (the mother) until the time when the cows are driven together". Therefore, when a calf is born, they do not milk (the mother) during ten days and it stays with (its) mother until the time when the cows are driven together. For that is what it chose. Therefore Rudra is desirous of killing the calf which has been led (to the cow) and sucks (her) (after that period). For (then) it sucks beyond the agreement.

— The preceding passage refers to the custom of bringing the calf into contact with the mother cow in order to make the milk flow. See also JB. 1, 39: "After having united the agnihotra cow (with her calf) he says: 'Those who are united, are Heaven and Earth.[9] The Rudras collect what has been milked by the Vasus'". For the milking itself see the following passage in the TB.:

TB. 2, 1, 8, 1–3: He (i.e. not the priest himself, but a helper who milks the cow) lets (the calf) go towards (the cow) on (or: from) the southern side. Thereby he wins the world of the fathers. He causes (the cow) to turn eastward. Thereby he wins the world of the gods. He milks (the cow) after having caused her to turn[10] northward. He should milk the two teats in front for a man who is the eldest son, the son of the eldest wife,[11] or who has obtained prosperity. He should milk the two teats at the back for a man who is the youngest son, the son of the youngest wife, or who is desirous of more prosperity. In order to avoid the mixing of what should be kept apart (in society),[12] he should not touch together (two teats).[12] (...)[13] Just as he satisfies the cow upon descent into a river (*tīrtha*), even so the cow of the agnihotra satisfies the sacrificer. He is satisfied with offspring and cattle, he knows heaven, he sees (i.e. lives to see) his son and his grandson, he is productive in offspring and cattle by pairings, he for whom, knowing thus, they offer the agnihotra, as well as he who thus knows this (agnihotra).

— VādhS. 3, 19 prescribes that one should milk the four teats, because they represent four sacrifices.

NOTES

1 Cf. (i.a.) ĀpŚS. 6, 3, 7. For the following passage on pouring water on the milk, omitted here, see Section 6.4.

2 See Caland's emendation *iyaṃ vai sā; na vā imam* ... etc., *Fs. Kuhn* (1916), p. 70.

3 The interpretation of *upasīdati* is not quite certain. In connection with cattle it seems to denote careful attention and waiting upon them (cf. AV. 3, 14, 6), perhaps especially by milking them.

4 The passage dealing with the spilling has been left out (like the other expiations).

5 I read with Caland (*ZDMG* 72, p. 7) *duhanty* instead of *duhaty*. The plural mostly denotes someone else than the priest. According to MS. 4,1, 3: 5.5 f. the *śūdra* may not milk the agnihotra.

6 The translation of *ūrdhvakapāla* given by M.-W.'s dictionary is untenable. See for this detail the sūtras, e.g. ĀpŚS. 6, 3, 7.

7 Perhaps because it is directed towards heaven and does not have rims which are turned down.

[8] The construction of this sentence (with the calf apparently as the object of the verb *duh*) has caused troubles to scholars. Böhtlingk, "Eine Absurdität", *ZDMG* 54, p. 514 proposed to emend to *dṛṃhān* and *dṛṃhanti*, but *dṛṃh-* does not mean "festhalten, einsperren, anbinden". Dumont observes in a note: "It is certain that the object of *dohan* is *mā jātám*, just as, in the other sentence of the same paragraph, the object of *duhanti* is *vátsaṃ jātám*. — *duh-* means 'to milk', but it also means 'to take advantage of', 'to frustrate', and consequently 'to take from somebody that which rightly belongs to him'." This semantic "tour de force" does not convince me. Moreover a rather satisfactory solution was found already long ago by Oertel, *Syntax of Cases*, p. 84 f., who based himself on Geldner, *Ved. Stud.* III, p. 111, n. 3. Indeed the accusatives *mā jātam* and *vatsaṃ jātam* "cannot depend as direct objects on the √*duh*". On the other hand the instances of an absolute accusative adduced by Oertel are not completely reliable. Are we to assume that *mā jātam* and *vatsaṃ jātam* "would thus be equivalent to the Absolute Locatives **mayi jāte* and **vatse jāte*"? The parallels quoted by Oertel in the locative refer to a particular moment (*putre jāte* "when a son is born"), whereas here the extension of time seems to be fundamental: They do not milk (the cow) all the while that the calf is no older than ten days old. Cf. the use of *jāta* at the end of a compound, e.g. *māsajāta* "one month old". Especially in *daśa mā rātrīr jātam* the word order seems to confirm my interpretation. However, in *vatsaṃ jātaṃ daśa rātrīr na duhanti* the accusative *daśa rātrīr*, which, in the accusative of the extension of time, should be taken with *jātam* and only secondarily with the verb *duh*, primarily belongs to *duhanti*. A shift may have taken place. At any rate a new, extensive study of the absolute accusative is required.

[9] For different identifications with the calf which should make flow the milk of the cow (= heaven) see *JB. I, 1–65*, p. 190 (n. 2).

[10] Read (with Dumont) *āvártya* instead of *āvṛtya*.

[11] According to Dumont's translation only two categories are mentioned. However, his rendering of *jyeṣṭhásya jyaiṣṭhineyásya* "For a man who is the eldest son of the eldest wife of his father" cannot be correct, since *jyaiṣṭhineya* means "a son of the father's first wife". So theoretically a translation "For a man who is the eldest son of the son of the father's eldest or first wife" is possible, but our rendering seems to be preferable.

[12] On touching together (*saṃmṛśati*) see Dumont, *Agnihotra*, p. 210. I doubt whether this is not done "in order to avoid confusion (i.e., in order to avoid a mistake)" (Dumont's translation of the present place). The term *vyāvṛtti* has nothing to do with the confusion of making mistakes, but refers to keeping distinct those people or those entities which should be kept separated in the conservative Indian view of life. See also *JB. 1, 1–65*, p. 51, n. 1.

[13] For the passage omitted here, the so-called *vaiśvadeva* of the milk, see Section 16.

6.2 *Transference of the fire from the gārhapatya to the āhavanīya and other preparatory actions.*

AB. 5, 26, 1–4: "Take (the fire for) the āhavanīya out (of the gārhapatya)" he (the sacrificer) says at the end of the day. All the good which he does during the daytime he thereby takes out and places in security.[1] (....).[2] The āhavanīya is sacrifice; the āhavanīya is heaven.[3] He who knows thus, places heaven in that heaven which is sacrifice.

— For the right time for taking out the fire according to the ŚB. see Section 4. This brāhmaṇa also deals with the entrance of the sacrificer:

ŚB. 2, 3, 3, 13–14: When (entering) from the east he (the sacrificer) has gone round the āhavanīya, he passes between (it and)[4] the gārhapatya. For the gods do not know this man. But when he passes here by them between (the fires), they know him, thinking "This is the one that now offers to us". Moreover, Agni (the fire or the fires) is the repeller of evil. These two drive away evil from him who passes between them. He whose evil has been repelled becomes a light by his glory and renown. On the north side is the door of (that house which is) the agnihotra.[5] This is like entering (a house) by a door. But if he should sit down (on his prescribed place) after approaching from the south, he would walk outside (the house) as it were.

— The next paragraph homologizes the agnihotra with a ship and in that connection a new passage on the direction taken by the walking sacrificer, follows:

ŚB. 2, 3, 3, 16: In that he walks up towards the east, thereby he steers that (ship) eastward to heaven[6] and he thereby wins heaven. It is ascended in the north. (Then) it makes him reach heaven. But if he should sit down (on his prescribed place)[7] after entering from the south, he would as it were try to come on board of a ship which has already gone to sea, he would be left behind and remain outside it.

— The same argumentation as used by the ŚB. in the first passage is found in the AB. The latter may be the source of the ŚB., since that brāhmaṇa is generally considered to be later than the AB. However, the passage under discussion does not belong to the oldest stage of the AB. and may be based on the ŚB. The JB. mentions the entrance of the sacrificer in a passage which has no parallels:

AB. 7. 12, 7: When he is going to offer, he should walk (in) between the gārhapatya and the āhavanīya. When he walks by this way, the fires know "He is going to offer in us". "When he walks by this way the gārhapatya and the āhavanīya repel his evil. After his evil has been driven away, he rises upwards to heaven" thus they quote a brāhmaṇa.[8]

JB. 1, 41: When he sits down to the south of the fires after having made a circumambulation in the west (i.e. round the gārhapatya) or in the east (i.e. round the āhavanīya, before passing between the two fires),[9] then he has become Prajāpati when he sits down, and (he recites) "I am happiness (*kam*),[10] happiness is mine".

— Of all the other introductory actions treated by the sūtras only pouring water round the fires is mentioned in the brāhmaṇas:

TB. 2, 1, 11: In the evening he (the performer) pours water round (all the three fires) with the formula: "I pour truth round thee, order".[11] In the morning with the formula: "I pour order round thee, truth". Order is Agni, truth the sun.[12] Thus in the evening he pours the sun round Agni, and in the morning Agni round the sun. As long as there will be day and night, so long will there be no distress, no damage, no end, no limit of[13] this world for him for whom, knowing thus, they offer the agnihotra and for him who knows this (agnihotra) thus.

— A rather extensive survey of these introductory actions is found in the only sūtra translated in this book, the brāhmaṇa-like VādhS. The passage seems to start with a discussion between Agni and Prajāpati:

VādhS. 3, 9: He (Agni) said: "I am afraid of the end (i.e. death)".[14] (The other, i.e. Prajāpati, said): "How should (something) be (done) about that?" He said: "They should take me out while I am (still) burning". Therefore they should take it (i.e. the fire) out (from the gārhapatya) burning. He does not come to his end[15] in this world and in yonder one, for whom they take it out burning. Therefore they should take it out, while it burns. He said: "I am afraid of loneliness." "How should (something) be (done) about that?" He said: "After having taken me out they should sit down near me".[16] Therefore after having taken it out they should sit down near it. He does not become lonely in this world and in yonder one, for whom they take out and sit near. Therefore they should sit down near it after having taken it out. He said: "I am afraid of nakedness". "How should (something) be (done) about that?". He said: "They should wipe around me and strew (grass) around me". Therefore they should wipe and strew (grass) around it. He does not become naked in this and yonder world, for whom they wipe and strew (grass) around it. Therefore they should wipe around it and strew (grass) around it. He said: "I am afraid of hunger". "How should (something) be (done) about it?". He said: "They should throw some burnt down pieces of wood on me and kindle them". Therefore they throw some burnt down pieces of wood on it and kindle them. He does not become hungry in this and yonder world, for whom they throw burnt down pieces of wood in the fire and kindle them. Therefore they should put some burnt down pieces of wood on it and kindle them. The taking out of the fire is (the offering of) an immortal oblation.[17] Real oblations of nectar are offered by him. A stream of nectar is thrown into the fire, when he (the priest) directly[18] kindles it for him. By one of the two either by the daily taking out or by the kindling he who knows thus overcomes repeated death (i.e. dying again in yonder world).

NOTES

[1] The sūtras (e.g. ĀpŚS. 6, 1, 7) have formulas which express that taking out the fire means taking out the evil done during the daytime, during the nighttime respectively.

[2] An identical description of the morning agnihotra has been omitted here. The texts always deal first with the evening performance.

[3] This is a very usual identification. Correspondingly the gārhapatya is identified with the earth.

[4] On this ellipsis see Minard, *Trois Énigmes* I, 88 *b* (see also o.c., 372 *c* on the entrance of the sacrificer).

[5] Eggeling remarks in a note: "I do not understand this, there being no door on the north side of the Āhavanīya fire-house". The problem is, however, solved, if we take this door metaphorically and not referring to the āhavanīya. The agnihotra, i.e. the complex of two or three fires used in that ritual, is described as a house. The entrance lies between the two fires. This metaphorical door or entrance has to be distinguished from the door or entrance to the sacrificial emplacement, which lies in the east. By that entrance the sacrificer comes in. The prescribed place to which he has to move is situated in the eastern quarter to the south of the āhavanīya fire (see the plan in Dumont's book on the agnihotra). He might go directly from the eastern entrance to his place, keeping the āhavanīya on his right side. The ritual, however, prescribes that he should keep the āhavanīya on his left and enter the agnihotra-house from the north side by the "door" which is formed by the space between the two fires.

[6] The eastern quarter is always brought into connection with heaven.

[7] Not: "in it" (i.e. in this ship) as Eggeling translates. Cf. n. 5. The ship is going from the north to the south-east, where the sacrificer should sit down. If he should go directly from the eastern entrance to his southern place without rounding the āhavanīya, he would miss his boat.

[8] The brāhmaṇa, to which the AB. refers here, seems to be the ŚB. See the introductory remarks to this passage.

[9] My translation of *JB. I, 1–65*, p. 95 has to be corrected.

[10] Prajāpati is also called *ka*.

[11] This formula is also recited in the *prāṇāgnihotra* ritual (see *JB. I, 1–65*, p. 334, n. 54).

[12] In fact the water which is poured out is identical with truth or with or-

der. This is the usual homology. Here the alternation of the night and the day aspect of the agnihotra has been forced into the classification.

[13] Dumont's translation "... so long, in this world, there will be no damage ...., for him (the Sacrificer) for whom ..." (cf. Caland's note on his translation of ĀpŚS. 6, 5, 4) does not account for the syntactic construction of the genitive *asya lokasya*.

[14] The end or death for Agni (= gārhapatya fire) means extinction. By taking out fire from the gārhapatya the chance of extinction of the fire is reduced.

[15] For this type of compound ending in *-bhāvuka-* with abstract meaning see also VādhS. 4, 60 and 64 *a*.

[16] According to Caland's translation "soll man (mit Sprüchen) mich ehrend in meiner Nähe sitzen". Now this passage belongs to the *agnyādhāna* (and not the agnihotra) section. Indeed, *upās-* may refer to worship, and the āhavanīya fire is worshipped with mantras in the *agnyādhāna* ritual. However, the whole passage constantly refers to actions to be performed continuously (since the *agnyādhāna*) in the agnihotra ritual. Moreover, loneliness forms the basic motif. Sitting near the fire during the whole ritual rather than worship seems to be relevant. So perhaps this refers to the sacrificer and his wife who sit near the āhavanīya fire during the ritual. In the agnihotra no *upāsana* or *agnyupasthāna* takes place immediately after the taking out. The only objection to this interpretation might be that the same passage states: "He does not become lonely .. for whom they sit down near the fire". The text as it stands should apply to the officiant who is doing something for the sacrificer. Perhaps the stock expression of this passage *yasyainam* .. inadvertently was not changed here.

[17] Taking out the fire means immortality (unendingness) for the fire according to the beginning of the passage. Moreover, the sūtras contain mantras to be recited on this occasion which mention the *amṛtāhuti* (e.g. ĀpŚS. 6, 1, 8 *amṛtāhutim amṛtāyāṃ juhomi*).

[18] *atraiva* implies that the fire is kindled (*samindh*) directly after (*anu*) being taken out. The *anvādhāna* takes place on the spot or at the same moment (*atraiva*). Together with the taking out (which is also an *amṛtāhuti*) a continuous stream of *amṛta* is produced in this way.

6.3 *The milk is put on the fire and cooked.*

KS. 6, 7: 56.15–20: The agnihotra is a creation (or emanation by Prajāpati). This observance (i.e. the silence of Prajāpati mentioned in the preceding context) is a creation. He (Prajāpati) made them (the creatures) come up (or: created them) with the thought "You are (my) production (or: coming up)". At the moment when there are bubbles, as it were (on the milk), then he should look upon (the milk with the formula): "You represent rising to prosperity.[1] May I reproduce myself with offspring and cattle".[2] The agnihotra (milk) represents coming up (or: forth), represents production.[3] He thrives with offspring and is productive in (rearing) cattle, for whom the agnihotra is offered thus. He looks upon (the milk) with a fire (i.e. with a burning grassblade). The agnihotra (milk) is the female generative organ.[4] The fire is the procreator who procreates. The agnihotra (milk) is seed. He should not cook it intensively. (Otherwise) he would make it thick[5] (i.e. produce a crust on the bottom of the vessel). Nor should he leave it uncooked. It should be in between.[6]

— The same formulas are found MS. 1, 8, 3: 119.12 ff. with the same introductory context. The order of the treatment of the ritual is more regular in the MS. In the KS. this passage seems to belong to a paragraph containing some addenda. If the assumption that the MS. is later than the KS. holds good, one may say that the MS. has corrected the redaction. It has added one detail:

MS. 1, 8, 3: 119.13 f.: Moreover he thereby sprinkles[7] (it) in order to make it sacrificially pure.

— Some elements of the passage of MS. are found again in the TB. The usual development of a theme in the Yajurvedic texts is KS.–MS.–TB

TB. 2, 1, 3, 1–4: The fire (or: Agni)[8] is Rudra. The pot (in which the milk is cooked) is the (sacrificer's) wife. If he should put in the middle of the fire, he would give the wife to Rudra. She would die prematurely. Having pushed the coals to the north out of the fire he puts it on them in order to protect the wife. He separates them (from the fire). Thus the wife does not die prematurely (...). The cooked oblation which has not been besprinkled with ghee has proceeded from this world without reaching the world of the gods. He illuminates it (with a burning grass-blade). (Thereby) he besprinkles it[9] and causes it to go to the gods. He carries fire round (the agnihotra pot) in order to remove the Rakṣasa demons. He carries it round thrice. For the sacrifice is threefold.[10] Moreover this is done for the sake of ritual purity.

— The purification of the milk by illuminating it is mentioned by the VādhS. Another Yajurvedic text, the ŚB., again refers to the identification of milk and seed.

VādhS. 3, 25: Now they say: "What is the purification of the agnihotra?" That he illuminates the milk after having poured water on it, that is the purification of the agnihotra.

ŚB. 2, 3, 1, 14–16: Having milked he puts that (milk) on (the gārhapatya) thinking: "Let it become cooked". Now they say: "He should offer it at the moment when it rises". He should, however, not let it rise. He would burn it, if he should let it rise. Burnt seed is not productive. Therefore he should not let it rise. Before offering it he should put it on the fire. In that it is Agni's seed, thereby it is cooked. And when he puts it on the fire (Agni), thereby it also becomes cooked. Therefore he should put it on the fire before offering it. He illuminates it with the intention "I must know whether it is cooked".

— The Ṛgvedic and Sāmavedic brāhmaṇas ŚāṅkhB. and JB. are completely independent in this passage and do not agree with the Yajurvedic texts quoted above.

ŚāṅkB. 2, 1: Having put (the milk) on the gārhapatya fire he should offer it in the āhavanīya fire. The gārhapatya is the fire for cooking and the āhavanīya for offering in (*āhavana*). Therefore he should put (the milk) on the gārhapatya and offer it in the āhavanīya. He separates[11] the coals (from the gārhapatya). Thereby he puts apart these two worlds. Therefore these two worlds though being together (as two complementary parts) still are, so to say, distinct. Now, in that he holds a burning grass-blade over (the milk)[12] after having put it on (the gārhapatya), thereby he cooks it. (...)[13] And in that he again illuminates (with the burning straw), thereby he boils the water (which had been added).[13]

JB. 1, 39: He pushes the coals out (of the gārhapatya, reciting:) "Ye are the prosperity bringers. Danger coming from abroad has been pushed away". Then he puts (the milk) on (these coals, reciting:) "Thou art put on Vaiśvānara's (fire). May Agni not burn thy lustre. For truth, thee". Then he illuminates (the milk with a burning grass-blade) reciting: "Light together with light". (...)[13] Thrice he passes a firebrand sunwise round (the milk, with the formula:) "Excluded is the race of the demons (rākṣasas), excluded are the powers of adversity".[14]

— As stated above, these two brāhmaṇas have not been influenced by the Yajurvedic texts in this section. On the other hand the latest of these Yajurvedic texts, the ŚB., seems to react to one view put forward by the ŚāṅkhB. Concerning the illumination it observes that this is only done in order to know whether the milk cooks (after a digression on the actual cooking and the symbolical cooking).

NOTES

1 The rising of the milk symbolizes by its *udbhava* ("coming up or forth") prosperity and procreation.

2 The expression *prajāyate prajābhiḥ* is already found ṚV. 2, 33, 1. In Vedic prose the instrumental of *prajā* is sometimes accompanied with the

instr. of *paśu*. See e.g. MS. 1, 8, 3: 119.5 f. . . *yajamānaḥ prajayā ca paśubhiś ca prajāyate*. The combination of these two data shows that this turn of phrase does not refer to rebirth in the son, but to being prolific (see Macdonell's rendering of ṚV. 2, 33, 1 in his Reader) in a more or less economic sense. In the present context *prajāyate* is replaced by *udbhavati* ("to come up, rise, come into existence" as well as "to be productive") in order to make a connection with the rising milk, which should represent rising welfare.

[3] From the *udbhava* of the formula the text arrives by way of *udbhūti* at *prabhūti*, the prosperity produced by the rising milk. Moreover a distinction between the instrumentals *prajayā* ("offspring") and *paśubhiḥ* ("cattle") is brought about in this way.

[4] Mostly *prajanana* is not the female (but the male) organ. Here, however, the context seems to require this rendering.

[5] See Section 3.1 (n. 4) on the parallel of MS. 1, 8, 2, which occurs in a rather different context. See also Caland, *WZKM* 26, p. 123 on *krūḍayati* "gerinnen machen, dick machen" (referring to milk) and "dick (unflüssig) machen" (referring to seed).

[6] Read with Caland, *ZDMG* 72, p. 13 *antar evaiva syāt*.

[7] Compare TB. 2, 1, 3, 3 (see n. 9). The parallel proves that looking at the milk is the action which takes place while the milk is illuminated.

[8] Agni is sometimes identified with Rudra. See e.g. JB. 3, 261. Without distinction Rudra and Agni occur at KS. 6, 7 and MS. 1, 8, 6. Both do harm to the cattle.

[9] The besprinkling (*abhighāra*) is a well-known element of most sacrifices. For the same identification in MS. see above (n. 7).

[10] This may refer to the morning, midday and afternoon offerings in the Soma ritual.

[11] Read *vyantān* instead of *dvyantān* of Lindner's ed. See Caland, *WZKM* 23, p. 61.

[12] For a criticism of Keith's translation see Caland, *AO* 10 (1932), p. 308.

[13] For pouring water on the milk (here omitted) see the following section.

[14] See author, *JB. I, 1–65*, p. 96, n. 8 on the correct punctuation of this passage.

6.4 *Water is poured on the hot milk.*

KS. 6, 3: 51.16–18: He should neither pour milk nor water to (the hot milk of the oblation). If he should pour milk on it, there would be no pouring on (of something different). By pouring water he would extinguish (the glow of the milk; i.e. he would cool it). He should leave some remainder of the milk (in the milking-pail). He should pour that[1] mixed with water on (the milk). Thereby neither milk nor water is poured on it.

— After this ingenious solution the text continues with a digression on the possibility of spilling milk while turning the milking-pail over into the agnihotra vessel.[2] It prescribes that the milking-pail should be the agnihotra vessel at the same time. In that case there is indeed no chance of spilling (the *sthālī* into which one milks being the earth itself), but there is no opportunity to pour the remaining milk (*saṃsrāvam*) mixed with water on the hot milk. So the text has to accept the pouring of water (now called *āpas* instead of *udaka*, which may make some difference) on the milk.

KS. 6, 3: 52.1 f.: He pours water on (the milk), For water is for pouring on. Therefore water and milk form a harmless combination.

— At the end of this passage the KS. again returns to the discussion on the disputed pouring of water on the milk.

KS. 6, 3: 52.7–13: To pour or not[3] to pour water on the milk is not a matter of indifference.[3] Pouring on is for the one who desires cattle; not pouring on for the one who desires splendour. The agnihotra pot is identical with the kettle of milk which is put on the fire in the suncharm of the Pravargya ritual.[4] If he offers (milk) on which (water) has not been poured,[5] he obtains splendour.[6] If he does not obtain milk, he may offer clarified butter. That of course does not admit of an additional pouring of water,[7] and is not favourable for cattle. There is a chance that it might burn his cattle with its heat. He who is desirous of cattle pours water on the milk. Water and milk form a peaceful mixture.[8] If he does not obtain milk, he may offer a rice-gruel. That of course admits of an additional pouring of water. Water and rice form a peaceful combination, which is favourable for (obtaining) cattle.

MS. 1, 8, 3: 118.10 ff.: There should not be poured upon by him who is desirous of lustre, the splendour of a learned brahmin, by him who wishes to spread his influence[9] or who desires: "May a strong male child be born to me". The hot milk (*gharma*)[10] on which no water is poured represents lustre and the brahmin's splendour. He obtains lustre and splendour. He overthrows whom he wishes to overthrow. There is born a male child to him. There should be offered with melted butter by him who does not pour water on. For there is not poured on it. There is no expiation for spilling and he does not obtain cattle. The milk of the cattle is thereby thrown into the fire. He causes heat (pain)[11] in the cattle. The glow being unappeased (unextinguished) burns away the cattle. Therefore there should be poured on. If he should pour on water, he would take away the glow. There should be poured on with the water used to remove the remainder of the milk.[12] For that is neither water nor milk. Now they say: "That is a spilling. At the moment when there is transfused from the milking-pail, then there is spilled".[13] There should be poured on with water while the mantra "The trees have disappeared"[14] is recited. With one drop he does not take away the glow, (but) appeases the pain of the cattle. The heat represents cattle and splendour. Water and milk form a couple. Out of a couple forsooth offspring and cattle are produced. These (i.e. water and milk) form a couple. On the basis of this couple the sacrificer is productive with offspring and cattle.[15] There should be offered with cooked rice by him who pours on. For this admits of pouring on, forms a harmless (peaceful) combination (couple), which is ritually pure and produces offspring.

— Following this version of the MS. which contains the same themes as the KS. in a different order,[16] the treatment of this subject in the TB. represents a small advance.

TB. 2, 1, 3, 2 f.: An indomitable Pravargya milk-offering is put on the fire every day in the form of the agnihotra milk.[17] For one who is desirous of cattle he should pour (water) on (the milk). For when tempered it yields cattle. He should not pour on for one who is desirous of splendour. For splendour is blazing as it were. Or rather there should be poured on. In that he pours on (the milk), it produces cattle. By the fact that he offers it, it reaches splendour.[18] He has done both.

— A short passage in VādhS. (3, 28), which unfortunately is rather corrupt, states that the evening agnihotra should be performed with cooled milk (i.e. cooled by the addition of water) and the morning agnihotra with hot milk. The other brāhmaṇas (at least the JB.) refer to another function of the water: the replenishment of what has been lost of the milk during the cooking:

ŚāṅkhB. 2, 1: That he pours water (on the milk), — whole and complete oblations are indeed waters —[19] is for the sake of the wholeness of the oblation.

ŚB. 2, 3, 1, 16: Then he pours water on it, for the sake of tempering (the heat) and of the completeness of the fluid. For when it rains here, then herbs are produced. After these herbs have been eaten and the water drunk,[20] this fluid (i.e. the milk) is produced out of it. Therefore this (pouring water) is also done for the sake of the completeness of the fluid.[21] Therefore, if it occurs to him that there is pure milk to be drunk,[22] he should order a drop of water to be sprinkled on it, for the sake of appeasement (or: tempering) and of supplementing the fluid.[23]

JB. 1, 39: Then he pours water on it (with the formula:) "Fill up thyself with thy sap which has entered into the waters". What the waters consume of it on this occasion, that he thereby pours on it again.

NOTES

[1] For the correct reading of the text (*ucchiṣya tenodakamiśreṇa* instead of *ucchiṣyeta nodakamiśreṇa*) see Caland, *Fs. Kuhn* (1916), p. 69.

[2] See Section 6.1.

[3] For the turn of phrase *anyad .. anyad* compare KS. 6, 3: 51.14 (Section 6.2 beginning).

[4] See n. 10 for the parallel of ŚāṅkhB. 2, 1.

[5] Read *yad apratiṣiktena juhoti* with Caland, *Fs. Kuhn*, p. 70.

[6] The term *brahmavarcasa* denotes splendour, especially that obtained by knowledge of the sacred texts. The splendour and brilliance of the hot milk, undiminished by the addition of cold water, correspond to human splendour.

[7] Otherwise Hoens, *Śānti*, p. 32: "The Agnihotra upon which nothing is poured does not bring any cattle".

[8] The sentence *tac chāntaṃ mithunam āpaśca payaśca* also occurs KS. 6, 3: 52.2, where *śāntam* has no relation to extinction. Perhaps here also (as at the end of this passage) *śāntaṃ mithunam* denotes a peaceful, harmless combination or mixture, and does not refer to the extinction of the hot milk which might magically burn the cattle.

[9] The rising milk, which represents an extension, produces an extension (of influence) for the sacrificer. Male offspring likewise is a form of extension (i.c. of the lineage).

[10] The *gharma* is the milk heated in the Pravargya ritual, on which see van Buitenen's publication *The Pravargya*, Poona 1968. For this identification of agnihotra and *pravargya* milk see also the preceding passage of the KS., as well as TB. 2, 1, 3, 2 (below) and (in a different context of the agnihotra section) ŚāṅkhB. 2, 1.

[11] The difficult root *vṛj-* in the verbal compound *pravṛj-* denotes on the one hand the placing of the *gharma* on the fire (in the Pravargya ritual). On the other hand it also plainly refers to throwing in the fire, as seems to be the case here (although the *gharma* was mentioned before). Thus, the pain or distress of the cattle is literally heat (both meanings represented by *śuc*).

[12] Read *godohasaṃnejanena* for *gāṃdohasaṃnejanena* with Caland, *ZDMG* 72 (1918), p. 7. See also the same, *Fs. Kuhn* (1916), p. 70.

[13] See the beginning of this section (n. 2) and Section 5.2 on this spilling. The version of the MS. proves that the digression on all kinds of spillings in the KS. disturbs the composition of that section (KS. 6, 3).

[14] There are no parallels of this mantra, which is even missing in Bloomfield's *Concordance*.

[15] See Section 6.3, n. 2.

[16] KS. deals with: a) objections against adding water or (cold) milk. — Conclusion: water mixed with the remainder of the milk is added; b) objection: this is a spilling. — Conclusion: milking-pail is used as an agnihotra pot; c) in that case there is no cleansing water. — Conclusion: water should be added; d) adding water or not depends on the aims of the sacrificer.

The MS. starts with d), continues with a) and b), and omits the prescription that the milking-pail should be used as an agnihotra vessel. Instead it directly suggests to pour water on the milk. The ingenious solution of pouring only some drops of water as well as the improved composition of this passage may be taken as indications that the version of the MS. is later than that of the KS.

[17] Dumont's "Verily the Agnihotra (-oblation) is the unappeased (not cooled) gharma (-oblation) . . . (Like the gharma-oblation) it is put on the fire day by day" seems to miss the point. The text wants to state that the daily heating of the agnihotra milk is identical with the heating of the gharma which only takes place when a *pravargya* is performed. Cf. also KS. 31, 7 and MS. 4, 1, 9 for another identification with the *gharma* milk (i.c. the cake which may burn the cattle by its heat; according to TB. 3, 2, 8, 5 it may burn the sacrificer himself).

[18] Dumont translates "one has made it holy", but splendour rather than holiness is relevant in this context.

[19] Keith, observing in a note that Lindner's text must be corrected and that "the insertion of *kṛtsnāḥ* before *kṛtsnāni* is easy and gives fairly good sense", translates: "In that he brings up the waters, and the waters are complete, all the oblations become complete; verily (they serve) to complete the oblation". Apart from the unfelicitous rendering "to bring up" of the verb *prati-ā-nī* (see Caland, *AO* 10, p. 308) the construction is debatable. Caland's suggestion (*WZKM* 23, p. 62) to omit *sarvāṇi* as a gloss and to replace it by *kṛtsnāni* is indeed (as Keith observes) a less easy corruption. I suggest to retain the text as it stands and in this connection refer to ŚB. 7, 2, 4, 25 (*virāḍ u kṛtsnam annaṃ sarvam evāsminn etat kṛtsnam annaṃ dadhāti*) for the combination of *kṛtsna* and *sarva*. The completeness of the waters may be based on a pseudo-etymology of *āpas : āpnoti, āpta* (complete).

[20] On the construction of the disjunct gerunds see Oertel, *Syntax of Cases*, p. 307 ff. (espec. p. 313).

[21] The completeness of the oblation is a motif borrowed from the ŚāṅkhB. (see above). The JB. (see below) has an entirely different conception of this completeness.

[22] Minard, *Trois Énigmes* I, 384 *b* criticizes Eggeling's translation and remarks on the syntax of this sentence that *kṣīram* should be subject ("si donc il se trouve ne boire que du lait . .").

[23] There is no indication that supplementing here implies restoring what has been lost during the cooking.

6.5 *The pot is removed from the fire and the milk is ladled out.*

KS. 6, 4: 52.14 ff.: In the agnihotra ritual husband and wife take a different course. If he should take off (the milk) eastward the husband would die first. If he should take off westward the wife would die first. He should take it off exactly to the north. Thus they become old together.[1] He should first ladle out a full ladle, then a reduced one, then (again) a reduced one, and then as last the most reduced one. His sons according to seniority will become prosperous. He might also first ladle out a reduced ladle, then more, then more and at last a full one. More and more food there is produced for him. But (in that case) the youngest of the sons becomes prosperous (first). He who may wish "May all my sons become equally prosperous", should ladle out all the ladles equally full. This father desires prosperity for all the sons. All of them become equally prosperous. No one surpasses the other. He ladles out four times. He (i.e. the priest)[2] [bestows on him (i.e. the sacrificer)][2] quadruped cattle.[2] [He first offers twice].[2] He bestows biped cattle on him.

— Later (KS. 6, 7) the same text again deals with the ladling out in the passage treating the silence during the agnihotra, especially prescribed for this part of the rite. The version of the MS. (1, 8, 4: 119.14 ff.) completely agrees with the direction of taking off the pot and with the decreasing amount of milk in the ladles. On the latter point it adds an objection:

MS. 1, 8, 4: 119.20 ff.: Now they say about this: "He performs a smaller (i.e. decreasing) sacrifice, he obtains smaller offspring, a smaller amount of cattle, a smaller quantity of food. He becomes inferior. He should start with a reduced ladling, then ladle out more, then (again) more and a full ladle at last, for the progress (i.e. success)[3] of the sacrifice.

— In a different paragraph of its agnihotra section the MS. mentions the warming of the spoon before ladling out the oblation:

MS. 1, 8, 5: 122.3–6: When he warms the agnihotra spoon, he (Agni) becomes unappeased. After having heated the agnihotra spoon, he must put his hand on it; or he should put the spoon on his hand after having warmed it. By this he appeases him (Agni); by this he propitiates him. Having been appeased and propitiated he does not harm him.[4]

— MS. 1, 8, 7: 126.14 states that during the ladling out the sacrificer should be standing (see Caland's note on ĀpŚS. 6, 7, 4 which has to be corrected). According to MS. 1, 9, 5: 136.8 ff. he should touch the milk which has been ladled out with the *daśahotṛ* formula. The treatment of the subject of this section evolves further in the TB.

TB. 2, 1, 3, 4–6: If he should take off (the milk) eastward, he would pierce the sacrificer with grief;[5] if southward, it would fall to the share of the *pitṛs*;[6] if westward, he would pierce the wife (of the sacrificer) with grief.[5] He should take it off to the north. That is the quarter auspicious for gods and men.[7] He takes it off in that direction for appeasement.[8] He makes a track,[9] for the sake of the continuity of the sacrifice. He purifies (the two ladles) by heating them. Thereby he makes a 'pouring under' (*upástaraṇa*)[10] in the ladles. He ladles out four times. The cattle have four legs. (So) he (i.e. the sacrificer) obtains cattle. He ladles out all[11] (four ladles) completely filled. For all[11] are auspicious and favourable.[12] He ladles out successively[13] in order that his (i.e. the sacrificer's) offspring may be born in successive order.[14] One after the other his offspring prospers. He touches simultaneously[15] (the *agnihotrasthālī* in which the milk has been cooked and the *agnihotrahavanī* into which four ladles have been ladled out) in order to make a distinction (between the milk in both receptacles).

— On the last action, and on the fourfold ladling out, see also the following passages in the same brāhmaṇa:

TB. 2, 1, 3, 9: Four times he ladles out, twice he offers. Therefore the biped (man) eats the quadruped (animal). And he causes the quadrupeds to be dependent on the biped.

TB. 2, 1, 5, 10: The gods who come in the evening and those who come in the morning come to the house of the performer of the agnihotra. If he should not satisfy them, they would keep aloof from[16] his offspring and his cattle. If he should satisfy them, they being satisfied would satisfy him with offspring and cattle. In the evening he touches simultaneously (both ladles), saying: "With the gods who come in the evening"; in the morning saying: "With the gods who come in the morning". (Thereby) he satisfies the gods who come in the evening as well as those who come in the morning. They being satisfied satisfy him with offspring and cattle.

— The ŚB. gives hardly any information on the actions performed after the cooking and before the offering, while a rather lengthy passage on the subject is found in the ŚāṅkhB. as well as in the JB.

ŚB. 2, 3, 1, 17: Then he ladles out four times. For this milk is divided into four parts.[17]

ŚāṅkhB. 2, 1: He should take off the milk which has to be offered, to the north, setting it down thrice, for the sake of threefoldness. For the worship of the gods is threefold.[18] He should take it away without making an interruption.[19] Thus the sacrificer does not decay. Then he touches the coals on the south side with a poke (and says:) "Homage to the gods". For the gods are not beyond homage. He should carefully push back the coals.[20] Thus no (cow) at all, even if she is walking at the tail of the herd,[21] gets lost. He should ladle out four times — this All is fourfold — in order to obtain this All.[22] He should (optionally) ladle out five times — the sacrifice is fivefold — in order to obtain the sacrifice.

JB. 1, 39: Then he takes off (the milk and puts it down with the formula:) "Establish heaven, establish the world between heaven and earth, establish the earth, establish offspring and cattle for me, the sacrificer".[23] He pushes back the coals (into the gārhapatya fire, with the formula:) "You bring welfare, danger coming from foreign people has been pushed back". Then he takes the dipping spoon (*sruva*) and the offering spoon (*sruc*) and purifies them by heating them over the fire (reciting:) "Burnt is the race of the Rākṣasas, burnt are the powers of adversity". Then he rubs the offering spoon in the evening (with the formula:) "Together with the gods coming in the evening" and in the morning (with) "Together with the gods coming in the morning". "Thee, the golden one, made of gold, (I rub)". "Thou art the channel which conveys the oblations". It becomes the channel for conveying the oblations. Then he says: "I shall ladle out". He[24] should speak: "Yes, I (shall send) myself to heaven".

JB. 1, 40: The first ladle lifted out is a representation of the Full- and New-Moon sacrifices. Full- and New-Moon sacrifices are performed by him who, knowing thus, ladles out the first time. The second ladle lifted out is a representation of the Four-monthly sacrifices. The Four-monthly sacrifices are performed by him who, knowing thus, ladles out the second time. The third ladle lifted out is a representation of the *iṣṭis* and *paśubandhas*.[25] (...) The fourth ladle lifted out is a representation of the *tryambaka*, the *vājapeya* and the *aśvamedha* sacrifices[25] (...).

VādhS. 3, 22: As to the first ladle which Prajāpati lifted out, thereby he lifted out three months of the year, one quarter of himself, and Agni among the deities. The second ladle which he lifted out, thereby (he lifted out) again three months, one quarter of himself and Vāyu among the deities. The third ladle (...) Āditya among the deities. The fourth ladle (...) the moon among the deities. With this same integrated self (or: body) in the form of the year and with this agnihotra, with these utterances[26] Prajāpati won heaven at once. He who knowing thus offers the agnihotra at once wins heaven with a body which is thus integrated, with the year and the agnihotra (thus integrated), with these utterances. Now those who know thus say on this point: "If someone dies after having offered at least one oblation,[27] who would have injured him, if he had reached one oblation? With the first oblation he would at once have won heaven". He who knowing thus offers the agnihotra and he for whom someone knowing thus offers the agnihotra wins heaven with the first oblation.

NOTES

[1] Evidently in *sam* .. *jīryataḥ* the meaning of *sam* is "together". Perhaps *sam* (meaning "completely") in *sampratyudīcīnam* is used for the foundation of the conclusion.

[2] The text has a lacuna here, which can easily be filled in on the basis of the parallel version of the Kapiṣṭhala Saṃhitā.

[3] The meaning of *abhikrānti* in this context is not "overpowering, bringing into one's possession" (Monier-Williams' Dict.). The "going forward, progress, success" is on the part of the sacrifice. So the genitive *yajñasya* is subjective rather than objective. Cf. TB. 2, 1, 3, 5 (below) *yajñasya saṃtatyai* "for the continuity of the sacrifice".

[4] For an explanation see Hoens, *Śānti*, p. 37.

[5] The sacrificer sits on the east side and his wife on the west side of the gārhapatya fire, as Dumont observes in a note. See also the plan of the place of sacrifice in Dumont's book on the agnihotra.

[6] The deceased forefathers (*pitṛs*) are connected with the south, which consequently is an unfavourable quarter. Moreover an oblation to be offered to the gods is not allowed to become *pitṛdevatya* ("sacred to the fathers").

[7] Hoens, *Śānti*, p. 34 translates: "That is the *faustus* direction, the direction of gods and men", whereas Dumont renders: "Verily that region is the appeased region (i.e., the cooler and more comfortable region) for gods and men". I have followed Dumont's construction (genitive dependent on *śānta*), but I am not quite sure about the meaning of *śānta* required here.

[8] Dumont adds between brackets: "i.e., in order to soothe the hurting heat of the fire". This may sound rather convincing; on the other hand there is an opposition between the southern quarter (which is unauspicious or *aśānta*) and the northern one.

[9] I.e. he draws the pot from the coals over the earth without lifting it and thereby makes a track. Thus a break in the continuity of the sacrifice (an important element) is avoided.

[10] The *upastaraṇa* consists of a layer of ghee poured out underneath the oblation in other rituals. The counterpart is the *abhighāra* (sprinkling over the oblation), to which TB. 2, 1, 3, 3 refers in another identification (see Section 6.3, n. 9).

[11] I have translated *sarvān* by "all (four ladles)" in order to make a distinction with the parallel verions which mention only one (i.e. the first or the last) full ladle. The argumentation, however, is remarkably flat.

[12] The commentary explains: "all people connected with the sacrificer become virtuous and rich". Dumont translates: "(Consequently) all virtuous men become fortunate". The argumentation is rather vague. Are we to assume that *sarva* means "complete, whole"? In that case "whole, complete ones" represent fortune and success.

[13] Perhaps *anūcaḥ* does not merely denote "successively, in order" (or: "in uninterrupted succession", tr. Dumont), which would hardly make sense, since of course with one ladle one can only successively ladle out. A succession of full and less full ladles may be implied. In that case an optional prescription (in opposition to *sarvān* "all of them (full)"?) is implied.

[14] Dumont: "For the uninterrupted succession of the (Sacrificer's) offspring". In an alternative interpretation (see n. 13) this might mean: "In order that the natural order of the offspring in connection with inheritance and prosperity in general is not disturbed".

[15] See Dumont's note, *L'Agnihotra*, p. 210.

[16] Delbrück, *Altind. Synt.*, p. 259 translates "so gehen sie ihm mit seinen Kindern und Herden davon". A correct rendering, however, is found on p. 131 f.: "würden sie sich von den Kindern und den Herden des Opferers abwenden". Cf. TS. 2, 5, 7, 5 ("... they would go away from the sacrificer's offspring and cattle", tr. Keith).

[17] This refers to the four teats of the udder.

[18] The Soma sacrifices have three daily sessions.

[19] For a criticism of Keith's translation see Caland, *AO* 10, p. 308. This refers to making a track (i.e. drawing the pot over the earth). See n. 9.

[20] See Caland, *AO* 10, p. 308 who criticizes Keith.

[21] Keith translates *antamacāriṇī* (which is not found in Monier-Williams' Dict.) by "the outermost (of his offering)" without explaining the feminine gender. Pushing back the outermost elements of the ritual (i.c. the coals) within the sphere of the sacrifice should (as usual) produce a counterpart in the non-ritualistic profane sphere. The coals correspond to cows (fem.) who have to be brought back to the herd, since they are in imminent danger of being lost. The verb *naś-* often refers to the loss of cattle.

[22] *idaṃ sarvam* may denote "all here" or "this all, this Universe". See author, *JB. I, 1–65*, p. 166 ff. The fourfoldness of the universe was a well-known motif ever since the ṚV. Moreover obtaining the All as an expression for becoming one with the totality of space and time, and being freed from the limitations of the transitory individual, is a current conception in the brāhmaṇas. See author, o.c., p. 167.

[23] Note that the sacrificer himself is mentioned in the formula pronounced by the priest. It is doubtful whether originally an officiant took part in the agnihotra ritual, which is a particularly individual rite. Establishing the pot of milk on the earth means in the formulas: establishing welfare for the sacrificer. The three parts of the cosmos mentioned in the formulas are connected with the fact that according to some sūtras (and brāhmaṇas) the milk is removed from the fire in three stages (i.e. it is put down thrice).

[24] The formula has no parallels. The supplement proposed by me (between brackets) implies that "he" should refer to the sacrificer himself. There are indeed some instances in the agnihotra ritual (especially in connection with the ladling out) in which the sacrificer himself also recites some formulas.

[25] For all these sacrifices see Hillebrandt, *Ritual-Litteratur* and Renou, *Vocabulaire du Rituel Védique*.

[26] The *vyāhṛtis bhūr, bhuvaḥ, svar* are recited according to some sūtras.

[27] Caland translates: "Wer vor der einzigen Spende stirbt" and remarks in a note that the phrase "vor der einen Spende" is not clear. Moreover the mss. read *ekahutyā* instead of *ekāhutyai*. For *arvāk* with instrumental perhaps ṚV. 10, 129, 6 may be compared (though some scholars interpret the instr. differently). At least the meaning of *arvāk* should be "after" and not "before". It denotes a *terminus post quem*. Having offered the agnihotra at least once one has obtained heaven through the ladling out. The actualization of this winning of heaven has to wait for the death of the sacrificer.

6.6 *The settings-down* I.

— At several stages of the agnihotra ritual the milk is placed down (near one of the fires). Some of the texts call this the *upasads*, a term taken from the *soma* ritual. In the latter ritual it denotes approach or worship. In the agnihotra it is connected with the causative *upasādayati* "to set down near". These settings down are to be regarded as some sort of worship of the fires near which the milk is placed down.

KS. 6, 4: 53.2 ff.: With the formula "Give me cattle" he should set it down to the west (of the gārhapatya). The gārhapatya is (to be homologized with) cattle; the milk is cattle. This is a control of the cattle. (Or) he should not set it down behind (the gārhapatya). The agnihotra (milk) is an oblation (*havis*). The sacrificer is an oblation. He drives away the sacrificer who has become the oblation. He should set it down to the north.

MS. 1, 8, 4: 120.5 f.: He should not set it down behind (the gārhapatya). That (would be) a retreat of the sacrifice.[1] He should set it down on the spot where it has been ladled out or (even) further, for the sake of the progress of the sacrifice.

TB. 2, 1, 3, 6 f.: He should not set down (the milk) near (a fire, i.c. the gārhapatya), when he does not intend to offer (in it). If he should set it down near (the gārhapatya) without going to offer (in it), it would be as if he should set down something for the one and present it to the other. He would be cut off from this (gārhapatya fire). In that he puts (the milk) on the gārhapatya thereby he (already) propitiates the gārhapatya.

— Strangely enough the same brāhmaṇa afterwards states (in the same agnihotra section) that the milk should also be set down near the gārhapatya:

TB. 2, 1, 5, 8: To him who knows the *upasads* of the agnihotra, the *upasads* show reverence. He finds a respectful attendant (*upasattṛ*). After having ladled out he sets (the milk) down near (the gārhapatya). (Thus) he propitiates the earth.

— This text as well as the ŚāṅkhB. mentions together the three occasions on which the milk may be set down. Perhaps TB. 2, 1, 5, 8 is based on the ŚāṅkhB., being a later addition.

ŚāṅkhB. 2, 2: The *upasads* in the agnihotra ritual must be learnt. After having ladled out he sets (the milk) down to the north of the gārhapatya. Thereby he obtains this world.

NOTES

[1] The movement of the agnihotra sacrifice is from west (gārhapatya) to east (āhavanīya). Setting down the milk to the west of the gārhapatya therefore marks a retreat. One should not return. See *JB. I, 1–65*, p. 162 and 165.

6.7 *The priest moves from the gārhapatya to the āhavanīya.*

KS. 6, 4: 53.4 ff.: The agnihotra (milk) is something impure. The fire (of the gārhapatya) is a means of purification. In that he takes (the milk which has been ladled out) through[1] the fire, thereby he purifies it. He (i.e. Agni, the fire of the gārhapatya)[2] misses it, when[2] after having placed it on the fire in the west (i.e. on the gārhapatya) he offers it in the east (i.e. in the āhavanīya). By taking it through the fire he pleases him and causes him not to miss it.[3] From this gārhapatya the eastern (āhavanīya) fire was produced. This here (i.e. the gārhapatya) was Prajāpati; that eastern one (i.e. the āhavanīya) was Agni. This one (i.e. Prajāpati) ran after him (Agni), having taken this (milk, i.e. the oblation of the primeval agnihotra), and offered it. Therefore, after having placed the agnihotra milk on the fire in the west they offer it in the east. In the east they cook the other oblations; in the east they offer them.

MS. 1, 8, 4: 120.6 ff.: He makes the western fire miss it, (or: jealous), when they heat it on the western fire, but offer it in the eastern fire. They take it (i.e. the milk which is transferred to the āhavanīya) through the fire (of the gārhapatya). Thereby he pleases it. Moreover this is a purification of the agnihotra milk. He purified it.[4] The eastern fire was emitted from the western one.[5] They made it stop within this limit.[6] Therefore he offers after having run eastward.

— TB. has only a small trace of the motif of the gārhapatya being jealous. It argues that the gārhapatya is already gratified by heating the milk on it, in the context of the discussion on the setting down of the milk (see the preceding section). For the recitation of the *daśahotṛ* formula by the priest on his way to the āhavanīya see TB. 2, 2, 1, 6.

ŚB. 2, 3, 1, 17: Then he takes a kindling-stick and runs to (the āhavanīya) in order to offer an oblation on the burning (stick).

JB. 1, 40: Having taken a kindling-stick he runs eastward.

NOTES

[1] The preposition *samayā* means "zwischen" (Delbrück, *Altind. Syntax*, p. 183), "zwischen, mitten durch" (Speyer, *Ved. u. S. Syntax*, p. 25), "near, about" (Speyer, *Sanskrit Syntax*, p. 134), "through, into the middle of or midst of anything (..) in the neighbourhood of" (Monier-Williams). It is used in the same context in the sūtras, where Dumont translates "juste au-dessus de la flamme" (*L'Agnihotra*, p. 56: ĀpŚS. 6, 8, 5 *samayārciḥ*), "à proximité de la flamme" (o.c., p. 98: HirŚS. 3, 7, 55), "à proximité de .."

(o.c., p. 143: MŚS. 1, 6, 1, 30), "au dessus" (o.c., p. 190: ŚŚS. 2, 8, 22). The meaning "near" seems to belong rather to the classical Sanskrit. ĀśvŚS. 2, 3, 15 *adhi gārhapatyaṃ hṛtvā* proves that the milk is not held in the nearness of the fire (Dumont, o.c., p, 168: "juste au-dessus de"). The *Śrautakośa*'s rendering "through the flame of the gārhapatya fire" (p. 104, BhārŚS.) suits the purificatory function. If *samayā* should mean "near", it denotes "so near as to touch it"; if "over, above", it implies "skimming". The central meaning may be "on a level with" "touching".

[2] In my translation *etat* has been taken as referring to the milk of the agnihotra oblation, and *yat* as "when". Perhaps one might as well interpret *anudhyāyati* as "to be jealous" or "to be offensed", with *etat* .. *yat* as "on that point that".

[3] Read with Caland, *ZDMG* 72, p. 13 *ananudhyāyinam* instead of *anudhyāyinam*.

[4] The use of the form *apupot* instead of a present may be an indication that the subject is not the ordinary performer of the agnihotra (as in *tenaivainaṃ prīṇāti*),but Prajāpati. In the version of the KS. Prajāpati plays a role in the primeval archetype of this agnihotra. The composition of this passage in the MS. makes a rather corrupt impression.

[5] Since *pūrvam* should refer to the eastern fire and consequently a masculine form is required, a disjunct construction has to be assumed in which the proleptic accusative *pūrvaṃ sṛṣṭam* is resumed by the pronoun *tam*. For this type of construction see Oertel, *Syntax of Cases*, p. 78 ff.

[6] Text and interpretation are doubtful. One expects a third person singular (referring to Prajāpati) instead of the plural. Probably traces of the well-known Prajāpati myths in which Agni (h.l. = āhavanīya fire) is emitted by Prajāpati, flees and is stopped (h.l. on the place of the actual āhavanīya), are to be found here.

6.8 *The settings-down* II.

KS. 6, 5: 53.18 ff.: "Give me life; give me glory; give me offspring" (with these formulas) he sets (the milk and the kindling-stick) down in the east (i.e. near the āhavanīya). The agnihotra is a creation.[1] If he should not set it down, the descendants[2] would go away without returning. In that he sets it down, therefore the descendants are restrained; therefore they are subservient.

MS. 1, 8, 4: 120.10–11: "Give me life" (with this formula) he sets (the milk) down. Thereby he bestows life on him (i.e. on the sacrificer). "Give me glory" (with this formula) he sets down. He bestows glory on him.

TB. 2, 1, 5, 8: Being about to offer he sets the milk down near (the āhavanīya). (Thus) he propitiates the space between heaven and earth.

ŚāṅkhB. 2, 2: Being about to offer in the āhavanīya (he sets it down) a second time. Thereby he obtains the space between heaven and earth.

JB. 1, 40: He sets (the milk and the kindling-stick) down (on the grass near the āhavanīya) silently (reciting) "The kindling-stick is indeed a man. He is kindled by food. Make me go to heaven by the energy of the food (of the oblation). Make my agnihotra go there where is the favourite domain of the gods and the seers"[3]

— An extraordinary position is taken in by the ŚB. which rejects setting down the milk before offering:

ŚB. 2, 3, 1, 17: He offers the first oblation without (first) setting down (the milk) near (the āhavanīya). If he should set it down, this would be as if one should take food to someone and set it down on one's way. But if (he offers) without previously setting it down, this is as if one first takes food to someone and only afterwards sets it down.[4]

NOTES

[1] The term *sṛṣṭi* does not just denote "creation". It refers to "emission (or emanation)" and "letting loose". In this context the "letting loose" is regarded as dangerous, since there is a risk that this movement does not stop. Therefore a "setting down" should be made in order to establish rest.

[2] The term *prajā* may be taken to mean offspring or (plural) descendants, but it may also refer to the subjects of a ruler. Perhaps the latter meaning is suitable here and *upasthā* does not simply mean "to be (or: remain) present", but "to be subservient". The "setting down" establishes law and order.

[3] See author, *JB. I, 1–65*, p. 96, n. 16 on some problems of the interpretation of this passage. The present translation does not follow the punctuation of the edition of this brāhmaṇa.

[4] He sets it down after the first and before the second libation.

6.9 *The function of the* samidh *(kindling-stick)*.

KS. 6, 5: 53.11 ff.: It is the kindling-stick which is the fuel of the agnihotra. When he lays the stick on (the āhavanīya), he thereby makes it fuel for the agnihotra.[1] Rudra besmeared the plants with poison. The cattle did not eat them while grazing. The gods wished to make an expiation for them. Prajāpati spoke: "I choose a boon and shall make those (plants) tasteful for you". He choose this kindling-stick. Therefore there is (only) one (kindling-stick). For there is (only) one Prajāpati. He let Agni loose upon them (the herbs).[2] Agni made them tasteful. When this (kindling-stick) has been laid on (the fire), the herbs become savoury for the sacrificer. For him who knows thus, food becomes savoury. Many people make it twofold (i.e. twice lay a stick on the fire) thinking "I must offer both oblations in a blazing fire". (But this is not necessary) for it (i.e. the fire) is kindled once for the whole sacrifice.

MS. 1, 8, 4: 120.11 ff.: The Rudras besmeared these herbs with poison. The cattle did not eat them anymore. The gods ran to Prajāpati (for help). Prajāpati said: "Let me choose a boon. There should be a share for me". "Choose a boon" they said. He said: "Let the kindling-stick be sacred to me". Therefore the kindling-stick is offered to Prajāpati. For it was choosen as a boon among the gods by him. Should he make two kindling-sticks since there are two oblations? He should make one, for there is only one Prajāpati. Forsooth the kindling-stick should be single. It even happens that many oblations are offered.[3] He scattered[4] Agni (or: fire) over them (i.e. those herbs). He made them savoury. They were born anew. At that moment when he lays on the kindling-stick[5] all herbs become savoury for the sacrificer of the agnihotra and for him who offers the Full- and New-Moon sacrifices. He has made savoury[6] all herbs for him.

— For a different story of the poisoning and making savoury of the herbs in connection with the agnihotra see TB. 2, 1, 1, 1–2, where, however, the context does not agree with the present one. It is remarkable that in connection with the kindling-stick the TB. does not have this myth, as appears below.

TB. 2, 1, 3, 7–9: Agni feared: "The oblations will pass me over (i.e. evade me)". He saw this kindling-stick (*samidh*). This he laid on himself. Thence forward the oblations remained fixed on the fire (or: on Agni). Because it condensed (*samayacchat*)[7] him, therefore the kindling-stick is called *samidh*. He (i.e. the priest) lays the kindling-wood on (the fire) and makes it (the fire) compact, so that it may be able to support the oblations. Moreover he makes the agnihotra provided with fuel, so that the oblation may have something to stand on.[8] Those who partake in the debates say: "If he puts one kindling-stick on the fire and offers two libations, on what kindling-stick should he offer the second libation?" (The answer should be:) If he should put two kindling-sticks on (the fire), he would produce a rival for him (i.e. for the sacrificer). He offers one (libation)[9] after having laid on a kindling-stick and a second (one) with the formula.[10] (Thus) he offers both libations provided with fuel. He does not produce a rival for him (i.e. for the sacrificer).

ŚāṅkhB. 2, 2: He lays on a kindling-stick consisting of Palāśa wood (= Butea frondosa). The Palāśa is equal to Soma. This is the first libation, and a Soma-libation at that.[11] It has the measure of a span. For these orifices have the (ultimate) distance of one span towards each other.[12]

ŚB. 2, 3, 1, 17: Then he takes a kindling-stick and runs to (the āhavanīya) in order to offer on the blazing (stick).

JB. 1, 40: Having taken a kindling-stick he goes eastward (to the āhavanīya), He puts (the stick and the milk) down (upon the grass) near (the āhavanīya) silently (reciting) "The kindling-stick is indeed a man (...)".[13] Then he lays the stick on (the fire, reciting) "I make thee a bridge to heaven, a golden cross-beam, *svāhā*".

VādhS. 3, 30: Now they say: "What is (the function of) the kindling-stick?" The kindling-stick is an oblation. When he lays (the stick) on (the fire), he offers by that (stick) all the days and nights that have passed before his birth.

— The text continues by stating that the first libation represents the offering of all the days and nights since the birth and before the establishment of the sacred fires. The second libation substitutes for the offerings after death. Probably the preceding paragraph (VādhS. 3, 29), which is rather corrupt, also refers to the *samidh*.

NOTES

[1] The other wood forms the fuel of the fire; the kindling-stick is the fuel which enables the transport of the oblation from earth to heaven.

[2] For the construction of *upasṛj-* + acc. + instr. see author, *JB. I, 1–65*, p. 69, n. 1.

[3] More than two libations are offered in rituals other than the agnihotra. In those cases as well there is not an unlimited number of kindling-sticks corresponding to the number of the libations. Probably the text has in view the New- and Full-Moon sacrifices mentioned in the same passage.

[4] The text reads *agninānvavākarot* and M.-W.'s dictionary mentions s.v. *anvavakṛ-* only "to despise, refuse" (with explicit reference to the MS.). This meaning of course does not fit here. Read °*kirat* for °*karot* (M.-W.: *anvavakṛ-* "to scatter or strew about (with instr.)"; only referring to Yājñavalkya).

[5] The translation does not follow the punctuation suggested by the edition of von Schroeder.

[6] Read *svadayām akaḥ* instead of *svadhayām akaḥ*.

[7] The verb admits of several other translations. One may also take into consideration "to shut, close". The most essential element required here is that of impermeability. Agni is afraid that the fire is too meagre and lets through the libation.

[8] In fact *āhutīnāṃ dhṛtyai* and *āhutīnāṃ pratiṣṭhityai* come to the same. The only difference is the starting-point, the fire, resp. the oblations. Therefore the genitive *āhutīnām* should be taken as an objective, resp. subjective genitive, as has been done in the translation.

[9] One may connect *ekām* with *samidham* (opposition to *dve samidhau*), or

(as has been done in the translation) supply *āhutim* (opposition to *anyām āhutim*). Dumont translates: "(Therefore) having put upon the fire only one stick, he pours one of the two libations with a formula (and the other silently)". It is to be doubted whether *anyām āhutim* is correctly translated by "one of the two libations".

[10] The argumentation is not completely clear. Perhaps the formula of the second libation, which according to some sūtras is not recited aloud (as indicated by the term *manasā*), should be pronounced (indicated by *yajuṣā*) by way of compensation for the lack of a second kindling-stick. Or are we to take the actual kindling-stick as intended for the first libation, and the formula of the first libation as the symbolical kindling-stick for the second libation?

[11] Keith's translation "This is the first Soma libation" seems more correct from a grammatical point of view, but does not make sense. For the interpretation of the kindling-stick as an oblation compare VādhS. 3, 30 (see below).

[12] Keith renders *prādeśamātraṃ hīma ātmano 'bhi (*read *adhi) prāṇāḥ* "for these breaths are a span over the body". Caland, *AO* 10. p. 308 suggests "for the mouth (or the nose) is a span (distant) from the body". Indeed *adhi* is the reading required here and denotes together with the ablative "from" rather than "over". However, the statement that the mouth "is a span (distant) from the body" has no meaningful function in the passage. Moreover the plural *prāṇāḥ* has to be accounted for. Obviously this refers to the organs of sense (the openings) rather than to the vital powers behind them. Probably a span is the ultimate distance between the openings themselves (*ātmano 'dhi* "away from themselves" with the regular singular of *ātman*). The kindling-stick represents the diameter of the head which eats the oblation. It is hardly imaginable that this *samidh*, on which there is offered, should stand for the distance between body (*ātman*) and the openings of the head.

[13] For this passage see also Section 6.8.

6.10 *The offering I: The first libation.*

KS. 6, 5: 53.20 ff.: (With the formula) "In Agni (be) light, light in Agni" he should offer the agnihotra in the evening. With a speech which has something in the interior[1] he produces an embryo;[1] with a speech which consists of a pair he impregnates. (With the formula) "Sūrya is the light, the light is Sūrya" (he offers) in the morning. With a speech that has something in the interior and consists of a pair he engenders it (the embryo). The expressed and the unexpressed[2] form a pair. That which is (recited) with a formula and that which is (recited) in thought[2] form a pair. Of the two oblations there is this variation: the evening oblation is sacred to Agni, the morning oblation to Sūrya. Agni is the one who inseminates, Sūrya the one who brings forth.[3] After the sun has just set, he should offer the agnihotra in the evening, just before sunrise in the morning. Agni, having poured out the sun as seed, impregnates the night. He engenders him in the morning with a speech which has something in the interior and consists of a pair. Along with and as a consequence[4] of his being born offspring are born. He for whom the agnihotra is offered thus becomes prolific with offspring and cattle.[5]

— The passage above especially deals with the formula of the first libation and its twofold (evening and morning) aspect. Since here we touch upon the most important moment of the ritual, the texts mostly give a digression on the esoteric meaning of the agnihotra. Procreation and fertility are essential aims in connection with this and other sacrifices. See also the parallel of the MS., which also refers to the three *vyāhṛtis* to be uttered before the first formula.

MS. 1, 8, 5: 120.21 ff.: "Earth, air, heaven"[6] he should say before offering. That (utterance) represents brahman. It is truth, it is order[7] (*ṛta*). For without (*ṛte*) this no sacrifice is (possible). Therefore there should be spoken thus. "Agni is the light, the light is Agni", with this speech which has something in its interior he impregnates. With this speech, which consists of a couple, he causes a couple to procreate. That he offers with speech and with a formula, that is a couple.[8] That he offers silently and in thought, that is a couple.[8]

MS. 1, 8, 5: 121.6 ff.: The evening libation is sacred to Agni. Thereby he pours out seed. That pouring of seed makes the night pregnant with an embryo. By the (oblation) sacred to Sūrya he engenders[9] that embryo in the morning.

— So far, the regular order of the description of the agnihotra as found in the KS. and the MS. has been followed. It should be noted that afterwards the MS. again deals with the three *vyāhṛtis* (in a rather short passage) and that the KS. even extensively takes up this subject in the addenda of 6, 7, whereas it was omitted in the systematical description of 6, 5. Has the later version of the MS. taken the two passages of the KS. (6, 5 and 6, 7) together in its more systematical treatment of 1, 8, 5?

KS. 6, 7: 56.5–14: Together with speech the human beings were born, without[9a] speech the gods and the Asuras. Whatever the human beings spoke, that they became. The gods and the Asuras said to Prajāpati: "These have become (all) this". He measured out the truth of speech, with the words "*bhūr*, *bhuvas*, *svar*". The fourth part, the untruth, he deposited with the human beings. What the human beings speak, that is the untrue part of speech. (With) "*bhūr*" he created this world, Agni, the Rathantara *sāman*, the Trivṛt *stoma*, the Gāyatrī metre. (With) "*bhuvas*" (he created) the space between heaven and earth, the god Wind, the Vāmadevya *sāman*, the Triṣṭubh metre, the Pañcadaśa *stoma*. (With) "*svar*" (he created) heaven, Sūrya, the Bṛhat *sāman*, the Ekaviṃśa *stoma*, the Jagatī metre. (With) "*bhūr bhuvas svar*. In Agni is the Sun, the Sun is in Agni" he should offer the agnihotra. That is the truth of speech. That is a couple. That is brahman. Thereby he offers. These are bricks which he puts down upon each other then.[10] Having placed these bricks he mounts to the highest vault of heaven. He becomes the highest among his equals, if the agnihotra is thus offered for him.

MS. 1, 8, 6: 124.10–11: "*bhūr bhuvas svar*" he should say before offering. Thereby he piles up bricks for these worlds, in order to reach heaven.

— For the identification of the evening with Agni and the morning with the sun, as well as for the procreative aspects of the agnihotra with the motif of the creative pair (*mithuna*) see als TB. 2, 1, 2, 7 ff., translated above in Section 4. The following passage was omitted there (see Section 4, n. 6):

TB. 2, 1, 2, 10–12: If he should offer to Agni in the evening, he would be cut off from the sun. If he should offer to Sūrya in the morning, he would be cut off from Agni. He would produce a strife between the gods. There should be offered with "Agni is the light, the light is Sūrya; hail" in the evening and with "Sūrya is the light, the light is Agni; hail" in the morning. Thereby there is offered to both in the evening, to both in the morning. He does not produce a strife among the gods. He says "Agni is the light". Agni indeed is the impregnator. He says (in fact) "The offspring is light".[11] He (the priest) produces[12] offspring for him (the sacrificer). He says (in the morning) "Sūrya is light". In the offspring which has been produced, he places seed (i.e. fertility). He says "Light is Agni". He (Agni) firmly establishes the offspring after his birth on earth.

— Besides this unusual form of the formula the TB. also prescribes the usual one in a different passage (dealing with an expiation for not having taken out the fire in time):

TB. 2, 1, 9, 2: He offers in the evening with "Agni is the light, the light is Agni; hail". Thereby he inseminates. In the morning (he offers with) "Sūrya is the light, the light is Sūrya; hail". He progenerates what has been inseminated.[13]

— The text continues by stating that the seed is not reproduced in case the sun rises over the agnihotra before it has been offered, and then further deals with the expiation.

ŚāṅkhB. 2, 1: He offers in the evening and at daybreak. In the evening to Agni, at daybreak to Sūrya. The day belongs to Sūrya, the night to Agni. Thus he gratifies night and day at their beginning.

— For the formulas used by ŚāṅkhB. (the usual ones) see Section 1, 3 (ŚāṅkhB. 2, 8). For an extensive passage of the ŚB. (2, 3, 1, 3–5) parallel to the KS. above, in which the procreative aspect is essential, see Section 13.2. On the interpretation of the first (and to some extent also of the second) libation and its formulas the following passage of the ŚB. gives elaborate information:

ŚB. 2, 3, 1, 22–38: It was one single oblation which Prajāpati offered there in the beginning.[14] And since these, namely Agni, the one that ventilates (Vāyu) and Sūrya, afterwards took efforts on this point,[15] therefore this second libation is offered. The first libation, that is the deity of the agnihotra.[16] To that (deity) it is therefore offered. And the second one, that is the equivalent for Agni Sviṣṭakṛt.[16] Therefore he offers it in the northern part (of the fire). For that is the quarter of Sviṣṭakṛt. Now the second libation is made in order to produce a couple. For a pair is a couple which produces offspring. These two libations form a pair: what has come to be and what is about to become, the born and the to-be-born, what has come true and what one hopes, to-day and to-morrow, according to that principle they are a pair. What has come to be is the self, for that which has come to be is certain and something certain is also the self. What is about to become is progeny; for that which is to be is uncertain and something uncertain is also progeny. (. .).[17] The first libation is offered for the sake of the self. He offers it with a *mantra*, for the *mantra* is something certain and something certain is the self. The second one is offered for the sake of progeny. He offers it silently (i.e. not uttering a formula, but having one in thought); for that which is silently (done), is something uncertain, and something uncertain is progeny. (In the evening) he offers (the first libation) with "Agni is the light, the light is Agni; hail", and in the morning with "Sūrya is the light, the light is Sūrya; hail". Thus there is offered with truth.[18] For when the sun sets, then Agni is the light; when the sun rises, then Sūrya is the light. What is offered with truth, that goes to the gods. Now it also happened that Takṣan once recited this same (formula) as follows for Āruṇi who wished to obtain lustre as a (learned) brahmin (*brahmavarcasa*): "Agni is lustre, light is lustre", "Sūrya is lustre, light is lustre". He who, knowing thus, offers the agnihotra obtains lustre as a (learned) brahmin. On the other hand "Agni is the light, the light is Agni; hail", is a form of generation. Thereby he encloses the seed which is the light on both sides with the deity. Now seed[19] enclosed on both sides is born. Therefore he causes it to be born by enclosing it on both sides. (...)[20] But on this point Jīvala Cailaki said: "Āruṇi produced just conception; he does not bring forth. He should offer with this (formula) in the evening. And in the morning with "The light is Sūrya, Sūrya is the light". Then he places the seed which is the light, outside by means of the deity, Now seed[19] is born outside (the body). Thus he causes it to be born". Now some people say[21] "In the evening he offers Sūrya in Agni, and in the morning Agni in Sūrya". Now this is the case with those who offer after sunrise. For when the sun sets, then Agni is the light; when the sun rises, then Sūrya is the light. On this point one cannot blame him. There is indeed (room for) criticism[22] in that there is not manifestly offered to the deity of the agnihotra. He says[23] "Agni is the light, the light is Agni; hail" and not "To Agni, hail"; and in the morning "Sūrya is the light, the light is Sūrya; hail" and not "To Sūrya, hail". He should offer (in the evening) with this (*mantra*) "Along with the divine Savitṛ". Thereby it becomes connected with Savitṛ, in order to have his impulse (*prasava*). "Along with the Night, who has Indra (as her husband)". Thereby he produces a coupling for the night. He makes it (the sacrifice) connected with Indra. For Indra is the deity of the sacrifice. "Agni should approach with delight, hail". Thereby he overtly offers to Agni.[24] And in the morning with "Along with the divine Savitṛ". Thereby it becomes connected with Savitṛ, in order to have his impulse. "Along with the Dawn, who has Indra (as her husband)" or "Along with the day ..". Thereby he produces a coupling for the days or the dawns. He makes it connected with Indra. For Indra is the deity of the sacrifice. "Sūrya should approach with delight, hail". Thereby he overtly offers to Sūrya. Therefore he should offer thus.

VādhS. 3, 25: There is an agnihotra (formula) with light (i.e. the word *jyotis* "light") in its interior, and one with light at the outside. He should offer in the evening with "Agni is the light, the light is Agni; hail". This is the agnihotra with the internal light. Therefore all (winged) beings pass the night with their wings retracted. For the two wings are lights. And in the morning he should offer with "The light is Sūrya, Sūrya is the light; hail". This is the agnihotra with the external light. Therefore all (winged) beings spread their wings when they arise and continue their migration. For the wings are lights.

— The formula proposed by the VādhS. has a parallel in the ŚB. (see above). For the alternative formula the ŚB. seems to have been inspired by the KS., which in its last paragraph of the agnihotra section suddenly introduces a new formula. The preceding passage, which seems to be corrupt[25], may refer to the expiation for offering too late.

KS. 6, 8: 57.20 ff.: (Reciting) "Agni along with heaven, with earth" he gratifies heaven and earth and Agni. He obtains them. (He recites) "Along with the divine Savitṛ". For no oblation can do without Savitṛ. "Along with Pūṣan, with the space between heaven and earth". Pūṣan means cattle, the intermediate space means cattle. He obtains cattle. "Along with the Night, who has Indra (as her husband)". Thereby he offers for the sake of the night. For no offering can do without Indra. The gods formerly offered the agnihotra. Out of that he was formerly born big and great. "Along with the Day who has Indra (as her husband), hail". The day is connected with the Bṛhatī;[26] the sun is connected with the Bṛhatī. Thereby the day and the sun are won by him, for the sake of them there is offered. The night is connected with the Anuṣṭubh metre, the day with the Triṣṭubh. Thereby he offers for the sake of night an day.[27]

— The MS. just like the KS. and the ŚB. has an alternative formula, but seems to apply it exclusively in emergencies (when Jātavedas injures the cattle). Cf. KS. 6, 7: 57.2 f.

MS. 1, 8, 6: 123.1 ff.: "Along with heaven, with earth, O Jātavedas, approach, enjoying this oblation, hail", (with this formula) he should offer.

— The formula shows that the milk of two cows is used in this expiation. See also Caland's note on his translation of ĀpŚS. 6, 14, 12. The JB. only mentions the ordinary formula (in a context which does not deal with the systematical treatment of the ritual).

JB. 1, 4: "Agni is the light, the light is Agni, hail", with this eight-syllabic formula he offers the oblation.

NOTES

[1] The formula is filled with (*garbhin*) the two words "light" (*jyotis*) in its interior, and thus contains an embryo (*garbha*).

[2] On the one hand the formula of the first libation itself consists of a pair. On the other hand, the first and the second libations form a pair or couple

(*mithunam*), since the first is offered with a formula which is expressed (i.e. recited aloud), whereas the second libation is accompanied by something which is not expressed and which is only recited in thought.

[3] The theme of night as pregnancy and daybreak as delivery is well-known in connection with the agnihotra. In the present passage, the role of the sun as the one who brings forth (*prajanayitṛ;* masculine) is rather strange in view of the fact that Agni has poured him out as seed according to the same passage (below). Most often the sun is regarded as being born at daybreak. This motif is often found in the discussion on the right time for offering the agnihotra (here this forms a minor point). See Section 4, where TB. 2, 1, 2, 7 ff. likewise refers to a couple (*mithunam*). Those parts of that discussion which mainly deal with this procreative aspect of the Sūrya-Agni offering have been included in the present section.

[4] On this interpretation of *anu* see Whitney, *AJPh* 3, p. 400.

[5] On this phrase see 6.3, n. 2.

[6] This translation of the formula *bhūr, bhuvar, svar* is the conventional one. Whatever the exact meaning of *bhuvar* may be, the three utterances denote the totality of the cosmos, and as such may be equated with brahman and cosmic order (*ṛta*).

[7] The present passage belongs to those which make the interpretation of *ṛta* as truth unacceptable.

[8] In fact the only couple which exists is that of the first libation (with the recited formula) together with the second one (which has only a mental, silent accompaniment). See TB. 2, 1, 2, 8 *yajuṣānyat tūṣṇīm anyat* (translated in Section 4). The KS. already makes this simple distinction confused by doubling it (*niruktam-aniruktam* = *yajuṣā-manasā*). The MS. makes the confusion complete by connecting the identical concepts in a couple (*vācā* = *yajuṣā* + *tūṣṇīm* = *manasā*).

[9] Pāṇini 3, 1, 42 signalizes this periphrastic construction *prajanayām akar* with the aorist as an auxiliary. It also occurs MS. 1, 6, 10.

[9a] Read *ṛte vāco* (Caland, *WZKM* 23, 58).

[10] The three utterances which are identified with the three parts of the cosmos become involved here in the symbolism of the piling of the fire-altar (*agnicayana*). See author, *JB. I, 1–65*, p. 290, n. 62 on the identification of three layers of bricks with the threefold division of the cosmos.

[11] Probably this means that the first half of the formula ("Agni is the light") is interpreted as referring to procreation. On the other hand a formula "Offspring is the light" is actually recited according to the sūtra of Baudhāyana (3, 6, 16) in a different ritual context (the priest eats the remains of the oblatory milk).

[12] Dumont translates: "he causes (Agni) to procreate offspring for him"; a doubtful interpretation of the causative *prajanayati*.

[13] Cf. the passage of the KS. and the MS. above. It may be noted that the present passage gives no arguments for the assumption that the evening agnihotra means impregnation and the morning agnihotra delivery. The text becomes clear only in the context of the total corpus brahmanicum consisting of borrowings, adaptations and polemics.

[14] This refers to Prajāpati's primeval sacrifice of ŚB. 2, 2, 4, 4 ff. (Section 1.1). Eggeling's rendering "Now the first of these libations, doubtless, is the same as that which Prajāpati offered in the beginning" does not correctly represent the original, since *ekā* means "one" or "single", but not "first". Moreover the syntactic interpretation is hardly acceptable.

[15] Eggeling renders *etat* ... *adhriyanta* by ".. continued (to sacrifice)".

Indeed *dhriyate* is often construed with an infinitive and "(to sacrifice)" may be supplied from the context, though the ellipsis is not necessary. However, the meaning "to continue" seems to be doubtful in this connection. Either *dhriyate* means "to continue living, remain alive" or (with inf. or acc.) "to undertake, set oneself to". In fact the other gods do not continue Prajāpati's sacrifice (as is the case in other contexts), but take their own efforts. The translation freely renders *etat* (acc. or adverb "here") by "on this point".

[16] Some sacrifices have a primary oblation to the deity of the sacrifice (i.c. Agni or Sūrya), and a secondary one to Agni "who makes the offering well-offered".

[17] ŚB. 2, 3, 1, 26–28, dealing with the other three couples in an identical way, has been omitted here. All the three couples deal with past and future in their own way. Therefore it is preferable not to choose the translations "past" and "future" for one of them, i.c. *bhūtam* and *bhaviṣyat*, since this does not specify enough. See Minard, *Trois Énigmes* I, 336 *a*.

[18] On the connection between truth and the agnihotra (its offering, its formula, the time of its offering) see Sections 1.1, n. 9; 1.3, n. 7 and 4, n. 21.

[19] Eggeling wrongly translates "and the seed, thus enclosed on both sides, is brought forth" and "and the seed thus brought outside he causes to be born". The two sentences should contain an argumentation: seed which is enclosed and does not flow away becomes an embryo; this seed having become an embryo is born outside the body. These two argumentations are preceded by the statements that the formulas enclose, resp. bring outside, the term "light" (= seed), and are followed by two conclusions. In Eggeling's interpretation the first conclusion is rather superfluous, since he had already transformed the argumentation into a conclusion. The second conclusion completely disappears, and is confused with (what in our view should be) the argumentation. Argumentations in favour of a certain ritual custom and discussions on these points with other schools or texts follow a fixed pattern (see author, *JB. I, 1–65*, p. 197, n. 2).

[20] ŚB. 2, 3, 1, 33, dealing with the morning version in an identical way, has been omitted here.

[21] For *tad āhuḥ* referring to objections of other schools or texts see Minard, *Trois Énigmes* I, 133. The concept of the sun entering the fire at sunset is quite current. See author, *JB. I, 1–65*, p. 39, n. 2. A different point is whether performing the agnihotra means offering the sun in the fire (and vice versa). On this symbolism see *Agn. and Prāṇāgn.*, ch. V A. It is to one of these views (even put forward in the ŚB. itself at 11, 6, 2, 2 f.) that the text refers here.

[22] *paricakṣā*. There is no question of "offence committed on his (the sacrificer's) part" (Eggeling). The text criticizes esoteric interpretations of the agnihotra. Provided one offers after sunrise there is no reason to criticize this interpretation on general grounds.

[23] Eggeling: "The author's object seems to be to show that those who offer the Agnihotra after sunrise, commit a mistake in not offering to Sūrya unmistakably; for while before sunrise, Sūrya is still reposing in Agni, and the oblation, in being poured into the fire, is consequently made to Sūrya directly, those offering after sunrise should rather use the formula 'To Sūrya Svāhā!'". In my view the only point of criticism is that the formula accompanying the offering (interpreted as Agni into Sūrya, resp. Sūrya into Agni) does not agree with its esoteric interpretation, since "Agni is the light, the light is Agni, hail" in no way expresses that Agni is offered into (or: to) Sūrya. The question of offering after sunrise was only mentioned as a sideline, as a conditio sine qua non for assuming the doctrine. The fact that the criticism also

applies to the evening agnihotra (where the formula should have been "To Agni, hail") proves that the question of the time of the agnihotra was regarded as having already been settled.

[24] The last formula, which manifestly refers to Agni (and in the next paragraph to Sūrya) as the deity, makes this set of alternative formulas acceptable for those who interpret the agnihotra as an offering of Sūrya into Agni and vice versa. See the discussion above (n. 23).

[25] Caland, *WZKM* 23, p. 58 proposes some emendations. The text, however, remains obscure and has no parallel in the MS.

[26] The adjective *bārhata* may either refer to the *bṛhat sāman* or to the *bṛhatī* metre. In this context the metre seems to be meant. On the other hand, the identification *bṛhat* = day, would seem to be attractive on account of the current homology of *bṛhat* and heaven in the brāhmaṇas. Is there any connection with the obscure sentence above which states that he (Indra?) was born as a big one (*bṛhat*)? Then *bṛhatī* would be the female belonging to *bṛhat* (= Indra).

[27] Probably this refers to the fact that the Bṛhatī metre combines the Anuṣṭubh with the Triṣṭubh.

6.11 *The offering II: The state of the fire and the method of offering.*

KS. 6, 7: 57.9 ff.: The flame which has a golden colour is sacred to Bṛhaspati. When it is neither golden nor red, then it is sacred to Mitra. When it is red, then it is sacred to Varuṇa. When it is enveloped in smoke, then it is sacred to the All-gods (or: all the gods). Where the fire flickers as it were in the coals, that is his (Agni's) mouth, Āvi by name.[1] That is brahman. Therein should be offered. By his mouth he (Agni) eats; (by his mouth) he impels his flames;[2] (by his mouth called Āvi) he becomes manifest (*āviḥ*) among the creatures. He for (or: by) whom the agnihotra is offered thus, becomes more prosperous day by day.

— The version of the MS. forms an exact parallel. Only at the end there are some differences:

MS. 1, 8, 6: 123.12–18: What flickers[3] and flares up in different directions, as it were, in the coals when they become extinguished, that is the mouth of the gods. Moreover they consider this to be the glow of yonder Āditya (sun) as well as of Agni. Therefore there should be offered at that moment. What he (the priest) places in the mouth (of the gods, i.e. Agni) that he (Agni) conveys (to them). This oblation is called Āvi by name. He who knows thus keeps being present (*āvirbhūyam*) before the eyes of gods and men. The kindling-stick is not to be offered upon.[4] That oblation would have no firm foundation. Nor (should there be offered) so that it (the offering) trickles asunder as it were. That (oblation) would be uncontrolled. There should be offered so that it diffuses[5] over the whole fire. For that (oblation) is controlled and has a good foundation. Therefore a large amount of fuel should be prepared for the agnihotra.

— An even more extensive classification of the several stages of the fire is found in the later texts TB. and ŚB.

TB. 2, 1, 10: When he takes out the fire, then the fire is the Vasus. The agnihotra of him for whom they offer in such a fire, is offered to the Vasus. (When) the fire having been placed on (the āhavanīya) keeps smoking, then the fire is the Rudras. The agnihotra of him for whom they offer in such a fire is offered to the Rudras. (When) the flame seizes the fuel for the first time, then the fire is the Ādityas. (....)[6] (When) the whole fuel becomes flaming on all sides, then the fire is the All-gods. (..)[6] (When) the flame becomes lower and a red glow as it were appears, then the fire is Indra. (..)[6] (When) there appear glowing coals and a flame arises from these glowing coals, then the fire is Prajāpati. (..)[6] (When) the coals become overlaid with a film (of ashes), then the fire is brahman. (..).[6] To the Vasus, the Rudras, the Ādityas, the All-gods, Prajāpati, brahman, to these deities without exception oblations are offered by him for whom, knowing thus, they offer the agnihotra, and who thus knows this (agnihotra and its stages of the fire).

ŚB. 2, 3, 2, 9–13: Now when it is just kindled and it only smokes as it were, then it (the fire) is Rudra. If anyone should desire "May I eat food", just as Rudra seeks to enjoy these creatures, as it were partly through lack of faithfulness, partly at random, partly hitting somebody intentionally,[7] he should offer then. He who knowing thus offers then obtains that food. And when now it becomes rather inflamed, then it is Varuṇa. If anybody should desire "May I eat food", just as Varuṇa seeks to enjoy these creatures, as it were partly taking[8] them, partly at random, partly hitting somebody intentionally, he should offer then. He who knowing thus offers then obtains that food. And when now it becomes fully ablaze and the smoke whirls[9] upwards with utmost force, then it is Indra. If anyone should desire "May I be like Indra in lustre and fame", he should offer then. He who knowing thus offers then, obtains that food.[10] And when now the flame of the extinguishing (fire) retires more and more and as it were goes sideways (instead of upwards), then it is Mitra. If anyone should desire "May I eat food here through friendship, (being one) of whom they say 'This brahmin is everybody's friend, he does not harm anybody'", he should offer then. He who knowing thus offers then, obtains that food. And when now the coals shine brightly as it were, then it is brahman. If anybody should desire "May I become a brahmin of brilliant fame (*brahmavarcasin*)", he should offer then. He who knowing thus offers then, obtains that food.[10]

— All these texts agree on this point, that the extinguishing fire should be connected with brahman. It is strange that the TB. contains another reference to the right moment for pouring out the libation (besides the passage quoted above) which on the one hand mentions *brahmavarcasa* (cf. the ŚB.), but on the other hand connects this with a blazing fire:

TB. 2, 1, 3, 9: He offers (in the fire) when it is flaming up. For glory (*brahmavarcasa*) is blazing forth. And it is also like waiting upon a guest after having given him a light.

— This appears to be the official point of view of the TB. (in fact 2, 1, 10 belongs to the addenda), since it is mentioned by the related VādhS.

VādhS. 3, 31: Now they say: "He should offer (on the kindling-stick) when it has flamed up. For glory is blazing forth as it were". The kindling-stick is also (to be regarded as) a boat. If he should offer on the flaming (kindling-stick), this would be like going on board of a ship which is full of water, and capsizing with it. "He (should offer) it (the oblation) before it (the kindling-stick) starts to flame" (this rule applies) for someone who desires to be successful. It would be like going on board of a ship which is not water-logged: it would make him go safely.

VādhS. 3, 32: Now Agni is also identical with Death. If he should offer in the blazing (fire),[11] he would offer the first libation in the mouth of Death and also the second one in the mouth of Death. Having laid the kindling-stick on that very spot where the coals are as it were manifold,[12] he should first offer a smaller quantity and then a greater one. Having suppressed Death with the first libation[13] he mounts up to heaven with the second one.

— For the end of the quoted passage see also the next section. The exact spot on the kindling-stick where the libation should be poured out, is mentioned by the ŚāṅkhB., which also refers to different stages of the fire for different aims.

ŚāṅkhB. 2, 2: He passes two finger breadths of the kindling-stick and offers on it, making a knot as it were (by means of the two oblations).[14] For food is placed here on a distance of two finger breadths from the face (measured from below).[15] He should offer when it smokes for one who desires to possess a village; when it flames for one who desires renown; on the coals for one who desires cattle. But[16] the established practice says (that there should be offered) only after having laid the kindling-stick on (the fire). For all these desires are obtained then,[17] they say.

NOTES

[1] The name Āvi here is applied to the special stage of the fire, whereas in the MS. it denotes the oblation. It plays a role in a 'wordplay'. Besides the evident connection with *āviḥ bhū* "to become manifest" it may also refer to *avati* ("to impel").

[2] The *aṅgāni* (literally "limbs") are Agni's flames as appears from several places in the ṚS.

[3] See Oertel, *Syntax of Cases*, p. 148 f. on the correct reading and interpretation of the verb.

[4] According to ĀpŚS. 6, 10, 12 this should refer to the second libation (see Caland's transl. and n.). However, the context of the MS. does not point to this interpretation. Rāmāgnicit's Vṛtti on the ĀpŚS. states: *kecid dhomadvayaṃ na samidhīti*, which may agree with the MS.

[5] This meaning of *vyava-i* is not found with M.-W.'s dictionary. For a different translation see Delbrück, *Altind. Syntax*, p. 349 ("dass sie das Feuer theile").

[6] The translation has been shortened by omitting repetitions.

[7] The punctuation and the interpretation of single words is doubtful. Should the comparison ("just as Rudra..") be included in the direct quotation? Eggeling translates *nighātam* by "in striking them down" and *sahasā* by "with violence", which hardly produces a useful distinction or opposition. Apparently the way of killing the creatures (picked out or just wholesale) is meant. In that connection *aśraddhayā* (Eggeling: "with distrust") is awkward. It seems improbable that Rudra's motive is "distrust". The cause of his action may be his unreliable character. Is there any parallelism with the rising fire, whose actions are unpredictable: now it seems to become fully ablaze, then again it produces some stray flames? See also n. 8.

[8] The verb *gṛh-* may refer to Varuṇa's nooses. It denotes the progress of the inflammation. The flames would catch the oblation (the food), if it should be offered at this point. Its opposite in the preceding stage of the fire was *aśraddhayā*. Should this be taken as a negated adverb *śraddhayā* (cf. *akāraṇāt* "without reason") meaning "without any longing, desire, appetite"? This would excellently suit the initial stage of the fire.

[9] See Minard, *Trois Énigmes* I, 246 *a*. The interpretation of *balbalīti* is uncertain (see Mayrhofer's etymological dictionary).

[10] In the stereotyped phraseology "food" was retained in the text. It does not suit the context.

[11] The gender of *jvalati* proves that it refers to the fire rather than to the kindling-stick (as Caland takes it).

[12] Probably the meaning is that in a fire which blazes forth the coals cannot be distinguished, i.e. all the burning wood (or coals) seems to form one glowing mass. The waning of the blaze makes single pieces of wood or coals visible again.

[13] The first libation more or less extinguishes the fire of the coals. On Agni-Death being subdued by the fluid (the milk or other libations) see JB. 1, 12–14.

[14] Keith's remark "The idea is that in some way the two finger breadths of the *samidh* are made into an outline of a human mouth" misses the point. If the two finger breadths were the mouth, the libation should be poured out on them, rather than past or beyond (*atihṛtya*) them. The double libation offered on the same spot (according to this brāhmaṇa) produces a mouth.

[15] Keith: "in two finger breadths of the mouth here food is placed". The point is that the kindling-stick represents a head or face (see also 6, 9, n. 12). The libation is offered at a distance of two finger breadths from below (Āpastamba's sūtra states: *dvyaṅgule mūlāt;* 6, 10, 4). The mouth is situated about two finger breadths from the lower side of the face. Here *mukha* means face, not mouth.

[16] The established practice or rule quoted here does not imply that the offering should be made "on the *samidh* as soon as it is put on" (Keith), but "at any case after a kindling-stick has been put on the fire, be it on the *samidh* itself or on the coals". The restrictive (*tu!*) remark therefore refers only to mentioning the custom of some people who offer on the coals instead of on the kindling-stick.

[17] Or perhaps: "on it" (*atra*).

6.12 *The offering III: The second libation. The stumbling-block in the agnihotra ritual.*

KS. 6, 5: 54.8 ff.: The stumbling-block in the agnihotra, that is the first libation. Passing it over he should offer (the second one). He avoids it. There should be offered with the right foot placed forward in the evening. He impregnates.[1] (There should be offered) with the right foot backward in the morning. He brings forth. Some people say: "There should be offered (in the morning also) with the right foot advanced. For by the advance in the ritual he gets advance in worldly affairs".

MS. 1, 8, 5: 121.4 ff.: The first libation is a stumbling-block. The second should be offered by jumping over the first libation. He misses (does not strike upon) the stumbling-block. The second libation to be offered should be larger, for the sake of the advance (progress, success)[2] of the sacrifice. By the first libation he wins cattle, by the second renown.[3] [The evening oblation is sacred to Agni. Thereby he pours out seed. The pouring of seed makes the night pregnant with an embryo. By the (oblation) sacred to Sūrya he engenders that embryo in the morning][3] (In the evening) this one libation is offered and then (the second) further on. But in the morning the second libation should be offered under (or: on this side of) the first one.[4] For the birth of offspring takes place in downward direction. For the oblation sacred to Sūrya means procreation. (However,) that should not be heeded. The libations should be offered forward[5] only, for the sake of the advance of the sacrifice.

— A new element is introduced by the TB. and later texts: the amount of the second libation. The discussion on the stumbling-block continues.

TB. 2, 1, 4, 1–4: The gods offered an increasing libation, the Asuras a decreasing one. Because of this the gods prospered and the Asuras were ruined. If he should wish (of the sacrificer) "May he become more wealthy (excellent)", then, after having offered a smaller (first) libation, he should offer the second one more copious for him. This is the increasing libation. This one the gods offered. On account of this they prospered. He for whom they offer thus becomes prosperous. If he should wish (of the sacrificer) "May he become worse", then, after having offered a larger (first) libation, he should offer a smaller second one. This is the decreasing libation. This one the Asuras offered. Because of this they were ruined. He for whom they offer thus becomes ruined. (. . .).[6] The agnihotra has a stumbling-block. He who strikes upon it, strikes upon the stumbling-block of the sacrifice.[7] The first libation is the stumbling-block of the agnihotra. If he should offer on it with the second one, he would strike upon the stumbling-block of the sacrifice. Jumping over the first libation he offers (the second). He avoids the stumbling-block of the sacrifice. And moreover, if he may once meet with an enemy, he overcomes him.

— On the increasing libation in the VādhS. see the preceding section (treating the question of whether both libations should be offered in the flaming fire which is identical with death). On the stumbling-block see below.

VādhS. 3, 33: Now they say: "The stumbling-block of the agnihotra should be recognized". The stumbling-block of the agnihotra is Death. If he should offer (the second libation) on the first libation, he would strike upon the stumbling-block of the agnihotra. Jumping over the first libation he offers. He avoids the stumbling-block of the agnihotra.

JB. 1, 21: Śāṇḍilya used to say "There are three stumbling-blocks in the agnihotra". Offering the libation on the kindling-stick before it has blazed up is a stumbling-block. Missing it (i.e. offering beside the stick) is a stumbling-block. Mixing up the two (libations by offering the second on the first) is a stumbling-block.[8] He offers on the fore part of the stick after it has blazed up. He offers the second libation jumping over (the first one). He who knowing thus offers the agnihotra increases his prosperity seventeen thousand-fold each time.

— The VādhS. has an esoteric discussion on the correct spot for the offering of the second libation.

VādhS. 3, 39: One (of Āruṇi's pupils) said: "The kindling-stick is a mouth, the oblation represents the food. If he offers the first libation on the kindling-stick and also the second, this is like food which, having been eaten in the mouth, satiates; it is of use. But if he offers the second libation beside (the stick), this would be like pouring afterwards in the eye or in the ear;[9] he would thereby injure him. Therefore these two should be offered together (in one line)". And another said: "The kindling-stick is a womb, the oblation represents the seed. If he offers the first libation on the kindling-stick and also the second, this is like seed which after having been shed into a womb is reproduced; it is of use. But if he offers the second libation beside (the stick), this would be like seed which is not shed in a womb and is spilled; it is useless. Therefore these two should be offered in one line (on the stick)". And a third said: "The kindling-stick is a ship, the oblation represents the sacrificer. If he offers the first libation on the kindling-stick and also the second, this is like placing the right foot on board and thereafter taking to ship; it safely transports him. But if he offers the second libation beside (the stick), this would be like placing the right foot on board and falling down with the other; he would thereby become turned upside down. Therefore these two should be offered in one line".[10]

— On the exact spot on the *samidh* where the second libation should be offered according to the ŚāṅkhB. see the preceding section. On the increasing libation see below:

ŚāṅkhB. 2, 2: He should offer increasing[11] libations. Thereby he obtains higher and higher heavens.

— An extensive discussion of the amount of the second libation is found in the ŚB. It is remarkable that a late brāhmaṇa like the ŚB. seems to have lost all interest in the motif of the stumbling-block which is found in all the Yajurvedic texts from the KS. up to the VādhS. and which even turns up in the JB.

ŚB. 2, 3, 2, 16–18: The first libation corresponds to the gods, the second to men, and what remains in the ladle to the cattle. He offers a smaller amount (of milk) for the first libation, a greater amount for the second and still more he leaves in the ladle. The reason why he offers a smaller amount for the first libation is that the number of the gods is smaller. The reason why he offers a greater amount for the second libation is that men are more numerous than the gods. The reason why he leaves still more in the ladle is that cattle are more numerous than men. He who knowing thus offers the agnihotra will have more cattle than (human beings) to be supported by him. For if someone has more cattle than (human beings) to be supported, this means prosperity.

— The second libation and the fact that it is not accompanied by a recited formula has already been partially treated in Section 6.10. See also the following small passage from the TB. on this silence:

TB. 2, 1, 2, 12: He offers a second libation silently, in order to produce a pair (together with the first), for the procreation of offspring.

— The KS. has an alternative formula for the second libation (just as in the case of the first libation).

KS. 6, 8: 58.7–8: He offers the second libation with the formula "O, Agni, you who cannot be deceived, enjoy (this offering), hail".[12] This is like cutting off[13] something for Agni.

NOTES

[1] The forward movement symbolizes the impregnation, the backward one the delivery (input and output). There is a to and fro movement along the same track.

[2] Cf. 6.5, n. 3.

[3] The passage between brackets has already been translated in Section 6.10. Here it is repeated in order not to disturb the context.

[4] The MS. seems to replace the forward and backward movement of the right foot of the priest (*abhikrāmam; pratikrāmam*) by the direction in which the two libations move over the kindling-stick. Or should one say that the MS. interprets (rightly or wrongly) *abhikrāmam* and *pratikrāmam* in this way? It should be noted that ĀpŚS. 6, 10, 5 reads *avakrāmam*, changed to *apakrāmam* by Caland who translates "zurückschreitend".

[5] *parāparā* denotes that in the evening as well as in the morning the second libation should be offered beyond the first. A backward movement is always criticized in the ritual. See e.g. *JB. I, 1–65*, p. 162.

[6] For the omission see Section 6.13.

[7] On the meaning of *sthāṇu* (stump on which chariots may strike) see

JB. I, 1–65, p. 70, n. 5. The *yajñasthāṇu* is not "a sacrificial post or stake (over which the priest stumbles)" (Monier-Williams' Dict.). It is not a supporting beam of the sacrificial 'building', which would, if struck, produce a ruin of the sacrifice. Dumont's rendering "pillar" does not make sense. It is an insidious obstacle, a cause of failure, which may produce an accident in the course of the sacrifice. In its progress the sacrificial action should jump (the text reads *atihāya*) over the first libation like horses with a chariot.

[8] Here the stumbling-block (*sthāṇu*) is not represented by something concrete. It is the possibility of being wrecked. A wrong ritual action means a failure or accident.

[9] According to Caland "*(a)kṣaṇvākarṇav(ā)* ist undeutbar". Read *(a)kṣan vā karṇe v(ā)*.

[10] Caland translates "auf einen Punkt gerichtet". The second libation, however, should be offered beyond the first (but on the same stick). See also Section 18 (end).

[11] Not "over one another" (Keith), as appears from TB. 2, 1, 4, 1 (mentioning an *uttarāvatī* libation).

[12] Cf. ĀpŚS. 6, 13, 5, where the formula is used differently.

[13] On this cutting off see Gonda, *Savayajñas*, p. 265 and 275.

6.13 *The setting-down III. Looking back at the gārhapatya and other actions between the two libations.*

— Other settings-down (*upasads*) have been treated above in Sections 6.6 (after the ladling out) and 6.8 (before the offering in the āhavanīya). This section deals with the setting down after the first libation.

TB. 2, 1, 4, 3: Having offered (the first libation) he should set down (the ladle) in order to avoid uniformity and to make a distinction. He looks back[1] at the gārhapatya. Thereby he prevents him (i.e. Agni of the gārhapatya) from being resentful.

— For the propitiation of the gārhapatya see also TB. 2, 1, 3, 6 f. (Section 6.6). For other ways of satisfying the gārhapatya see 6.7 (where the KS. and the MS. mention that the gārhapatya has become *ananudhyāyin*, the same term as used here). See also the incidental references to the gratification of the gārhapatya by looking back from the āhavanīya in Sections 6.15 (ŚB. 11, 5, 3, 6; GB. 1, 3, 12) and 6.17 (MS. 1, 8, 5). In another passage the TB. (as well as the ŚāṅkhB.) mentions a third setting down after the offering, i.e. probably after the first libation:

TB. 2, 1, 5, 8 f.: After having offered he sets (the milk) down. He gratifies heaven. These are the (three) *upasads* of the agnihotra. To him who knows thus the *upasads* show reverence. He finds a respectful attendant (*upasattṛ*).

ŚāṅkhB. 2, 2: Having offered (he sets down) a third time. Thereby he wins yonder world.

ŚB. 2, 3, 1, 17: (He makes) the second (libation) after having set it down. Thereby he causes the forces of these two to be different. Now these two libations are mind and speech. Thus he differentiates mind and speech here. Therefore mind and speech though being one and the same are still separate.[2]

— Another action which takes place between the two libations is the wiping off of the ladle (see e.g. ĀpŚS. 6, 10, 10). Some texts (e.g. the KS.) do not mention it, others refer to it by stating that he offers, wipes off and eats (of the milk) twice (e.g. ŚB. 2, 3, 1, 18). Moreover the *vaiśvadeva* passages of Section 6.16 contain references to this action. See further the texts translated below:

MS. 1, 8, 5: 121.12 ff.: In the evening he wipes off downward. Therefore dew falls at night. In the morning he wipes off upward. Therefore dew lifts in the daytime.[3] The agnihotra (oblation) turns away as it were (on account of this wiping off). That he first recites the *yajus* (*bhūr bhuvaḥ suvar;* i.e. probably before the first libation) is in order to keep it and not wipe it off.

TB. 2, 1, 4, 4: He wipes off downward at night. Thereby he inseminates. He wipes off upward in the morning. Thereby he procreates.

NOTES

[1] On *pratīkṣ-* meaning "to look back, respect, have regard for" see Section 6.17, n. 4.

[2] The same sentence is found ŚB. 11, 3, 1, 1 (in an agnihotra passage).

[3] Cf. ŚāṅkhB. 2, 2 translated in Section 6.15 (connection with setting and rising sun).

6.14 *The views of the Praiyamedhas on the offering.*

KS. 6, 6: There were some brahmins called Praiyamedhas by name.[1] They knew everything. This knowledge they had in common. Upon the agnihotra (however) they did not agree. Among them one offered the agnihotra once, another twice, a third one thrice. Him among them who offered once the other two asked: "To whom do you offer?" "What is single in this world" he said "that is Prajāpati. To Prajāpati I offer". Him among them who offered twice the other two asked: "To whom do you offer?" "To Agni in the evening, and also to Prajāpati" he said "and to Sūrya in the morning, as well as to Prajāpati". Him among them who offered thrice the other two asked: "To whom do you offer?" "To Agni, Sūrya and Prajāpati" he said. "To them I offer in the evening, to them in the morning".

He among them who offered twice became successful.[2] He became the most important. He surpassed the other two with offspring and prosperity. The offspring of the two others came to acknowledge the authority of his offspring in the clan.[3] Therefore two (libations) have to be offered, (one) with a formula and (another with a formula recited) in thought .The same prosperity which he (i.e. the one who offered twice) obtained is obtained by him.

— The same passage is found with a few variations in MS. 1, 8, 7: 125.1–9. The rather simple passage which closely follows KS.[4] need not be translated here.

TB. 2, 1, 9, 1–2: There were three Praiyamedhas. One of them offered the agnihotra thrice, another twice, and again another once. He among them who offered thrice, offered with an *ṛc* (verse).[5] He who (offered) twice, with a formula.[6] He who (offered) once, silently. He who offered with a formula and he who offered silently, those two became successful. Therefore the first libation should be offered with a formula and the second silently. He obtains both prosperities (i.e. the success of both).

GB. 1, 3, 15: The Priyamedhas, who belong to the family of Bharadvāja, thought themselves to be knowers of the sacrifice. They did not become the pupil of any knower of the Veda. They knew everything. They had this knowledge in common. On the subject of the agnihotra they did not agree.

— The rest of the passage rather closely follows the KS.[7] A change is introduced in connection with the threefold offering, which according to the GB. should be made to Agni, Prajāpati and Anumati (evening) or Agni Sviṣṭakṛt (morning).[8]

NOTES

[1] These descendants of the old sage Priyamedha are called Priyamedhas in the version of the GB. below.

[2] This way of performing the agnihotra prevails. The second, silent libation is always connected with Prajāpati.

[3] On the difficult term *sajātatva* (MS. *sājātya*) see Rau, *Staat und Gesellschaft*, p. 55. See also A. C. Banerjea, *Studies in the Brāhmaṇas*, Delhi 1963, p. 61–72.

[4] There are some differences. The MS. reverses the order of the three types of offering. Moreover the sentence *ekadhaivedam* . . *prajāpatiḥ, prajāpataye* . . (KS.; cf. GB. *ekadhā vā idaṃ sarvaṃ prajāpatiḥ, prajāpataye* . .) has been changed into *ekadhā vā idam, prajāpataye* . . The nominative Prajāpati, indispensable in the argumentation "onefold is this universe = Prajāpati; so the onefold offering is sacred to Prajāpati", has been omitted. The changed

order involved the connection of this world (*idam*) with *tredhā*. There are no arguments for this world being threefold, nor for the association with the three gods. The passage of the MS. is obviously secondary. Instead of *agnihotreṇa samarādhayan* (cf. KS. *agnihotra eva na samarādhayan*) read *agnihotre na samarādhayan* (Caland, *WZKM* 23, p. 53).

[5] This may refer to one of the alternative mantras mentioned in Section 6.10.

[6] The offering is twofold since the usual formula is twofold (substitution of Agni by Sūrya in the morning performance).

[7] Note that the GB. (reading *idaṃ sarvam*) proves that *idam* should refer to the universe in the KS. The passage of the GB. is based on the KS., not on the MS.

[8] These deities also play a role in the twilight offerings of the *gṛhya* ritual.

6.15 *The agnihotra is connected with other gods and powers through actions after the offering* (vaiśvadeva).

— In some of the preceding sections it was explicitly stated that the agnihotra is not only sacred to Agni, but also to the sun (or even Vāyu). ŚB. 2, 3, 1, 16–18 (see Section 6.12) even connected the first libation with the gods, the second with men and the remainder with cattle. Most of the actions after the offering are explained as gratifying several other gods as well. In some texts the term *vaiśvadeva* is used in this connection in order to denote that all gods are the deities of this sacrifice.[1]

KS. 6, 5: 54.11–13: What he offers, that is for the gods. That he points (with the ladle) to the north, thereby he appeases Rudra.[2] What he rubs (from the ladle), that is for the forefathers. What he eats (of the rest of the milk), that is for the human beings. Therefore the agnihotra is called sacred to all the gods.

KS. 6, 7: 56.20 ff.: (With the formula) "Rudra, be gracious, O Anārbhava, have mercy. Homage to you, O Dhūrta[3]" he should point to the north (with the ladle) after having offered. These are the inauspicious names[4] of Rudra. With these he injures the creatures, because he wants to have a share in the agnihotra (oblation). These (names) of his he drives away; these he appeases. When this god[5] may threaten the creatures, he should perform the agnihotra during twelve nights (and days) with the formula "Together with heaven and earth, O Jātavedas, accept (?) this oblation, hail". The form of Agni which is Jātavedas,[6] by means of this he (i.e. Rudra) injures the creatures, desirous of having a share in the agnihotra. That form of his he gratifies. To that he offers.

— The MS. introduces the second half of this passage in a completely different context (MS. 1, 8, 6: 123.1 ff.). It does not connect the regular with the incidental propitiation of Rudra. Being more or less an expiation the version of the MS. (which does not differ much from the KS.) has not been translated here.

MS. 1, 8, 5: 121.10 ff.–122.6: He points to the north (reciting) "Anābhu,[7] have mercy. O Dhūrta (rogue), homage to you. Have mercy, Rudra". These are the inauspicious forms of Rudra, these are his names. With these he destroys[8] the cattle. These he appeases[8] by means of his share (which he now receives from the ladle which points northwards). (. . .)[9] He who knows how all kinds of deities are involved in the agnihotra, him the lord of the cattle (Paśupati) does not hurt, the lord of the cattle does not hurt his cattle.[10] He offers sitting with his face towards the east. Thereby he gratifies the gods. Having offered he leaves (some milk) as a remainder. Thereby he leaves (i.e. reserves) some cattle for the sacrificer. He points (with the ladle) to the north. Thereby he puts off Rudra. He rubs off (the ladle) to the south. Thereby he gratifies the herbs and the *pitṛs* (forefathers).[11] He eats (the remaining milk of the oblation). Thereby he gratifies the human beings. He eats by means of his finger (i.e. he wipes off the ladle). And while eating[12] this he should not make it touch his teeth. If he should make it touch his teeth, the serpents would hurt him. He appeases the serpents in order not to be hurt. He should recite the formula "You are Pūṣan".[13] Pūṣan represents cattle. He obtains cattle. If he is not propitiated, he is unappeased. He expects a human sacrifice with the sacrificer as an oblation. When he purifies (by heating) the agnihotra ladle, he (Pūṣan) becomes unappeased thereby. After having purified the agnihotra ladle the hand should be put down (into it). Or the hand should be put down in the agnihotra ladle after he has heated it. Thereby he appeases him. Thereby he gratifies him. Appeased and gratified he does not hurt him.

TB. 2, 1, 4, 4–8: Those who take part in esoteric discussions say: "Four times he ladles out, he offers twice. Where are the (other) two libations?" One should say: "In Agni Vaiśvānara". The brahmin indeed is Agni Vaiśvānara. Having offered he eats twice. He offers two libations in (or: to) Agni Vaiśvānara. He offers twice, twice he rubs off (the ladle), twice he eats (the remaining milk which sticks to his finger). These (actions) amount to six. Now there are six seasons. He gratifies the seasons. Those who hold debates on ritualistic subjects say: "What is the deity of the agnihotra?" He should say: "It is offered to all the gods". What he offers with a formula, that is sacred to Indra and Agni.[14] What silently, that to

Prajāpati. What he wipes off, that is sacred to the herbs. What the second time, that to the forefathers. What he eats, that is for the embryos. Therefore the embryos grow without eating.[15] What he sips (i.e. the purificatory water), that is for the human beings. Having turned to the north he sips (something of the remaining oblation) in order to protect himself. He cleanses (washes) (the ladle, the *agnihotrahavaṇī*) for the sake of purity. He heats (it) for the sake of the Svagā exclamation.[16] He points northwards (with the ladle and) gratifies the seven Ṛṣis.[17]

— The TB. also contains a special passage on the connection between the wiping off, the herbs and the *pitṛs*. Since it is in the form of an aetiological myth, it is placed before the systematical treatment of the ritual. It even precedes the myth of the primeval agnihotra performed by Prajāpati, and may form a later addition (which is usually put either at the end or at the beginning of a section).

TB. 2, 1, 1, 1–2: The Aṅgirases[18] performed a long sacrificial session. Their cow which provided the milk for the hot-milk offering (*gharma*) was Pṛśni.[19] She lived on the residue (the pressed out stalks) of the Soma plant. They said: "Wherefore do we perform the sacrificial session, if we are not able to produce herbs for her?" They made rain fall from heaven. As many drops as fell down, so many herbs were produced. As soon as they had been produced, the *pitṛs* besmeared them with poison. Having eaten of them she continuously suffered pain. They said: "Who did this thus?" "We did it" the *pitṛs* said "wishing a share". "What share should be yours?". "In the agnihotra there should be a share for us" said the fathers. To them they gave this share, namely what, after having offered, he wipes off. Thereupon they made the herbs palatable. For him who knows thus the herbs become savoury.[20]

— The ŚāṅkhB., which contains an extensive *vaiśvadeva* of all kinds of gods and powers to be pleased or gratified by several actions after the actual offering, opens its agnihotra section (2, 2) with the following remark on the sun's role (beside Agni) in this agnihotra.

ŚāṅkhB. 2, 2: The agnihotra which is put on the fire is identical with the hot milk (*gharma*) (of the Pravargya ritual).[21] The one who gives out heat here, that is the *gharma*. Him he thereby gratifies. (.....) Twice he stretches out the ladle to the north. Thus having gratified Rudra in his own quarter[22] he sends him off. Therefore one should not stand to the north of the offering which is being made (thinking) "Lest I would be in the nearness of that fearful god".

In the evening he wipes off the ladle which points to the west, (standing) to the north (of the fire). Thereby he causes the sun to set. At daybreak (he wipes off) the ladle which points upwards, (standing) to the south (of the fire). Thereby he leads the sun upwards. What[23] he wipes off the first time, that he smears down on the grass (the *kūrca* bundle). Thereby he gratifies the herbs. When[23] (he wipes off) the second time, he lays down his hand, with the backside down,[24] to the south of the grass bundle. Thereby he gratifies the *pitṛs*. And when he eats twice with his forefinger, he gratifies the foetuses with the first. Therefore the foetuses breathe without eating food.[25] With the second (he gratifies) the birds. Therefore the birds eat much (different food), now this, then that, (but) they (always) make white water.[26] When he eats with the ladle, he thereby gratifies the past and the future. When he licks out the ladle, he thereby gratifies the serpent-demons[27] and when he cleanses the ladle, he thereby gratifies the Rakṣas-demons.[27] When he pours out water to the north-east, he thereby gratifies the Gandharvas and Apsarases. When he points the ladle to the north-east, he thereby places Rudra in his own quarter. Thus he gratifies all beings by means of the agnihotra.

ŚB. 2, 3, 1, 19–20: What he offers in the fire, that he offers to the gods. On account of this the gods exist.[28] What he wipes off, that he offers to the fathers and the herbs. On account of this the fathers and the herbs have existence there. And what he eats after having offered, that he offers to the human beings. On account of this the human beings can exist. Those creatures who do not participate by association in the sacrifice are lost.[29] In this way[30] now he makes those creatures who are not lost participate in the beginning of the sacrifice. And thereby also the cattle receive an associated share in that they are associated with the human beings.[31]

— In its eleventh book, which mostly deals with esoteric discussions as far as the agnihotra is concerned, this same brāhmaṇa has another *vaiśvadeva*. Uddālaka Āruṇi is interrogated by Śauceya Prācīnayogya. For that part of the answer which deals with the *vaiśvadeva* of the milk see Section 16. The passage translated here for the greater part (though not exclusively) covers the actions after the offering.

ŚB. 11, 5, 3, 6–7: The kindling-stick which I place on (the fire), that is the foundation for the libations. With the first libation I gratified the gods. When I set (the milk of the oblation) down, it thereby became sacred to Bṛhaspati. When I looked back (towards the gārhapatya), I thereby joined this and yonder world.[32] By the second libation I placed myself in heaven. And when, having offered, I tossed (the spoon), it (i.e. the milk) thereby became sacred to Vāyu.[33] When, having rubbed off the ladle, I wiped it on the bundle of grass, I thereby gratified the herbs and the trees. When, having rubbed off a second time, I placed my hand to the south (of the fire), then I gratified the *pitṛs*. When I ate of the milk the first time, then I gratified myself. When a second time, then I gratified my offspring. When, having withdrawn (from the place of the sacrifice), I drank (water), then I gratified the cattle. When, having poured water in the ladle (*sruc*), I sprinkled, then I gratified the snake-demons.[34] When a second time, then the Gandharvas and the Apsarases. When a third time, I thereby opened the door of heaven. When I poured down water behind the āhavanīya fire, I thereby gave rain to this world. When I closed (this sacrifice), I thereby completed everything which is deficient in this world.

— The same passage is found in the GB. (which often borrows from the ŚB.). Uddālaka's answer, however, is different on some points.

GB. 1, 3, 12: 79.5 ff.: The first libation which I offered, thereby I placed myself in heaven. That I looked back towards the gārhapatya, was for the sake of keeping contact with this world. The second libation is sacred to Prajāpati. Therefore it is fuller and (with a formula recited) in thought. When, having offered, I lifted up the ladle three times to the north, I thereby gratified the Rudras. When, having put down the ladle on the bundle of grass and having rubbed off (the ladle), I wiped off my hands (on the grass) to the north (of the ladle), I thereby gratified the herbs and trees. When, having rubbed off a second time and having made the investiture with the thread sacred to the *pitṛs*, I made an offering to the *pitṛs* (by wiping off the milk) to the south (of the ladle), I thereby gratified the *pitṛs*. When I ate the milk the first time, I thereby gratified the (own) breaths. When the second time, the embryos. Therefore the embryos live without eating food. When at the end I ate all the milk, I thereby gratified the All-gods (or: all gods). When I poured out water with the ladle which still had not been washed, I thereby gratified the serpents and the "other beings" (*itarajanāḥ*).[35] When with a cleansed ladle, I thereby (gratified) the serpents and the "good beings" (*puṇyajanāḥ*). When I poured out water with the ladle behind the āhavanīya fire, I thereby gratified the Gandharvas and Apsarases. When I heated the two ladles (the *sruc* and the *surva*) I thereby gratified the Seven Seers.

— A very elaborate treatment of this subject is found in the JB. All these appeasements and gratifications of all kinds of powers are not mere speculations of the brāhmaṇas. They have partial counterparts in the actual ritual as described in the sūtras in the form of formulas which accompany these actions. For references to the sūtras concerning the following passage see author, *JB. I, 1–65*, p. 97 f.

JB. 1, 40 (end): With the first (libation) which he offers he reaches the gods. And with the second which he offers he reaches the Seers.

JB. 1, 41: Then he wipes off (the ladle). When he wipes off the first time, he thereby gratifies the Gandharvas and the Apsarases. To him the Gandharvas and Apsarases say: "Thy faith must not disappear. Become satisfied with all one may wish. Reach the world of heaven". When he wipes off the second time, he thereby gratifies the house[36] and the *pitṛs*. To him the house and the *pitṛs* say: (..).[37] When he eats twice by means of his finger, when he eats the first time, the *prāṇa* and *apāna* (ex- and inhalation) thereby are satisfied. To him (...).[37] When he eats the second time, the *udāna* and the *apāna*[38] are thereby satisfied. To him (...).[37] When he eats (the remaining contents of the ladle) by means of the ladle (i.e. by drinking it out), he thereby gratifies the *samāna*, the *vyāna* and the embryos. To him (...).[37] When he empties (i.e. licks out) the ladle, he thereby gratifies the divine hosts (*devajanāḥ*). To him (..).[37] When he pours out the cleansing-water of the ladle, he thereby gratifies the birds. To him (...).[37] The waters which he tosses upwards towards the north out of the ladle after he has washed it, thereby he gratifies the Seers. To him (...).[37] When he pours out the cleansing-water of the cauldron (*agnihotrasthālī* in which the milk was cooked), he thereby gratifies the hosts of serpents (*sarpajanāḥ*). To him (...).[37]

— The variety of propitiations in the passages translated above in this section shows some agreement. The oldest passage (KS. 6, 5) has the simplest *vaiśvadeva*. It is followed by the other texts, which merely make additions. The following survey makes the agreements and disagreements clear.

Oblation	– Gods (KS.; MS.; ŚB. 2, 3, 1, 19; TB., with specification)
First libation	– Gods (ŚB. 2, 3, 1, 16; ŚB. 11, 5, 3, 6; JB.)

<table>
<tr><td>Second libation</td><td>– Prajāpati (TB.; GB.). No agreement between the other texts</td></tr>
<tr><td>Remaining milk</td><td>– Cattle (MS.; ŚB. 2, 3, 2, 16; ŚB. 2, 3, 1, 20)</td></tr>
<tr><td>Eating of the remaining milk</td><td>– Human beings (KS.; MS.; ŚB. 2, 3, 1, 19); Agni Vaiśvānara, the deity within human beings (TB.); embryos (TB.)</td></tr>
<tr><td>Eating with finger</td><td>– Serpents (MS.)</td></tr>
<tr><td>a) first time</td><td>– Embryos (ŚāṅkhB.); prāṇāpāna (JB.)</td></tr>
<tr><td>b) second time</td><td>– Birds (ŚāṅkhB.); udānāpāna (JB.)</td></tr>
<tr><td>Drinking the milk</td><td>– Himself (TB.); past and future (ŚāṅkhB.); samānavyāna and embryos (JB.)</td></tr>
<tr><td>a) first time</td><td>– Himself (ŚB. 11, 5, 3, 7); the (own) breaths (GB.)</td></tr>
<tr><td>b) second time</td><td>– Offspring (ŚB.); embryos (GB.)</td></tr>
<tr><td>Licking out</td><td>– Serpents (ŚāṅkhB.); All-gods (GB.); devajanāḥ (JB.)</td></tr>
<tr><td>Pointing northward</td><td>– Rudra(s) (KS.; MS.; ŚāṅkhB.; GB.); Vāyu (ŚB. 11, 5, 3, 7)</td></tr>
<tr><td>Wiping off</td><td>– pitṛs (KS.); herbs and pitṛs (MS.; ŚB. 2, 3, 1, 19)</td></tr>
<tr><td>a) first time</td><td>– herbs (TB.; ŚāṅkhB.); herbs and trees (ŚB. 11, 5, 3, 7; GB.); Gandharvas and Apsarases (JB.)</td></tr>
<tr><td>b) second time</td><td>– pitṛs (TB.; ŚāṅkhB.; ŚB.; GB.); the house and the pitṛs (JB.)</td></tr>
<tr><td>Heating of the ladle</td><td>– Pūṣan (MS.); Seven Seers (GB.)</td></tr>
<tr><td>Sipping water</td><td>– Human beings (TB.); cattle (ŚB. 11, 5, 3, 7)</td></tr>
<tr><td>Cleansing of the ladle</td><td>– Rakṣases (ŚāṅkhB.)</td></tr>
<tr><td>Pouring water</td><td>– Gandharvas and Apsarases (ŚāṅkhB.)</td></tr>
<tr><td>a) first time</td><td>– serpents and other hosts (sarpadevajanāḥ/sarpetarajanāḥ) (ŚB.; GB.); birds (JB.)</td></tr>
<tr><td>b) second time</td><td>– Gandharvas and Apsarases (ŚB.); serpents and puṇyajanāḥ (GB.); Seers (JB.; with ladle pointing northward)</td></tr>
<tr><td>Pointing northward</td><td>– Seven Seers (TB.); Rudra (ŚāṅkhB.)</td></tr>
<tr><td>Pouring water behind the āhavanīya</td><td>– Gandharvas and Apsarases (GB.)</td></tr>
<tr><td>Pouring water out of the sthālī</td><td>– Serpents (sarpajanāḥ) (JB.)</td></tr>
</table>

Conclusion:
The elaboration of the subject runs parallel to the chronology of the texts: KS. – MS. – TB. – ŚāṅkhB. – ŚB. – JB. – GB.[39] Originally the eating of the remaining milk (in opposition to the offering in the fire which had the gods, especially Agni and Sūrya, as its aim) was merely an offering to man, an *ātmayajña*. The later texts have differentiated this simple dedication, more and more in agreement with the great variety of actions

connected with the consumption of this milk. To what extent this variety of ritual actions is a later development as well, is difficult to ascertain. The offerings into man himself are connected with the human beings, the internal deity called Agni Vaiśvānara, man himself, his own breaths, the several *prāṇāḥ*. This foreshadows the later *prāṇāgnihotra* ritual. Partially due to the fact that some of these actions were twofold, partially under the influence of the rising water doctrine which culminated in the theory of the five fires (*pañcāgnividyā*), the nourishing of the own person was extended to the production of offspring. There is a dualism of man and embryo, the self and the offspring, past and future. Eating food, i.e. offspring milk into oneself, maintains the own *prāṇāḥ*, but also produces the seed for offspring. A completely different background underlies the dedications to the serpents (already in the MS.), the birds, the Viśve Devas and the Devajanas. These are powers to be gratified at the end of an offspring. On the function of the last two groups see author, *JB. I, 1–65*, p. 97, n. 23. All these powers receive the *ucchiṣṭa*, the remains. The other concluding actions have the same function, sometimes with the aspect of repulsing a dangerous power ("Abfindung"). This is also the case with Rudra. In the ŚB. the ladle is tossed through the air and therefore Vāyu is honoured. Perhaps this action should be distinguished from the pointing northward. This pointing northward takes place twice: first after the offering (to Rudra), afterwards with a ladle filled with water (to the Seers, who often have this concluding function, or the Seven Seers). ŚāṅkhB. secondarily connects this action with Rudra as well. Summarizing, one may say that the whole range of actions can be reduced to three basic elements: the offering as such (to the deities), the offering into the brahmin himself (*ātmayajña*; forerunner of the *prāṇāgnihotra*), the *ucchiṣṭa* as the conclusion of the rite.

NOTES

[1] For a different form of the agnihotra *vaiśvadeva* see Section 16. The *vaiśvadeva* is also the name of a ritual described in the gṛhya sūtras. See the Appendix.

[2] The appeasement of Rudra forms a special subject in the agnihotra section. It is more or less an expiation. See KS. 6, 7 (quoted below; the agnihotra of twelve days) and MS. 1, 8, 6: 123.1 ff. See also Hoens, *Śānti*, p. 39.

[3] The meaning of the first epithet is not clear. The second means rogue. See also Caland, *WZKM* 23, p. 52.

[4] The names are the representations of the power of the gods. They form his aspects. See also Gonda, *Notes on Names and the Name of God in Ancient India*, Amsterdam Academy 1970.

[5] Read *devaḥ* for *devāḥ*. Rudra is meant. Some sort of expiatory agnihotra is introduced here. The starting-point is Rudra in the preceding context.

[6] The epithet Jātavedas seems to be used here on account of the etymology "who finds (*vid*) the creatures (*jāta*)" (for a different interpretation of this compound see Whitney, *AJPh* 3, p. 409). Agni/Rudra kills the creatures (*prajāḥ*). Hoens, *Śānti*, p. 39 (and elsewhere) translates *prajā* by "offspring (of man and cattle)". Rudra would afflict here "the young cattle and the

children of the yajamāna". Indeed Rudra often does harm to the cattle, but I see no reason why he should especially kill the young cattle. "Creatures" may include all kinds of living beings. Rudra causes epidemics which injure especially cattle, but human beings as well.

[7] The exact meaning of this epithet, which in the version of the KS. is Anārbhava, is uncertain. Indeed ṚV. 1, 51, 9 has *anābhū* ("not helpful"). The vocative *anābho* of the present text, however, points to *anābhu*. Perhaps *anābhava* should be the reading in the version of the KS.

[8] Note the use of *śamāyati* ("to kill") and *śamayati* ("to appease") side by side in this passage. The etymology of both verbs is different. See Hoens, *Śānti*, p. 36.

[9] MS. 1, 8, 5: 121.12–15, dealing with actions without any relation to the *vaiśvadeva*, has been omitted here.

[10] See n. 2.

[11] He smears the milk on the herbs. As to the *pitṛs*, these are always brought into connection with the south, which is the region of death.

[12] The gerund (here ending in *-tvāya* and not in *-tvā*) does not always refer to actions in time preceding the action of the predicate, as is very obvious here. See also Minard, *Trois Énigmes* II, 143 ff.

[13] On not touching the teeth and its association with serpents on the one hand, and Pūṣan (the toothless god) on the other, see Hoens, *Śānti*, p. 37.

[14] Here Indra is identical with the sun. Cf. TB. 2, 1, 2, 7 (in Section 4 on the right time for the performance) stating that the night is sacred to Agni and the day to Indra (4, n. 2). See also 16, n. 14.

[15] Cf. ŚB. 2, 3, 1, 4 ".. and because he offers for that (sun) in the state of an embryo (i.e. nourishes it by the night performance), therefore embryos here live without taking food". Note that the context (though likewise dealing with the agnihotra) is different.

[16] Nothing is known about *svagā* in connection with the agnihotra. Dumont observes: ".. in the opinion of the author of the Taittirīya-Brāhmaṇa, the formula uttered by the Adhvaryu when, having heated the *agnihotrahavaṇī*, he points out the northern direction with that ladle, i.e., the formula *saptarṣibhyas tvā, saptarṣīn jinva* "to the seven Ṛṣis, thee; do thou quicken the seven Ṛṣis", was preceded or followed by the exclamation *svagā*". This is highly hypothetical. Probably *niṣṭapati svagākṛtyai* means that the final heating of the ladle functions as the *svagākṛti* of other rituals. Compare KS. 6, 8: 58.9 on the conclusion of the agnihotra by throwing a grassblade into the fire. This is a termination (*saṃsthiti*), but also a "farewell" (*svagākṛti*).

[17] The Seven Seers (*saptarṣis*), whose names are not fixed in tradition, in the sky are represented by the seven stars of the Great Bear.

[18] The Aṅgirases are famous forefathers from primeval times. They are the first sacrificers. On the one hand a priestly family originates from them, on the other hand they are also deified and as such they sometimes are distressed by other groups of beings, as is the case here. See also Lévi, *Doctrine*, p. 68.

[19] Pṛśni ("the dappled cow") as a deity is variously explained (e.g. as the mother of the Maruts). Here she seems to have no cosmic dimensions. Dumont translates "a spotted cow", which seems to miss the point.

[20] Compare the passage on the poisoning of the herbs by Rudra or the Rudras in a different context (Section 6.9). There are some agreements.

[21] Cf. 3.1, n. 5 and 6.4, n. 10. ŚB. 14, 3, 2, 26 identifies the Pravargya with (i.a.) the Agnihotra.

[22] Cf. TS. 2, 6, 6, 6 "verily he appeases Rudra in his own quarter" (tr. Keith).

[23] In these *vaiśvadeva* passages it is often difficult to decide whether *yad* ..

(*tad/tena*) means "in that, when" or "what". KS. 6, 5 has side by side *yaj juhoti tad devānām* (i.e. *yad* is "what") and *yad uddiśati tena rudraṃ śamayati* (*yad* meaning "in that; when"). MS. *prāśnāti manuṣyāṃs tena prīṇāti* points to a construction *yat prāśnāti* .. "in that he ..". In the TB. I have translated *yad* by "what", because constructions such as *yan nimārṣṭi tad oṣadhīnām* hardly admit of a different interpretation. In the present passage of the ŚāṅkhB. *yad* in *yad dvitīyaṃ tad dakṣiṇena kūrcam uttānaṃ pāṇiṃ nidadhāti* obviously means "when" (to be correlated with *tad* as well as with *tena* in *pitṝṃs tena prīṇāti*), whereas *yad* in *yat pūrvam upamārṣṭi tat kūrce nilimpati* seems to mean "what". In cases where the direct correlate of *yad* is *tena* the meaning of *yad* is probably "in that; when". See e.g. *yat srucaṃ mārjayate rakṣodevajanāṃs tena prīṇāti*, where *yat* cannot be interpreted as "what". In the passage of the ŚB. I have translated *yad* .. *tad* by "what .. that", whereas JB. *yad* ... *tena* has been taken as meaning "when .. thereby".

[24] *uttāna* does not mean "outstretched" (Keith), but "on the back, with the hollow side above".

[25] On this sentence see n. 15. The passages of the TB. and the ŚāṅkhB. agree.

[26] I read *prasrāvayanti*. The form *prasrāpayanti*, accepted by Keith, seems to me quite doubtful.

[27] The compounds *sarpadevajanāḥ* and *rakṣodevajanāḥ* may be taken (with Keith) as *karmadhārayas*, the more so since here the general term *devajana* occurs twice. For a different interpretation of *devajanāḥ* as a separate group side by side with *sarpadevajanāḥ* (which would point to a different analysis of the compound *sarpadevajanāḥ*, i.e. as a *dvanda*) see author, *JB. I, 1–65*, p. 97, n. 23. If the *devajanāḥ* should be some kind of demons (specified as *sarpa* or *rakṣas*), this would imply a shift of the function of the term *deva*, in Iran denoting the evil powers, in Vedic India originally the positive counterparts of the Asuras. Perhaps, however, the evil aspect is expressed by the second element (cf. the term *itarajanāḥ*), and *deva* only refers to the divine or heavenly origin. See also Arbman, *Rudra*, Uppsala 1922, p. 151.

[28] Eggeling assumes that "*anvābhaktāḥ* ('allowed to share in the sacrifice') has probably to be supplied here from the next paragraph" and translates "and thereby the gods are (admitted to the sacrifice)". This kind of ellipsis is rather strange. Moreover *anvābhakta* does not just mean "admitted to the sacrifice". The prefix *anu* implies participation through association, which is excluded in the present context. Evidently *santi* in this paragraph forms the opposition to *parābhūtā(ḥ)* of the next one. The brāhmaṇas often use the verbs *as-* and *parābhū-* in connection with the sacrificer who knows the esoteric implications of the rite as expounded by the brāhmaṇa, in opposition to his enemy or rival (*bhrātṛvya*) who will be lost.

[29] The preceding paragraph deals with the creatures who directly participate in the sacrifice on account of ritual actions dedicated to them. By association (i.c. with the human beings) other creatures (i.c. the animals) are able to participate. Those who would not be associated at all are lost.

[30] Eggeling: "to those creatures that are not forlorn he thus offers a share". The interpretation of *evam eva* forms a problem. Eggeling's "thus" remains obscure in the context. Cf. ŚB. 1, 5, 2, 4 *evam evaitad imāḥ prajā aparābhūtās tā yajña ā bhajati*, where Eggeling translates ".. and therefore he makes .. take part ..". This parallel, in which Eggeling wrongly translates "therefore", seems to give the clue to the solution of our problem. If *evam eva* is taken to mean "in this way, in the following way", it can be connected with the following clause *manuṣyān anu paśavo devān anu vayāṃsy oṣadhayo vanaspatayo*

yad idaṃ kiṃ ca. Thus, on account of these associations (*anu*!!), those creatures which are not lost can be made to participate in the sacrifice (*evam u tat sarvaṃ yajña ābhaktam*). See also ŚB. 3, 6, 2, 26 (the preceding paragraph forms an interesting parallel of the present passage), which is quite identical. In the present passage the stereotyped phraseology of these related passages caused *evam eva* to be retained, while the description of the way in which all these creatures are associated in the participation in the sacrifice was changed. The version of the Kāṇva recension, quoted in translation by Eggeling ("Behind men are beasts; behind the gods are birds, plants, trees, and whatever else exists here. Thus he makes these creatures share in the sacrifice, those that are not forlorn here"), is superior for two reasons. First, it retains the possibility to connect *evam eva* with the detailed description of the association of all kinds of creatures. Secondly it makes *evam eva* follow instead of precede these associations. The version of the Kāṇva rec. definitely is more original.

[31] On *anu* in this connection see Minard, *Trois Énigmes* I, 190–192.

[32] The āhavanīya, where he stands, represents heaven, the gārhapatya earth.

[33] The ladle moves through the air which is the domain of Vāyu.

[34] *sarpadevajanāḥ* (see n. 27).

[35] See *JB. I, 1–65*, p. 97 f.

[36] I read *gṛhāṃś ca* instead of *grahāṃś ca.*

[37] The stereotyped repetitions have been left out here.

[38] The usual number of the *prāṇāḥ* is five. In this group *apāna* mostly denotes the wind which leaves the body through the anus. However, in the combination *prāṇāpānau* the *apāna* refers to the inhalation. This same combination is replaced by *prāṇodānau* in other texts. In this case *udāna* means inhalation. In the total group, however, the *udāna* seems to denote the air which is directed upwards in opposition to the abdominal air which is directed downwards or backwards (*apāna*). So in the present passage *apāna* first means inhalation and afterward *flatus ventris.*

[39] On this chronology, which concerns the agnihotra sections only, see *JB. I, 1–65*, p. 13.

6.16 *Actions after the offering which do not belong to the* vaiśvadeva.

KS. 6, 8: 58.8 ff.: With the formulas "You have pleased your own body, Agni. You have honoured with sacrifice[1] heaven and earth. Put vigour in us" he anoints a blade of grass (with milk or ghee) and throws it after (the oblation into the fire). This is the conclusion[2] or the Svagā exclamation.[3] If something of the agnihotra is not yet appeased, as a result of this he (i.e. Agni) injures the creatures.[4] When he anoints the blade of grass (with milk or ghee) and throws it after (the oblation), he thereby appeases it. (. . .)[5] A performer of the agnihotra is born among his offspring and he becomes more wealthy day by day, if the agnihotra is thus performed for him.

MS. 1, 8, 7: 126.8–11: They reflect upon the agnihotra: "Should it be concluded or not?" If he should conclude it, he has to anoint a blade of grass (with ghee) and throw it after (the oblation in the fire). For that is the conclusion of the agnihotra. Now they say concerning this: "When he is defeated, when he dies, when he falls into calamity, then the agnihotra is concluded".[6] Therefore it should not be concluded (by throwing the grass blade).

TB. 2, 1, 4, 9: He does not throw a blade of grass after (the oblation). The agnihotra is a sacrifice without a conclusion. If he should throw after, he would interrupt the sacrifice. Therefore there should not be thrown after, for the sake of the continuity of the sacrifice. He pours out water (after having washed the *agnihotrasthālī*). Thus he has made a representation of the final bath (*avabhṛtha*).

— The continuity of the lifelong agnihotra, as described above, is a well-known motif in the speculations on the agnihotra.[7] Some other actions performed at the end of the agnihotra are mentioned below.

MS. 1, 8, 5: 122.6–7: He turns round in this way.[8] For thus the sacrifice turns round. Moreover he thereby turns along with the course of the sun.

TB. 2, 1, 4, 8–9: He turns round to the right. He turns along his own strength.[9] Therefore the right half of the body is stronger. Moreover he turns along with the course of the sun.[10] After having offered he kindles the flame of the fire, in order to kindle his glory.

ŚāṅkhB. 2, 2: Having offered the two libations he mutters: "The blessing of a successful sacrifice, for which one may pray,[11] should be fulfilled for me". The blessing of a successful sacrifice falls to the share of the sacrificer.

ŚāṅkhB. 2, 2: He touches the coals with the lowest part of the ladle. Then he places the sacrificer in heaven.

ŚāṅkhB. 2, 4: When, after having offered, he honours[12] the fires, he expresses his purpose among the gods after having gratified them. And in that he also touches the calf, on account of this it is called Vātsapra.[13] Thus the cattle are not desirous of leaving the sacrificer. When he releases his vow after having sipped water,[14] he places this vow in the waters. They guard his vow until his next offering.

— Concerning the eating of the remaining milk by the brahmin priest something has already been said in the preceding section (dealing with the *vaiśvadeva*). The ŚB. has an explanation of the fact that a brahmin priest should eat these remains.

ŚB. 2, 3, 1, 39: They (the gods)[15] said: "Who shall offer this to us?". "The brahmin". "Brahmin, offer this to us". "What will be my share?" "The remains of the agnihotra". What he leaves in the ladle, that is the remainder (*ucchiṣṭa*) of the agnihotra. And what remains in the pot, is as (the rice which) one scatters out (offers) from the receptacle of the cart. If any one should drink, none but a brahmin must drink it. For it is put on the fire and therefore none but a brahmin should drink it.

NOTES

[1] ĀpŚS. 6, 14, 2 reads *ayāḍ* instead of *ayān*.

[2] See Caland's note on ĀpŚS. 6, 14, 3: "Gerade so wie das eigentliche Voll- und Neumondsopfer durch das Hinterdreinwerfen der in dem Löffel gesalbten Streu ... abgeschlosssen wird".

[3] See 6.15, n. 16.

[4] See also Hoens, *Śānti*, p. 38. However, the version of the MS. invites to take *agnihotrasya* with *saṃsthiti* and *svagākṛti*.

[5] For the passage omitted here see the next section.

[6] The agnihotra is not concluded at every performance, but forms a continuum. The night and the day performances cannot be taken as separate unities. Without interruption this alternation of the two performances goes on just as the cosmic alternation of night and day. For the unlimitedness of the agnihotra see MS. 1, 8, 7: 126.4 ff. (in the context of the question why the agnihotra does not have a fasting): "It is something continuous, unlimited, unconcluded". See also ŚB. 2, 3, 1, 13: "Now they say: 'Other sacrifices come to an conclusion, but the agnihotra does not come to a conclusion'. Even that which lasts for twelve years has a limitation, but this is unlimited. For having offered it in the evening he knows that he will offer in the morning. And when he has offered in the morning he knows that he will again offer in the evening. Therefore this agnihotra is unlimited and along with and in consequence of its unlimitedness the creatures are born unlimitedly. He who knows thus the unlimitedness of the agnihotra, is unlimitedly productive of prosperity and offspring." JB. 1, 4 states (in the context of the equation of the agnihotra with all kinds of great sacrifices): "Therefore this agnihotra is unlimited".

[7] The agnihotra is called *jarāmarya* (*JB. I, 1–65*, p. 155, n. 2) and *avyavachinna* (Section 1.3, n. 1). See also 4, n. 53.

[8] How is turned, is described in the TB. (see below). The MS. shows traces of oral transmission by just stating "in this way", which must be accompanied by a gesture.

[9] Dumont's "(By doing so) he turns around his own strength in the same way (i.e. to the right)" does not completely correspond to the Sanskrit. For parallels see TS. 5, 2, 1, 3; 5, 2, 5, 4, (with Keith's correct rendering and his reference to his own translation, *Śāṅkhāyana Āraṇyaka*, p. 25, n. 5).

[10] Again Dumont's translation, which seems to make the turning of the sun dependent on the turning of the priest instead of the reverse, has to be rejected (*anu* being a postposition here). I follow Keith (see n. 9).

[11] Keith renders *āśīḥ* by "blessing", which gives a good construction with the genitive. However, *samṛdhyatām* favours the interpretation adopted here.

[12] The worship of the fire(s) (*agnyupasthāna*) is not obligatory according to most texts, and if performed at all it should mostly be connected with the

evening performance. Its description (which mainly consists of a long list of mantras and formulas) is omitted in the present work. The worship is performed by the sacrificer himself. The *agnyupasthāna* mentioned here, may be a rather short one, performed just after the pouring out of the libations. See Dumont, *Agnihotra*, p. 171 (quoting the *prayoga* of the ĀśvŚS.). On the distinction between the very short and the long *upasthānam* see Eggeling's note on ŚB. 2, 3, 4, 9. The reference to the name Vātsapra (i.e. composed by Vatsaprī, the author of ṚV. 10, 45 = TS. 4, 2, 2) for this worship shows that the long *mahopasthāna* is meant.

[13] The wordplay or 'etymology' is based on *vatsa* "calf" and the root *prī* ("to gratify"; see *prītvā* above) which is evident in the name of the ṛṣi Vatsaprī rather than in the derivation Vātsapra (i.e. the *upasthāna* consisting of hymns composed by Vatsaprī or of the *sāman* ascribed to Vatsaprī). Keith assumes a play on *vatsaṃ spṛśati* ("he touches the calf") and Vātsapra.

[14] For this action performed by the sacrificer himself see ŚŚS. 2, 12, 12 (mentioning the mantra "By truth I descend to the (water for the) final bath of the sacrifice. The vow is in the waters"). See also JB. 1, 4 (*JB. I, 1–65*, p. 27 f.).

[15] The subject can only be the gods, who are not mentioned, however, in the immediate context. The composition of the passage seems to have been disturbed.

6.17 *Should there be offered in other fires than the āhavanīya?*

KS. 6, 8: 58.11 ff.: "O, Agni, lord of the house, enjoy (it)", with these words he offers in the gārhapatya fire by means of the small ladle (*sruva*), just as he performs the Patnīsaṃyājas.[1] It (i.e. the fire of the gārhapatya) takes offense in that after having put (the oblation) on the fire in the west (i.e. on the gārhapatya) he offers it in the east (i.e. in the āhavanīya). When he offers in the gārhapatya with the small ladle (*sruva*), he thereby gratifies it and brings about that it is not jealous.

MS. 1, 8, 5: 122.7–16: They reflect on the question whether there should be offered in the gārhapatya or not. It is jealous and harsh (if one does not offer). (Therefore) there should be offered. With "O, Agni, lord of the house, earning our worship, enjoy (this), hail" he should offer. Thereby he appeases it, thereby he gratifies it and thereby he brings about that it is no more jealous and harsh.[2] Moreover when, after having offered the first libation and being about to offer the second,[3] he looks back (towards the gārhapatya),[4] he thereby appeases it, thereby gratifies it and thereby brings about that it is no more jealous and harsh.[5] And when in his house is given by him (i.e. the sacrificer) that which people who sit near the fire beg from him,[6] he thereby appeases it, thereby gratifies it and thereby brings about that it is jealous and harsh no more.

VādhS. 3, 23: Then he looks back in view of the oblation which is offered in the gārhapatya.[7] He offers it with "To Agni, the lord of the house, hail. Yonder sun (Āditya) among the gods ..".[8] This is the thirteenth month. He for whom this (libation) is offered looks back (towards the gārhapatya), but also he for whom this is not offered looks back.[9]

Śāṅkh B. 2, 3: Some people say "Only in the āhavanīya he should offer". He should, however, offer in all the fires, for these were established in view of the offering. He offers four libations in the *gārhapatya*, four in the *anvāhāryapacana*, two in the *āhavanīya*. These amount to ten. The Virāj[10] consists of tens. The Virāj is prosperity and food.[11] For the sake of obtaining the Virāj in the form of prosperity and food (he offers these libations). He who thus offers the agnihotra which is homologized to the Virāj[12] obtains all things he desires.

AB. 7, 12, 4: They say: "When he is putting fuel on the fires, should he also procure the *anvāhāryapacana*, or should he not procure it?" "He should procure it", they say; he who establishes the fires establishes the breaths (*prāṇāḥ*) as counterparts on the personal level.[13] The *anvāhāryapacana* eats the most of them. In it he offers the libation with "Hail to Agni, the eater of food, the lord of food". He who knows thus becomes an eater of food, a lord of food; he obtains food with his offspring.

ŚB. 2, 3, 2, 6–8: The *gārhapatya* has the sacrificer as its deity and the *anvāhāryapacana*[14] (= *dakṣiṇāgni*, the southern fire) has his rival as its deity. Therefore they should not take it out (of the gārhapatya, every day. He for whom, knowing thus, they do not take out the *anvāhāryapacana* every day has no competitor. This is indeed the *anvāhāryapacana*. They should take it out only on the fast-day (before the new and full-moon sacrifices), on which occasion they will sacrifice in it.[15] Thus it has not been taken out for (or: by) him in vain[16]. Or they may also take it out in case there is occupied a new dwelling-place.[17] Then they should cook (food) on it. The brahmins should eat this. If he should not be able to procure anything to cook, he must order the milk of a cow to be put on it and the brahmins to eat it. His rivals will become more miserable, for whom, knowing thus, they act thus. Therefore he should wish to do thus.

— The offering in three fires is mentioned by ṢaḍvB. 4, 1, 9 in an identifi cation with the threefold Soma *savana*.

NOTES

[1] On the particular way of pouring out the libation in the Patnīsaṃyāja ritual see e.g. ĀpŚS. 3, 8, 6 ff. This oblation forms part of the New-moon sacrifice.

[2] Hoens, *Śānti*, p. 38 translates: "But he also achieves that he shall lack nothing and not grow thin". The parallel turn of phrase *ananudhyāyy akṣodhukaḥ* (MS. 1, 6, 4: 93.11; 1, 6, 5: 93.18–19; 1, 6, 11: 103.16) and the occurrence of *rūkṣa* meaning "emaciated" at PB. 5, 8, 1 (for both references see Hoens, o.c., p. 38, n. 161) may support his rendering. However, the essential point is the feeling, rather than the actual lack of something (which is not expressed by *anudhyāyin*). The actions which make the gārhapatya *arūkṣa* do not produce any nourishment (e.g. in the case of the looking back), but remove the jealousy and annoyance in the agnihotra context.

[3] On this propitiation see also 6.13, n. 1.

[4] Obviously he neither looks at the second libation (Delbrück, *Altind. Syntax*, p. 373), nor just at the gārhapatya (Hoens, *Śānti*, p. 38). He looks back towards the gārhapatya. This meaning of *pratīkṣ-* is not mentioned by M.-W. (but *pratīkṣa-* "looking backward" is found in this dictionary). Looking back also implies showing regard, respect, attention, consideration for.

[5] Cf. 6.6 (TB. 2, 1, 3, 6 f.) and 6.7 for other devices used to avert the wrath of the gārhapatya fire.

[6] Differently Hoens, *Śānti*, p. 38: "Then by the fact that a sacrifice takes place in his house and that they call on him (Agni Gṛhapati) for help, though they are close to that fire (Āhavanīya), he appeases him, he propitiates him".

[7] According to Caland "blickt er (wohl der Yajamāna) auf jene Spende hin, welche im Gārhapatya dargebracht wird". All the sūtras state that the priest (not the sacrificer) looks back at the gārhapatya after having offered the first libation in the āhavanīya. On the other hand, the subject of *pratyavekṣ-* ("to look back"), *sa yasyaiṣā hūyate* ("he for whom this is offered"), at the end of this passage seems to point to the sacrificer rather than to the priest. Probably, however, *sa yasyaiṣā hūyate* does not refer to the inactive sacrificer who has a priest for the performance and who looks at the offering by that priest in the gārhapatya. It should be noted that *sa yasyaiṣā hūyate* and *yasyaiṣā na hūyeta* imply an option: his agnihotra oblation is offered in the gārhapatya or not. The one who looks back at the gārhapatya after having offered in the āhavanīya is the performer, who may be either the priest or the sacrificer himself. The decision to offer in the gārhapatya as well rests with the sacrificer, not with the priest. Therefore, the phrase *sa yasyaiṣā hūyate* ("In the case of the sacrificer whose agnihotra is also offered in the gārhapatya") may have been chosen. By looking back at the gārhapatya the performer reminds this fire that he is aware of the offering which is offered (*hūyate*), or rather "will be offered", in the gārhapatya.

[8] The second formula has no parallel in the sūtras.

[9] According to Caland the end of this passage is not clear. The point is that according to KŚS. 4, 14, 16 (*hoṣyann asmin*) the performer only looks at the gārhapatya, if he is actually to offer in it afterwards. The other sūtras do not mention this restriction. The VādhS. explicitly states that he should always look back. See also n. 7.

[10] The Virāj, which represents totality and the hypostatization of the universe, is also a Vedic metre consisting of *Pādas* of 10 syllables each.

[11] Food is frequently identified with the Virāj. In this identification food stands for shortage of nothing, fullness, abundance.

[12] For a different homology with the tenfold Virāj in the context of the agnihotra see ŚB. 2, 3, 1, 18. According to KS. 6, 8: 57.13 ff. the five fires *odanapacana* (= southern fire, *dakṣiṇāgni*, or *anvāhāryapacana*), *gārhapatya*, *āhavanīya*, *madhyādhidevana* (probably the *sabhya* fire; M.-W.'s dictionary mentions only the meaning "middle of a playing-ground", which points to the *sabhā*, where the gambling takes place; for a threefold Virāj connected with gārhapatya, āhavanīya and again *madhyādhidevana*, cf. KS. 8, 7: 90.8) and *āmantraṇa* (apparently the *āvasathya* fire) are to be equated with a Virāj of three *pādas*. See Caland, *WZKM* 23, p. 58 on these fires.

[13] Keith translates *abhyātmam* by "in himself". See also *ātmany asya hitā bhavanti* "on his self are the (fires) placed" (tr. Keith) in the same passage. Perhaps *adhyātmam* is meant.

[14] The *gārhapatya* belongs to the house, the sacrificer himself, one's own domain, whereas the *anvāhāryapacana*, on which the *anvāhārya* (the dish of rice presented as a *dakṣiṇā* to the priests at the new- and fullmoon sacrifices) has to be connected with the other party. Perhaps this reflects the preclassical ritualistic situation as assumed by Heesterman, "Brahmin, Ritual and Renoncer", *WZKSO* 8 (1964), p. 1–31 (and other publications).

[15] I.e. in the *anvāhāryapacana*, not in the *āhavanīya* as Eggeling assumes. See n. 16.

[16] Not: "in order to prevent failure on his (the sacrificer's) part" (Eggeling). The *anvāhāryapacana* is taken out only on the day when there is actually offered in it, and consequently its being taken out makes sense. See n. 15.

[17] Not: "take it over to a new dwelling" (Eggeling). The fire is taken out in case the sacrificer moves to a new dwelling; *navāvasita* is not identical with *navāvasāna* (thus hesitatingly M.-W.), but a participle (here loc. abs.) with *nava* denoting either "anew" or "newly, recently". See also ĀpŚS. 6, 2, 16.

7 *The sacrificer (*yajamāna*) and the performer of the agnihotra.*

— "L'étude de l'origine des rites d'un sacrifice, de leur signification primitive, de leur histoire, de l'interprétation qu'en ont donnée les prêtres, offre certainement plus d'intérêt que leur simple description". These words put forward by Dumont in his introduction to *L'Agnihotra* are especially relevant in connection with the personages involved in the agnihotra. Here we may touch upon the question of the origin of the rite and its later transformations. A study of these problems lies beyond the scope of the present work, which primarily tries to give an annotated translation of the relevant passages in the brāhmaṇas. These texts perhaps do not represent the original situation. The performance of the agnihotra by a priest on behalf of a yajamāna who is present (and who according to some texts cannot be a kṣatriya) raises some questions. If the yajamāna is a brahmin, why does not he perform this rite himself? Several formulas to be recited by the priest and several comments in the brāhmaṇas on actions of the priest make sense only in connection with a sacrificer who performs the rite himself. BaudhŚS. 3, 5, 13 e.g. contains a formula *ahaṃ yajamāno mā riṣam*, to be recited by the priest. See also 6.5, n. 23. The performance on behalf of someone else (especially a kṣatriya) points to a later development. The original, much simpler agnihotra, performed by the sacrificer in his own fire(s), may be compared to the *gṛhya* version, which in its description is based on the śrauta agnihotra, but may be a continuation of an older form of fire ritual.

7.1 *The kṣatriya and the agnihotra.*

KS. 6, 6: 56.1 ff.: There is no agnihotra (performed) for the kṣatriya, for he does not observe religious obligations and kills.[1] One should not interrupt one's observance (as the kṣatriya does).[2] He may offer (for him) in the night (and day)[3] of the full moon and of the new moon, for during these two he (i.e. the kṣatriya) keeps his observance.[4] During those days when he does not offer (for the kṣatriya), they should first (i.e. before his own meal)[5] present (food) to a brahmin in his (i.e. the kṣatriya's) house.[6] The brahmin is identical with Agni.[7] Thereby he offers in Agni. What has been tasted by him, thereby has been sacrificed.

MS. 1, 8, 7: 126.17 ff.: They raise the question: "Should the agnihotra be offered for a kṣatriya, or not?" The kṣatriya is someone who eats raw meat as it were. He is engaged in much which is profane and impure. He eats food which should not be eaten.[8] He oppresses the brahmin. Therefore the agnihotra should not be offered for a kṣatriya. The agnihotra is order and truth.[9] The brahmin is order and truth. Therefore there should be offered for the brahmin. But they should first (i.e. before the kṣatriya's meal) give (food) to a brahmin in his house. Thereby the agnihotra is offered for him. And whosoever may be engaged in order and truth, for him there should be offered continuously.[10]

— In its *agnyādhāna* section the MS. gives another explanation for the fact that the kṣatriya is excluded from the agnihotra:

MS. 1, 6, 10: 102.13 ff.: The Devas and the Asuras were in conflict. But Indra established his fire. The Devas feared: "In yonder place that one will keep guarding his fire, guarding his agnihotra. He will not come to our side. They will defeat us". They said: "Whatever you make, whatever you kill, whatever you win, whatever you find, that we (will) make an agnihotra for you. Come". He did come. Therefore the agnihotra should (or: need) not be offered for the *rājanya*. For whatever he makes, whatever he kills, whatever he wins, whatever he finds, whatever attendance he receives from the people, that is the agnihotra of the *rājanya*.

— The text continues with a discussion on the agnihotra of the *rājanya* similar to the one found in the agnihotra section (translated above).

MS. 1, 6, 10: 102.19–103.4: They raise the question: "Should the agnihotra be offered for a kṣatriya, or not?"[11] If after having offered one should not offer (anymore), one would interrupt the sacrifice.[12] He (the kṣatriya) would be defeated or would perish. There should be offered every night of the full and the new moon.[13] He (the kṣatriya) should be made to recite the mantras of the *agnyupasthāna* (during the days in between).[14] Thereby his New and Full Moon sacrifices form a continuity and are not interrupted (by a period without offerings).

NOTES

[1] For this passage cf. ĀpŚS. 6, 15, 10 f. with Caland's translation and notes. Caland translates "er zerstört die Observanz". Caland's construction *hanti vratam* is at variance with the regular order of words. It is true that MS. 1, 8, 7: 126.19 *atty anannam, jināti brāhmaṇam* seems to have a similar construction, but the exceptional position of the verb is due to the enumeration of actions.

[2] Caland (see n. 1) renders: "Er unterlasse es (aber für einen solchen) nicht (gänzlich)". The point, however, is that the kṣatriya cannot remain pure every day.

[3] The night refers to the most important evening performance of the rite, of which the morning agnihotra forms only a counterpart which is connected with the day-time.

[4] Caland (see n. 1) translates: "Denn diese beiden Tage bewacht die Observanz".

5 Cf. HirŚS. 3, 7, 118 *mukhataḥ* (Dumont, *L'Agnihotra*, p. 88: "d'abord (c'est-à-dire avant que le kṣatriya ait mangé)".

[6] The brahmin(s) receive(s) food in the house of the kṣatriya. According to the sūtras food seems to be sent from the kṣatriya's house.

[7] See also *Agn. and Prāṇāgn.*, ch. III, n. 14 on the brahmin as a substitute for the sacrificial fire. It is remarkable that in the preceding portion of the KS. and the MS. a passage is found in which a symbolical sacrifice is described. VāsDhŚ. 30, 2 ff. connects the feeding of a brahmin with symbolical sacrifices. This text refers to KS. 6, 6 (*agnir vai brāhmaṇa iti śruteḥ*) and uses the same set of identifications as are found in *ātmayajñas*, where the sacrifice is not performed in the fire.

[8] Read *atty anannam* (with Caland, who translates "er isst, was keine Speise ist" in a note on ĀpŚS. 6, 15, 10). On *ananna* "impure food" see *Agn. and Prāṇāgn.*, ch. IX B, n. 28.

[9] This is one of the places which show that *ṛta* "order", here occurring together with *satya* "truth", does not mean "truth", as Lüders assumes in *Varuṇa* II. On the relation between agnihotra and truth see *Agn. and Prāṇāgn.*, ch. V B.

[10] This sentence seems to prove that the MS. has carelessly worked out (or borrowed) the passage of the KS. The latter explicitly states that in the nights of the new and full moon the agnihotra may be performed for a kṣatriya, whereas in the intervening periods food presented to brahmins replaces the offering. The MS. does not mention the incidental agnihotra of the new and full moon, but abruptly states that for some kṣatriyas the agnihotra may be performed continuously (cf. MŚS. 1, 6, 1, 54 *nityam*), i.e. also between the two mentioned performances to which the MS. does not refer at all (at least in this passage; see, however, below).

[11] The same sentence is found in MS. 1, 8, 7. In the present passage von Schroeder's punctuation has to be corrected.

[12] At first sight this might support Caland's interpretation of the parallel passage in the KS. (see n. 2), but the situation is not wholly similar.

[13] This statement was missing in the passage of MS. 1, 8, 7.

[14] Read *agnyupasthānaṃ vācayitavyaḥ* instead of .. *vā cayitavyaḥ*. Cf. ĀpŚS. 6, 15, 12.

7.2 *Only the brahmin may consume the remains of the oblation.*

— The passage dealing with this subject in ŚB. (2, 3, 1, 39) has already been translated at the end of Section 6.16. See also TB. 2, 1, 4, 4–8 (in Section 6.15) mentioning the identification of the brahmin and Agni Vaiśvānara. Giving food to brahmins forms a substitution for the kṣatriya's agnihotra (7.1). In fact there is offered into a brahmin who replaces the fire.

7.3 *Should the brahmin perform the rite himself or should someone else?*

ṢaḍvB. 4, 1, 13–14: One oblation performed by a pupil is better than a hundred oblations performed by others. One oblation performed by a son is better than a hundred oblations performed by pupils. One oblation performed by oneself is better than a hundred oblations performed by a son. For he (the sacrificer) should offer[1] himself, he should milk himself, he should attend on[2] the agnihotra himself.

NOTES

[1] Bollée following the commentary translates *svayaṃ hotā* by "He ... should invoke (the gods at the sacrifice) himself". Although *hotṛ* as a technical term denotes one of the officiants who recites formulas and may invoke the gods in the systematized Vedic ritual, its etymology does not point to *āhū-* "to invoke", but to *hu-* "to pour out, sacrifice". Originally and in its non-technical sense — it should be noted that the agnihotra does not have a *hotṛ* officiant — it refers to the officiant, the priest, or in general to the one who performs the oblation. See also Schlerath, *Fs. Lommel* (1960), p. 131.

[2] Does *upasthā* ("to attend") refer to the ritual of the *agnyupasthāna*, the worship of the fire? In that case *agnihotra* should mean (as in later texts) the fire in which the libation is offered. See e.g. the opening of the Sāvitrī story (*agnihotrāt samutthāya* .., vs. 7) on this meaning of *agnihotra*.

7.4 *Should a sacrificer without a wife perform the agnihotra?*

AB. 7, 9, 9 ff.: They say: "Should a man without a wife also offer the agnihotra, or not?" "He should offer", they say; "if he should not offer (it), he would be a barbarian". "What is a barbarian?"[1] "One who (offers) neither to the gods, nor to the *pitṛs*, nor to men". Therefore a man without a wife also should offer the agnihotra. As to this the following verse is sung:[2] "Even he who is without a wife and does not drink *soma* should sacrifice the Sautrāmaṇī.[3] Thus is the rule of the scriptures on account of the prescription 'Sacrifice for the sake of being without debt towards father and mother'". Therefore he should act as a priest for someone who is acquainted with *soma*.[4]

AB. 7, 10: Now they say: "How[5] does a man without a wife offer the agnihotra?"[5] "(If) the wife has died or has disappeared after he (the agnihotrin) has married,[6] how does he offer the agnihotra?" "Sons, grandsons, great-grandsons (he wins)",[7] they say, "in this world and in yonder world. In this world is this heaven. By way of (this eartly) heaven[8] he mounts to the world of Heaven (in yonder world)". He maintains the continuity of his lineage in yonder world who does not desire a wife.[9] Therefore they establish the fires for someone who has no wife. How does someone who has no wife offer the agnihotra? His wife is faith, the sacrificer truth.[10] Faith and truth, that is the supreme couple. By faith and truth as a pair he wins the worlds of heaven.

NOTES

[1] See Rönnow, *MO* 23 (1929), p. 151 on *anaddhāpuruṣa*.

[2] For this verse (*gāthā*) inserted in the prose passage see Horsch, *Die Vedische Gāthā- und Śloka-Literatur* (Bern 1966), p. 77, whose translation of the end of the verse "weil er dadurch seine Schuld gegenüber Vater und Mutter abträgt, und weil '*yaja*' (= opfere) eine Aufforderung der Śruti ist" is not followed by me. I agree with Keith that the quotation of the prescription is not just *yaja*. In Horsch's interpretation a *ca* is missing between the two arguments. In defence of Keith's and my translation, it may be observed that Aufrecht has pointed out that *anṛṇī* is the origin of the gloss *anṛṇārthāt*. So the oblative *anṛṇārthāt* is not original and does not represent a separate argument apart from *yajeti vacanāt*.

[3] This rite, in which *soma* is not used, has no relation to the context. Apparently an existing verse intended for a different application has been quoted here. It is, however, not quite certain whether the text is sound.

[4] Again an obscure point, here formed by *saumya* "someone acquainted with *soma*". What does this mean in the context? Does the term want to say that at least for someone who is a *soma*-sacrificer the sacrifices (including the agnihotra) should continue to be offered after the death of his wife, since there is even authority (in the quoted verse) for sacrifices on behalf of non-*soma*-sacrificers? TB. 2, 2, 2, 6 (quoted by Horsch, p. 78) states that someone without a wife should also be without sacrifices. The last sentence of AB. 7, 9 as well as AB. 7, 10 apparently are later additions. They are not found in every ms.

[5] In this later added (see n. 3) paragraph, in which the text is "clearly in part at least corrupt" (Keith), several problems are met with. Keith translates *katham* by "why" here, but later on in an identical turn of phrase by "how". It has to be admitted that both renderings find support in the context. If *katham* is translated by "how", one has to wait till the end of the passage (where indeed the question is repeated) for an answer. On the other hand the direct answer seems to argue why a man without a wife may have reason to sacrifice. A second problem is raised by the repetition of the question (in a new formulation) at the beginning of AB. 7, 10 (apart from the repetition at the end of the passage and the fact that AB. 7, 10 deals anew with a point which had been concluded in AB. 7, 9). I am under the impression that two kinds of *apatnīka* sacrificers have to be distinguished here. On the one hand the term *apatnīka* seems to denote someone whose wife has disappeared, by death or otherwise (second formulation of the question). The text explicitly refers to the fact that this *apatnīka* has been married (*niviṣṭe*; see n. 5). This term, however, may also denote someone who does not marry, who does not take a *patnī* at all. This *apatnīka* is someone who has never had a *patnī*; this may be an *apatnīka* in its literal sense. In the same way a man who is *aputra* is a person who has never obtained a son, rather than someone who has lost his son(s). This may explain the difficult *vācā* at the beginning of this sen-

tence (*vācāpatnīkaḥ* ..). Keith translates: "Why does a man without a wife offer at command the Agnihotra?", which hardly makes sense. Does *vācā* mean "verbally, in the true sense of the word"? The one who is *vācāpatnīka* (note the order of the words) is set against the one whose wife has died/vanished (*mṛtā/naṣṭā*) after marriage (*niviṣṭe*).

[6] For the correct interpretation of *niviṣṭe* (and a criticism of Keith's translation) see Oertel, *Syntax of Cases*, p. 46. The construction of the beginning of this sentence is an "independent paratactical clause equivalent in sense to a hypotactical conditional sentence".

[7] The ellipsis is as strange as it is at AB. 7, 9 ("One who (offers) neither to gods, nor to Manes, nor to men"). Although following Keith in both cases, I still have some doubts.

[8] Agreeing with Keith that this chapter is rather corrupt, I propose to read *svargena* instead of *'svargena*. The point seems to be that continuation of offspring may be obtained in this world as well as in yonder world. One may live on here as well as in heaven (i.e. in eternity?). In the former case there is a heaven on earth ("In this world is this heaven"; Keith's translation "in this world is yonder (world) of heaven" mistranslates *ayam*). By means of this earthly 'heaven' the heavenly heaven may be obtained, i.e. by producing children and (indirectly) grandchildren one may safeguard living on in heaven. This might refer to the fact that in yonder world the deceased subsist on the offerings of the offspring on earth. It is a standard view in Indian literature that one cannot live on without a son.

[9] The alternative way of living on in heaven is by sacrifice. Those people who do not marry (who are *apatnīka* in the true sense of the word, see n. 4) safeguard the continuation of their race (i.e. their living on) by sacrificing. The context seems to point to people who do not marry, perhaps even to *ātmayājins* (see *Agn. and Prāṇāgn.*, ch. X, p. 304 ff.). Indeed the text seems to be corrupt. Still I do not follow Keith's conjecture ("perhaps *yasyaiṣā patnī naśyet*"), but would prefer to retain *icchet* ("people who desire a wife") without being able to suggest a smooth emendation of this evidently corrupt text.

[10] Truth and faith form a stereotyped couple, also in connection with the agnihotra. See VādhS. 3, 36 (*satya* and *śraddhā* are the *gati* and *pratiṣṭhā*, the refuge and support, of the agnihotra) and JB. 1, 19 and its parallel ŚB. 11, 3, 1, 4 (if all oblatory material should be missing, the oblation may consist of truth which is offered in the fire of faith; the substitution is comparable to the present passage). Cf. also VādhS. 3, 1 (context: *agnyādhāna*), where *satya* and *śraddhā* are two fires, and the two identifications *satya* = *cakṣus* and *śraddhā* = *śrotra* prove that *śraddhā* in combination with *satya* does not mean "Opferwilligkeit" (as sometimes Caland freely translates) but "confidence (in what is not seen, but only heard, e.g. from the priest)". For the substitution of the wife by faith (*śraddhā*) compare MNU. 543 (where the sacrificer is the self, the *ātman*; or should one translate: "he is himself the sacrificer"?). In the parallel passages dealing with the so-called *ātmayājins* who have no wife ("those who offer in themselves by eating the oblation, or who offer to the self") the wife is also substituted by other entities in these symbolic sacrifices, e.g. by *buddhi* (intellect; see VaiSmS. 2, 18 and PrāṇāgnU. 38). The inserted passage in the AB. may form a starting-point for this sort of identifications.

7.5 *The agnihotra has only one officiant.*

TB. 2, 3, 6, 1: Prajāpati, after having created the creatures out of himself,[1] collapsed. He lay down, being just heart.[2] He called upon (his own body) with the words "O, body, alas". The waters answered (his calling). They turned towards him with the agnihotra sacrifice. They brought near the trunk (of his body). Therefore the agnihotra has only one officiant.[3]

NOTES

[1] The creation in fact is an emanation (*sṛj-* "to emit out of oneself"). This explains why Prajāpati was exhausted.

[2] I.e. only life, or the soul, remained of his functions and elements.

[3] The passage continues with Prajāpati's fourfold calling for his body. Four deities answered the call and came to him with the new and full moon sacrifice. Therefore these sacrifices have four officiants. In this way ultimately Prajāpati's whole body is restored to him and the number of the officiants of several sacrifices is explained.

8 *The keeping silent during the rite*

KS. 6, 7: 56.14–15:[1] He should restrain his speech while the milk is ladled out. Prajāpati created (emitted out of himself) the creatures by means of penance. In that he did not speak, thereby he performed penance. The agnihotra is a creation. A creation is that observance (of restraining speech).

MS. 1, 8, 4: 119.8 ff.: Prajāpati created the creatures. He created them by means of penance. He restrained his speech. He who restrains his speech performs penance. The agnihotra is a creation of creatures (or offspring).[2] He creates offspring from two sides, from this side and from yonder side.[3] After the sun has set, speech should be restrained. And when the cow is being milked. And when the milk is on the fire. When it is being ladled out, then indeed it should be restrained.[4] That is the most correct (moment to restrain speech).

NOTES

[1] The preceding passage (the beginning of KS. 6, 7) also deals with speech. See Section 6.10.

[2] On the one hand *prajā* (especially in the plural) denotes the creatures, but on the other hand it may also refer to offspring, which elsewhere often is said to be produced by the agnihotra.

[3] Does *itaś cāmutaś ca* point to the twofold aspect of the agnihotra (sunset/daybreak)? Or should *amutas* as usual be connected with yonder world and does the text want to say that the heavenly production of creatures (*prajāḥ*) has a corresponding earthly production of offspring (*prajā*) by means of the agnihotra?

[4] Read *yantavyā* (sc. *vāk*) with Caland, *ZDMG* 72, p. 7.

9 *Why the agnihotra has no fast (upavāsa)*

MS. 1, 8, 7: 126.3 ff.: "They fast before other oblations, but why does not one fast before the agnihotra?" say those who are engaged in theological-ritualistic debates. This (rite) is extended, unlimited, endless. (During all these days before the daily performances) he eats meat, he sleeps with his wife. Therefore they do not fast before (the agnihotra). One should behave like cattle. The cattle perform their coitus in silence. They are ritually pure. When one silently has sexual intercourse with a woman,[1] one thereby becomes more pure. One should (only) make the sound *him* during the intercourse — for thus the cattle have intercourse — in order to be ritually pure.

NOTES

[1] Cf. KS. 6, 6: 55.20 "He should not speak during the coitus. He should become an animal (or: a cow), when he has intercourse. Day after day the animals have intercourse and still they are ritually pure". In the KS. the passage is almost too concise to make clear what is its purpose. The comparison with the MS. shows what is meant. Something may have fallen out in the original version of the KS.

— The agnihotra takes in a particular position among the *śrauta* rituals. In fact, its nature agrees more with the *gṛhya* rites (among which a duplicate of the *śrauta* agnihotra is found) than with most of the elaborate Soma sacrifices. It is a simple sacrifice and compulsory for those who have established the sacred fires. It forms the daily confirmation of the relationship between the *āhitāgni* and his fire(s). Indeed, the agnihotra may have several cosmological implications in the brāhmaṇas. However, it is essentially a personal ritual with at least partially personal aims. The priest who may act as the officiant temporarily or incidentally replaces the "owner of the fires", who may also use his own son or pupil as substitute. This private rite was often identified, partly or as a whole, with the more impressive great sacrifices, which had a totally different background. Glorification of the simple rite forms one of the aspects of this phenomenon.[1]

KS. 6, 6: 55.14–15: (Of) the two roads, the new- and full-moon sacrifices, on which he has stepped the path in the middle (of them) is the agnihotra. Thus the world of heaven similarly[2] shines for the sacrificer of the agnihotra and the sacrificer of the new- and full-moon sacrifices.

— The parallel passage of MS. 1, 8, 7: 126.1–3 is so close as to make a translation superfluous. This text, however, has another passage on the agnihotra and other sacrifices, which is found neither in the older KS. nor in the later texts:

MS. 1, 8, 6: 124.13 ff.: By the *agniṣṭoma*[3] he wins the realm of Yama, by the *ukthya*[3] the realm of Soma, by the Sixteenfold (*ṣoḍaśin*)[3] the realm of Sūrya, by the Overnight (*atirātra*)[3] sovereignty. Indra became all these. He who sacrifices with these (rites) becomes all these (worlds). Some offer libations, others sacrifice to the gods, others perform a sacrifice in which a thousand (cows) are involved (as *dakṣiṇā*, present for the officiants). He who offers the agnihotra is an offerer of libations (*haviṣmat*); who offers the new- and full-moon sacrifices is a sacrificer to the gods (*devayājin*);[4] who performs the Fourmonthly sacrifices is a sacrificer of thousand. In the agnihotra all sacrifices are (included). He obtains all sacrifices who knowing thus performs the agnihotra.

— In the sections on the setting down of the ladle an identification with the Soma ritual is found in the versions of TB. 2, 1, 5, 8 and ŚāṅkhB. 2, 2. See e.g. Section 6.6. The TB. also has a passage which seems to belong to the section on the symbolic sacrifices. However the ritual entities mentioned in the identifications belong to the Soma ritual rather than to the agnihotra:

TB. 2, 1, 5, 9: He who knows the calling out (*āśrāvita*)[5] and the response (*pratyāśrāvita*),[5] the *hotṛ*[6] and the *brahman*[6] and the *vaṣaṭ-kāra*[7] of the agnihotra, by him is (truly) offered. The exhalation (of the performer) is the *āśrāvita*, the inhalation[8] the *pratyāśrāvita*, the mind the *hotṛ*, the sight[9] the *brahman*, the shutting of the eye[10] the *vaṣaṭ*-call of the agnihotra. By him who knows thus there is offered.[11]

— By means of identifications the TB. tries to make up for the lack of *sāmans* in the agnihotra. There is no *udgātṛ* in this ritual. However, the sacrificer himself may belong to the Sāmaveda. In this case *sāmans* may be sung. See author, *JB. I, 1–65*, p. 98, n. 28.

TB. 2, 1, 5, 6 f.: That (sacrifice) which is without Sāmans is not a sacrifice.[12] He ladles out four times. The Rathantara Sāman has four syllables. This (ladling out) is a representation of the Rathantara. He holds (the ladle with the milk and the *samidh*) upwards as it were. The intermediate space[13] is (homologized to) the Vāmadevya Sāman. This is a representation of the Vāmadevya Sāman. He offers twice. The Bṛhat Sāman has two syllables. This is a representation of the Bṛhat. Thus he makes the agnihotra supplied with Sāmans.

— In the following passage (not belonging to the regular agnihotra section of the TB.) numbers again form the starting-point for identifications of the agnihotra with other rites:

TB. 2, 3, 7, 1 ff. Prajāpati created the Puruṣa.[14] Agni said: "This should be my food". He (the Puruṣa) feared: "He will burn me completely". He saw (i.e. discovered and produced) these *catur-hotṛ*[15] litanies which could save himself. When he offered (or: when nowadays the priest offers) the agnihotra, then he obtains a sacrifice of one *hotṛ* in the form of this agnihotra. And he saves his own trunk.[16] And he comes to communion with Āditya. He ladles out four times. He obtains a sacrifice (with the litany) of four *hotṛs*, in the form of the New- and Full-moon sacrifices. And he saves the four limbs of himself and comes to communion with Āditya. He ladles out four times. The firewood is the fifth. Thereby he obtains a sacrifice (with the litany) of five *hotṛs*, in the form of the Fourmonthly sacrifices. And he saves of himself (of his body) the following: hair, skin, flesh, bone, marrow. And he comes to communion with Āditya. He ladles out four times, he offers twice.

Thereby he obtains a sacrifice (with a litany) of six *hotṛs*, in the form of the the animal sacrifice (*paśubandhu*). And he saves of himself the following elements: the two breasts, the two testicles, the penis and the anus.[17] And he (...). He ladles out four times, he offers twice; the firewood is the seventh. Thereby he obtains a sacrifice (with a litany) of seven hotṛs, in the form of the Soma sacrifice. And he saves of himself the seven vital functions (*prāṇāḥ*) which are found in the head. (..). He ladles out four times, he offers twice, he wipes off twice and eats twice (the remaining material of the oblation). Thereby he obtains a sacrifice (with a litany) of ten *hotṛs*.[18] And he saves all of himself without any exception and comes to communion with Āditya.

— Some passages emphasize the particular position of the agnihotra with respect to the other sacrifices.

TB. 2, 1, 5, 1: Those who hold debates on religious and ritualistic subjects say: "The sacrifices have the agnihotra as their introduction.[19] What introduction has the agnihotra (itself)?" (He should say) "The calf (of the cow which produces the milk) is the introduction[20] of the agnihotra; the agnihotra of the sacrifices".

— VādhS. 3, 10 has an *anvākhyāna* (some sort of afterthought) on this passage. Unfortunately the text is not sound in all respects. Apparently the āhavanīya fire, which is kindled at every performance, has the same role as the calf. It is a starting-point or introduction, since with its birth (i.e. when it is set to fire) the ritual starts. For another reference to the position of the agnihotra as the *prāyaṇa* of the sacrifices see MNU. 527.

ŚB. 2, 3, 3, 10: Like the arrow-head for the arrow is the agnihotra for the sacrifices. For the way in which the arrow-head flies, in that way the whole arrow flies. And by this (agnihotra) his sacrifices escape that death.

— For this section the ŚāṅkhB. does not provide much material. It has an identification of the agnihotra milk with the hot milk of the Pravargya (see 6.15, n. 21). Further, it interprets the laying on of the *samidh* as a Soma libation (see 6.9, n. 11). The AB. has one extensive passage on the subject of this section (identifications with i.a. the Mahāvrata and the Agnicayana):

AB. 5, 28, 7–11; By the evening libation for Agni he begins the Āśvina (Śastra).[21] Speech responds in recitation with "Speech, speech".[22] By Agni, by the night the Āśvina is recited by him who knowing thus offers the agnihotra. By the morning libation for the sun he begins the Mahāvrata.[23] Breath responds in recitation with

"Food, food". By Āditya, by the day, the Mahāvrata is recited by him who knowing thus offers the agnihotra. This agnihotra has seven hundred and twenty evening libations in a year, and also seven hundred and twenty morning libations in a year. Agni (i.e. the altar construed at the Agnicayana) has as many bricks accompanied by Yajus verses. He who knowing thus offers the agnihotra has sacrificed with the year, with the piled up fire (the Agnicayana rite).

— For another homology with the Agnicayana see the following passage from the ŚB.:

ŚB. 2, 3, 3, 17–20: The firewood which he lays on the fire is a brick.[24] The mantra with which he offers is the formula with which he lays down the brick. When a brick is laid down, then a libation is offered. Therefore those libations of the agnihotra are offered on his piled up bricks. The fire is Prajāpati and Prajāpati is the year. Every year his agnihotra is accomplished with a fire which has been piled up, if knowing thus he offers the agnihotra. Seven hundred and twenty are the Ṛc verses (to be recited in the agnihotra during a year). Since he offers the agnihotra in the evening and morning, there are two oblations. These oblations of his amount to seven hundred and twenty in the course of a year. Every year his agnihotra corresponds to[25] the Great Chant (*mahad uktham*).[26] Every year he obtains the Great Chant whosoever knowing thus offers the agnihotra. And this agnihotra[27] of his also corresponds to the Great Chant. He obtains the Great Chant.

— See also 6.10 (n. 10) on the identification of the *mahāvyāhṛtis* with the *agnicayana* (KS. 6, 7: 56.12 f.; MS. 1, 8, 6: 124.10 f.). Several elements of the agnihotra are correlated with elements of great Soma sacrifices in the following passages:

ṢaḍvB. 4, 1, 6: That he cleanses the *gārhapatya* fire, that is the sacrifice of initiation. That (he cleanses) the Southern fire and the *āhavanīya*, that is the introductory sacrifice. That he lays pieces of firewood on the fire, those are the *upasad* rites.

ṢaḍvB. 4, 1, 9–11: That he offers in the gārhapatya, that is the morning libation of Soma. That he offers in the southern fire, that is the midday libation of Soma. That he offers in the *āhavanīya* fire, that is the third libation of Soma. That he (i.e. the sacrificer) cleanses himself,[28] that is the final bath (*avabhṛtha*)[29]. That he gives food, thereby[30] the obtainment of the *udayanīya* and *udavasanīya*[31] is intended.[30]

ṢaḍvB. 4, 1, 15–16: The remainder of the oblation is the gift to the priest. He who knowing thus performs the agnihotra has sacrificed with all[32] sacrifices.

JB. 1, 4: When he (i.e. the sacrificer) touches water[33] before (the sacrifice) — water is truth, the consecration (*dīkṣā*) is truth[34] — then this is his consecration. "Agni is the light, the light is Agni, *svāhā*" with this eight-syllabic formula he offers the oblation. The *gāyatrī* metre has eight syllables. That is the morning libation of Soma.[35] He offers the second libation reciting (a formula) in thought only.[36] That is the midday libation of Soma.[36] He wipes off (the spoon) and eats. That is the third libation; for that third libation of Soma is licked at as it were.[37] After (the sacrifice) he (i.e. the sacrificer) touches water. This is his final bath (*avabhṛtha*). When he offers these two evening oblations, all those sacrifices are performed by him on account of these two oblations. And when he offers these two morning oblations, all those sacrifices[38] are performed by him on account of these two oblations. Therefore this agnihotra is unlimited.

TB. 2, 1, 4, 9: He pours out water. He has made a representation of the final bath (*avabhṛtha*).

VādhS. 3, 25: They say: "What purification (purificatory grass)[39] has the agnihotra?" When he illuminates the milk with (burning) herbs after having poured water to the milk, that purification the agnihotra has. They say: "What is the final bath (*avabhṛtha*) of this sacrifice?" That he cleanses himself inside the place reserved for the *vedi* (sacrificial ground), that is the final bath of this sacrifice. They say: "What is the sacrificial post (*yūpa*) of this sacrifice?" He should say: "The yajamāna". The sacrificer is the *yūpa* of this sacrifice. When he sits down to the south of the āhavanīya with the intention of offering the agnihotra oblation in it, he (i.e. the sacrificer) should sit there till the offering in the evening, till sunrise at daybreak. From that moment the sun becomes the *yūpa* during the whole day.

— The identification of the sacrificer (or the sun) with the *yūpa* is also found in the symbolical, cosmological sacrifices of Section 12 (n. 8).

VādhS. 3, 34: They say: "What gift (to the priests) has the agnihotra?" The food that is cooked together with (the oblation),[40] that is the *dakṣiṇā* (gift). What he cooks during the daytime (i.e. in the morning), that is the *dakṣiṇā* of the morning oblation. What he cooks at night (in the evening), that (is the *dakṣiṇā*) of the evening oblation. He should (however) not consider it thus. The agnihotra is the cooked food. The four ladles which he ladles out, these are the pouring under (*upastaraṇa*)[41] and the besprinkling (*abhighāra*)[41] of the agnihotra. What he cooks in the daytime (in the morning), that is the agnihotra. The second libation of the morning performance he pours under this. By means of the first evening libation he besprinkles (this morning agnihotra). What he cooks at night, that is the agnihotra. The second libation of the evening performance he pours out under (this evening agnihotra). With the first libation of the morning performance he besprinkles (the food, i.e. agnihotra, of the night before). Thereby the agnihotra receives an *upastaraṇa* and an *abhighāra*. Indeed he (i.e. a priest) may pour out milk into the fire for him who knows thus, but whenever he (i.e. the sacrificer as a host) permits anybody to wash his feet and hands and puts (some food) down for him, then it is as if he would have performed the agnihotra himself.[42]

TB. 2, 1, 5, 2 f.: When he offers in the evening, he thereby makes the night fit for giving a *dakṣiṇā*. When he offers in the morning, he thereby makes the day fit for giving a *dakṣiṇā*. What he gives thereafter is a *dakṣiṇā*.

VādhS. 3, 35: They say: "What gift (to the priests) has the agnihotra?". The agnihotra has the own self of the sacrificer as its *dakṣiṇā* (gift). The daytime of his life is the *dakṣiṇā* of the morning libation, the nighttime of his life (is the *dakṣiṇā*) of the evening libation. With a body in the form of good conduct,[43] free from sin, with all his limbs, having a soul,[44] he comes into existence in yonder world, having become the offered agnihotra.

— For the eschatological implications of the agnihotra as described in this passage see also Section 13.5. VādhS. 3, 19 identifies the four teats of the cow with the *agniṣṭoma*, *ukthya*, *atirātra* and *aptoryāma* at the end of a myth in which the āhavanīya fire copulates with the cow produced out of Prajāpati's primeval offering. The conclusion:

VādhS. 3, 19: Every night and morning the agnihotra cow enters (the place where the sacrifice takes place) with these four sacrifices. Therefore he should milk the agnihotra (milk) out of all four teats. Every night and morning there is offered with these four sacrifices by him who knowing thus offers the agnihotra (or) for whom[45] someone knowing thus offers the agnihotra.

— JB. 1, 38 also connects four sacrifices (*agniṣṭoma*, *vājapeya*, *aśvamedha*, *puruṣamedha*) with the agnihotra. The agnihotra of twelve days (performed after the establishing of the fires) forms the context. Four times three days with variant oblatory material produce the representations of these sacrifices. For the identification of the fourfold ladling out with several sacrifices in JB. 1, 40 see Section 6.5. A connection with the *vājapeya* is made by two parallel passages of JB. and VādhS. The agreement is again rather far-fetched and merely based on numbers:

VādhS. 3, 37: This is the seventeenfold[46] agnihotra. The *vājapeya* is seventeenfold; it has seventeen *stotras*. He who knowing thus offers the agnihotra (or) for whom someone knowing thus offers the agnihotra wins both worlds, the one won by offering the agnihotra and the one of the *vājapeya* sacrificer. And he who knowing thus sacrifices with the *vājapeya* wins both worlds, the one of the agnihotra offerer and the one of the *vājapeya* sacrificer.

JB. 1, 21: This is the seventeenfold agnihotra. Seventeenfold is also the *vājapeya*. He who knowing thus offers the agnihotra wins both worlds, the world of the agnihotra offerer as well as that of the *vājapeya* sacrificer. (...) He who knowing thus offers the agnihotra increases his prosperity seventeen thousand-fold each time.

— The reversal of the two roles, i.e. the identification of other sacrifices with the agnihotra, of which we have seen a glimpse in the passage of the VādhS. above, is treated at length in VādhS. 4, 39 (outside the agnihotra section). In connection with the offering to Vāstospati TS. 3, 4, 10, 1 f. refers to an identification of the agnihotra with the *agnicayana* (the evening and morning libations are bricks piled up). Baudhāyana (14, 19; for a translation see *Śrautakośa* I, p. 100) quotes this brāhmaṇa. TS. 1, 6, 9, 1 states that among the sacrifices created by Prājapati the *agniṣṭoma* had the same size as the agnihotra. Consequently one achieves the same by both sacrifices.

NOTES

[1] For this and other aspects see *Agn. and Prāṇāgn.*, ch. II.

[2] In *anubhāti* the prefix *anu* denotes parallelism (heaven shines for the sacrificer of the New- and Fullmoon rites together with the agnihotrin) or succession (M.-W. gives "to shine after another" with the accusative). Cf. PB. 17, 14, 1, on the relation between agnihotra and New- and Fullmoon sacrifices.

[3] On these sacrifices see Hillebrandt, *Ritual-Litteratur*, p. 124 ff. (*agniṣṭoma*) and p. 137 f. See also Renou, *Vocabulaire du Rituel Védique* s.v. These four rites are the basic patterns (*saṃsthās*) of the Soma sacrifice called Jyotiṣṭoma and (apart from the preparations) take one day (*ekāha*).

[4] The term *devayājin* is the opposite of *ātmayājin* in other contexts (see *Agn. and Prāṇāgn.*, ch. X, p. 304). In the present context its function is less clear. Apparently the *devayājin* is higher than the *haviṣmat*, who just pours out an oblation (as in the *gṛhya* ritual). On the other hand, the New- and

Fullmoon sacrifices as well as the Fourmonthly sacrifices belong together with the agnihotra to the category of the *śrauta haviryajñas*.

5 On the *āśrāvita* (or *āśrāvaṇa*, uttered by the Adhvaryu priest to the Āgnīdhra priest with the words *o3ṃ śrāvaya* "ask (the *hotṛ*) to let hear (the *vaṣaṭ* exclamation)") and the answer *pratyāśrāvita* (or *pratyāśrāvaṇa* with the words *astu śrau3ṣaṭ* "Alright, he should hear") see Hillebrandt, *Ritual-Litteratur*, p. 99 and Renou, *Vocabulaire*.

6 Like all the other items of this identification the *hotṛ* and the *brahman* do not belong to the agnihotra which has only one officiant, the *adhvaryu*.

7 The exclamation *vaṣaṭ* ("that (Agni) may convey (the oblation)") is the final formula of the *yājyā* (the "honouring" verses to be recited by the *hotṛ*). On this and the preceding technical terms see Minard, *Trois Énigmes* I, 282.

8 The *apāna* (undoubtedly the inhalation when connected with *prāṇa* "exhalation") corresponds (as the air which is taken in backwards) to what is said back (in reply).

9 The *brahman* priest has the supervision of the great sacrifices and consequently is connected with sight here.

10 The shortness (and swiftness) of the exclamation *vaṣaṭ* matches the short twinkling of the eyes. The problem of this passage is the double identification. The agnihotra is equated to other sacrifices; the elements of this identification, however, are not taken from the agnihotra ritual, but from the bodily functions. Perhaps, however, these bodily functions should be connected with one particular moment of the agnihotra, when the officiant lays a firestick on the fire and starts offering. See ĀpŚS. 6, 10, 1 *samidham ādhāya prāṇya (= āśrāvaṇa), apānya (= pratyāśrāvaṇa), nimīlya (= vaṣaṭkāra*, here identified with *nimeṣa), vīkṣya (= brahman), hutvā dhyāyed* (= *hotṛ*, here identified with mind) *yatkāmaḥ syāt*. See also Sāyaṇa's commentary.

11 This may imply that knowledge of these identifications between bodily functions and the sacrifice replaces the actual performance. On these so-called *ātmayajñas* see e.g. *Agn. and Prāṇāgn.*, ch. VII, n. 8. If, however, we take these bodily functions as integrated in the agnihotra ritual (see n. 10), this would imply that *tasya hutam* here means "by him has been offered indeed; he has performed a true and correct sacrifice". See Sāyaṇa: *asyaiva homo mukhyo* ("excellent") *bhavati*.

12 Cf. TS. 1, 5, 7, 1. On the compound *áyajña* see Minard, *Trois Énigmes* II 470 b.

13 The *gārhapatya* fire represents earth, the *āhavanīya* heaven. After having ladled out the milk the priest runs from the *gārhapatya* to the *āhavanīya*. While taking (*harati*) the milk to the *āhavanīya* he passes the space between heaven and earth (the *antarikṣa*) and holds the milk high (*upari*), or, as some texts state, "on a level with the *prāṇāḥ* (the breaths, i.e. mouth or nose)" (ĀpŚS. 6, 8, 8). The *prāṇāḥ* are the microcosmic counterpart of *vāyu* (the wind), which represents the *antarikṣa*. The formula recited on this occasion runs *urv antarikṣaṃ vīhi* "Reach the broad space between heaven and earth" (ĀpŚS. 6, 8, 6). In the sūtras *upari* in this connection (together with *samidham* and *dhārayati*) refers to the fact that the firestick should be carried above (*upari*) the ladle with the milk. See e.g. KŚS. 4, 14, 12 *upari samidhaṃ dhārayan .. āhavanīyaṃ harati mukhamātre dhārayan* "Holding the firestick above (the ladle) .. he takes (the ladle and the stick) to the āhavanīya, holding (them) on a level with the mouth". Obviously the present passage does not refer by *upari* to this particular position of the firestick, since it uses the verb *harati*, which denotes the movement towards the āhavanīya. On the other hand, *upari* together with *dhārayati* seems to imply that the milk and

the stick are taken above or over the gārhapatya fire according to ĀpŚS. 6, 8, 5 (*upari dhārayan gārhapatyasya*).

[14] Here *puruṣa* seems to be the primeval Man or Giant, the Universe, which represents Prajāpati's body and has a counterpart in the human body.

[15] The *caturhotṛ* formulas consist of mystical identifications of priests and other entities. See P. Rolland, "La litanie des quatre oblateurs (Maitrāyaṇī Saṃhitā I, 9)", *JAs* 1970, p. 261 ff.

[16] In the preceding context (TB. 2, 3, 6, 1 ff.) it was said that Prajāpati was completely exhausted after the creation (emission) of the creatures and asked for a body. All kinds of powers successively build up his body by means of sacrifices. The agnihotra produces the trunk (see Section 7, 5), the other sacrifices the other parts of the body. In the present passage the agnihotra itself is again connected with the trunk, but the other parts of the body are now connected with elements of the agnihotra. I.e. the agnihotra incorporates the powers of all the other sacrifices.

[17] The text speaks of the *avāñc prāṇa* "the downward air, or, rather, the air which leaves the body in a downward direction", which is identical with the *apāna* (the air leaving the body as well as the anus itself). It is noteworthy that *prāṇa* denotes air in general, but especially that which goes out (*pra-*), i.c. the exhalation. In opposition to *prāṇa* the *apāna* is the air which is taken in. In the total series of the five *prāṇāḥ* the *apāna* is no longer the inhalation (this function seems to be adopted by the *udāna*), but the air which leaves the body in a backwards direction, and may even denote the anus.

[18] See also KS. 9, 13; MS. 1, 9, 5; TB. 2, 2, 11, 6 on *daśahotṛ* and agnihotra.

[19] Cf. TS. 1, 6, 10, 2 on the agnihotra as the beginning of sacrifice.

[20] The calf is the starting-point since it causes the milk of the *agnihotrī* (cow) to flow by its presence.

[21] The opening verse of this Śastra is addressed to Agni. See e.g. AB. 4, 9.

[22] See Keith's note. The passage is not too clear.

[23] On this rite see now Rolland, "Le Mahāvrata. Contribution à l'étude d'un rituel solennel védique", *NachrAkadGött.* 1973, nr. 3. The connection between the Mahāvrata and the sun (and the morning performance) is to be explained by the role of the sun in this ritual of which the solstice "constitue le fondement même" (Rolland, p. 58 [= 8]). The daily return has a counterpart in the annual one.

[24] See also the very end of this section on the agnihotra and the *agnicayana*.

[25] Eggeling translates: "Thus, indeed, his Agnihotra is accomplished, year after year, with the great chant". However, *sampad-* on the one hand means "to amount to" (as above), on the other hand "to correspond to (mostly on account of a numeral *sampad*, a correspondence)". See also Minard, *Trois Énigmes* I, 202 (observing that afterwards Eggeling adopted the rendering "to correspond" in his translation of ŚB. 9, 1, 1, 43).

[26] The *mahad uktham* (the conclusion of the agnicayana) amounts to 720 verses, i.e. 3 × 240 (= 3 × 80).

[27] Eggeling does not translate the concluding words *etad u hāsyāgnihotraṃ mahatokthena sampadyate mahad uktham āpnoti*. Probably this means that not only does the yearlong agnihotra of two times 360 performances correspond to the *mahad uktham*, but also that this single agnihotra (which forms the subject of this teaching) may be said to equal that *mahad uktham*. The correspondence is achieved by a year of agnihotras, but since it is a daily rite which does not know of any distinctions among the daily performances, every agnihotra obtains the same result.

[28] See ĀpŚS. 6, 14, 6, which likewise uses the verb *marjayate* (probably referring to the cleansing of the hands).

[29] For the same identification with the *avabhṛtha* see VādhS. 3, 35 (below). Different identifications are made by JB. 1, 4 and TB. 2, 1, 4, 9.

[30] Bollée's translation "That he gives food-sacrifices is (done) for the completion of the udayanīya and the udavasānīya" does not account for the difficult *tena*. The normal syntactical sentence would be *yat* .. *tena* .. "that ... thereby .." (see Delbrück, *Altind. Syntax*, p. 583). How can this be connected with the final dative *samāptyai* (for that matter "obtainment" rather than "completion")? My rather free translation tries to solve the problem of the crippled syntax, which seems to be due to a blend of two constructions.

[31] Giving food is equated to two concluding oblations of the Soma ritual. On the two terms see Renou, *Vocabulaire*.

[32] Here *sarva* means "all" and not "complete" (Bollée). It refers to all these great sacrifices which were equated with elements of the agnihotra in the preceding passage. Moreover the same sentence occurs at the end of ṢaḍvB. 4, 2, 1, where the successive reductions of the mythical sacrifice of thousand years to the daily agnihotra are "all" those sacrifices which are included in the performance of the agnihotra.

[33] See *JB. I, 1–65*, p. 27, n. 7 and 8 on this ritual act which seems to be performed by the sacrificer himself rather than by the priest (though the information provided by the sūtras permits a different interpretation).

[34] The connection between water and truth is the same as between water and the oath which is taken while water is touched. The *dīkṣā* is a consecration, an act of truth, a solemn oath. On *dīkṣā* and truth see also AB. 1, 6, 6.

[35] Gāyatrī verses are sung then.

[36] "In thought only" (*manasā niṣkevalyena*) is connected with the *niṣkevalya śastra* of the midday libation.

[37] The third pressing of Soma is licked at or sucked out according to the brāhmaṇas, since Suparṇa took it in his mouth according to the myth (see Caland, *Jaiminīya Brāhmaṇa in Auswahl*, p. 57, n. 4).

[38] This refers to the sacrifices mentioned in the preceding passage (see Section 1.2).

[39] The *pavitra* is a means of purification such as a strainer, e.g. made of straw. It may also (as here) denote leaves of *kuśa* grass for sprinkling and purifying the ghee (melted butter).

[40] The term *sapakvam* does not occur in M.-W.'s dictionary, but is quite clear. Together with the oblation one cooks the rest of the food. All this forms the *dakṣiṇā*. The second view of the sūtra interprets this non-oblatory food as the agnihotra itself, for which the official oblations form the underlayer and besprinkling. Caland did not translate this passage.

[41] On the technical terms *upastaraṇa* and *abhighāra* (mostly denoted by *abhighāraṇa*) see Renou, *Vocabulaire*. These actions have no function in the actual agnihotra.

[42] Caland (as was observed in n. 40) did not translate this passage of which especially the end contains some problems ("Die schwierige Stelle, deren Text besonders am Schlusse sehr unsicher ist, wage ich nicht zu übersetzen"). *Agn. and Prāṇāgn.*, ch. 4, n. 3 gives some suggestions on the solution. In the translation of the present passage the offering of hospitality in the form of food (with some ceremonial accompaniments) is considered as the agnihotra itself.

[43] The translation of *nītiśarīra* is only tentative. The text may also be corrupt. On account of JB. 1, 2, one might suggest *āhutiśarīra* as emendation.

[44] This is the translation of *ātmanvat* proposed by M.-W.'s dictionary. Cf. also the double negation of the Sāvitrī episode *nānātmavantas* (5, 24, ed. Caland). On the other hand VādhS. 4, 65 *a* and 4, 109 have *ātmanvin* translated by Caland with "im Besitze eines (normalen) Rumpfes" (Caland translates the present passage with *ātmavān* "mit dem Rumpfe").

[45] I do not follow Caland's translation. His argumentation, for which see VādhS. 3, 3, n. 4, does not convince me.

[46] This refers to the seventeen stages of the agnihotra milk treated in the preceding passage. See Section 16.

11 *Substitution of the oblation, the fire or other ritual elements*

— The oblation usually consists of milk, sometimes of ghee. If these are not available even rice-gruel may be used. See Section 5 (KS. and MS.). The mentioned section also refers to other substitutes, e.g. water, and ultimately to truth (to be offered in faith, the substitute of fire). This symbolic agnihotra (in the ŚB. and the JB.) is an esoteric interpretation rather than an incidental substitution. On this point see *Agn. and Prāṇāgn.*, ch. III (p. 223). Its parallel in VādhS. 3, 40 interprets the offering of the sun in the fire and the fire in the sun as the ultimate substitute. This is again a mere interpretation of the agnihotra. However, its application in the context of an emergency seems to be based on the following passage in the TB. (which has been completely translated in Section 1.1):

TB. 2, 1, 6, 5: He (Prajāpati) became afraid of death (brought about by Agni). He shaped out of himself yonder sun. Having offered this he fled away. (..) Therefore if they do not offer for one who knows thus during one or two days, there has been offered (all the same). For the agnihotra (oblation) is yonder sun.

— Similarly ŚāṅkhB. 2, 8 allows some esoteric interpretations to take in the place of the actual agnihotra:

ŚāṅkhB. 2, 8: These six (sun and fire, day and night, inhalation and exhalation) offer themselves in each other. He who knows that these six offer,[1] by him there is offered, even if he does not actually offer. And if he (actually) offers, there is offered twice by him who knows thus.

— The offering of truth in faith (*śraddhā*) mentioned above formed an esoteric doctrine. However, the substitution of the milk which is spilt by faith (*śraddhā*) is found in a purely ritual passage which deals with expiations:

AB. 5, 27, 10: If, however, all should be poured out (at the spilling), then he has to ask for another (cow), milk her and offer with that (milk). But there should be offered anyhow, even if only faith forms the oblation.

— The immediately following symbolic sacrifice originally had no connection with this mental *śraddhā* sacrifice (see Section 12). Offering *śraddhā* means evidencing one's good intentions. See also *Agn. and Prāṇāgn.*, ch. V (p. 239). It may also happen that the fire which had been consigned to the two sticks from which it should be produced fails to be churned out in time. In that case for the time being another fire may be taken, if available. If not, other substitutes should be found:

TB. 3, 7, 3, 1–5: If he should not obtain an other (fire), there should be offered into (the ear of) a she-goat, for the goat is sacred to Agni. The agnihotra has been offered by him in Agni. However he should not eat of a goat. If he should eat of a goat, he would eat the oblation offered in Agni. Therefore there should not be eaten of the goat. If he should not obtain a goat, there should be offered into the right hand of a brahmin. For the brahmin is Agni Vaiśvānara.[2] In Agni the agnihotra has been offered by him. However he should not refuse hospitality to a brahmin. If he were to refuse hospitality to a brahmin, he would deprive the fire in which he offers the oblation from its share. Therefore the brahmin should not be refused hospitality. If he should not find a brahmin, there should be offered on a bunch of (*kuśa*) grass. The bunch of grass contains Agni. In Agni the agnihotra has been offered by him. He should, however, not sit upon this grass. If he should sit down upon the grass, he would sit down on the oblation offered in Agni. Therefore he should not sit upon the bunches of (*kuśa*) grass. If he should not find bunches of holy grass, there should be offered into water. The waters are all deities. In all deities the agnihotra has been offered by him. Water, however, he should not (or: no longer) despise. If he should despise water, he would despise the oblation offered in the water. Therefore water should not be despised.

— A much simpler parallel is found in the ṢaḍvB. See also Bollée's extensive note on this passage in his translation:

ṢaḍvB. 4, 1, 12: If someone's fire is being churned out but fails to be produced, he should fetch another (i.e. profane) fire and offer on the same place.[3] Or he should offer in the hand of a brahmin, or in the ear of a (he-)goat, or on a bunch of (*kuśa*) grass, or in water.

— The fires may also go out during the rite and expiations are then required. ŚB. 11, 5, 3, 8–12 has a long esoteric, rather than ritualistic, passage on this subject, in which Uddālaka is interrogated by Śauceya. Uddālaka turns out to be aware of the identification of the fires and *prāṇāḥ*, and explains the extinction of one of these fires as the transition of the one *prāṇa* into the other. Even if all the fires should go out, one may just churn out a new *gārhapatya* and take out fire (for the *āhavanīya*) in the direction in which the wind blows (since the wind is identical with the totality of the *prāṇāḥ*). If, however, no wind at all blows, then one produces a new fire for the gārhapatya, takes out the āhavanīya and drinks the oblation oneself. The brahmin performer offers into himself, i.e. into his *prāṇāḥ* which on this occasion substitute for the fires. The fires are simultaneously reproduced, but their total absence might create the impression that the continuity of the fires had been disturbed. However, the fires are connected with the sacrificer's breaths. By offering into the breaths the identity of fires and breaths is emphasized, the temporary disappearance of the fires explained (as a transition into the breaths) and the continuity saved. In its explanation the text bases itself on the identity of brahmin and fire:[4]

ŚB. 11, 5, 3, 12: Having at once churned out the fire and taken out the (fire for the) āhavanīya eastward, and having sat down behind the āhavanīya, I would drink it myself. I would know that my agnihotra would be successful since it belonged to all deities. For all beings enter into the brahmin (= Brahman) and are again produced from him.

— The parallel of GB. 1, 3, 13, borrowed from the ŚB.,[5] has some differences in its expiatory section which are of no interest here. The end of the passage, however, is important. The question is raised as to what should be done in case all fires have gone out, no wind is blowing[6] and the new fire fails to be produced (cf. the TB. above; this point was not mentioned by the ŚB.):

GB. 1, 3, 13: Having smeared all round the fire-places with a lump of cow-dung, having put down the oblation he should offer it into himself with the verse "Let the wind blow hither".

— Again the fires are identified with and replaced by the *prāṇāḥ*, though less clearly than in the ŚB. In distinction to the ŚB., however, GB. 1, 3, 14 adds a long passage which describes this offering into the sacrificer himself as a *prāṇāgnihotra*. We leave the domain of the expiations and the incidental substitution of the fires by the *prāṇāḥ* and enter the esoteric sphere of the permanent substitution of the fire ritual by an *ātmayajña*.[7] In the present publication the expiations generally have been left out of account. However, sometimes the difference between real expiation, esoteric interpretation and substitution is difficult to ascertain. JB. 1, 20 (and its parallel in the ŚB.) refers to the incidental agnihotra of the sacrificer who stays abroad. His actual agnihotra is performed at home. His *prāṇa* temporarily forms the substitute of his fire; he offers in the breath and the inhalation forms the oblation. On the one hand the agnihotrin performs a mental agnihotra abroad, on the other hand the text refers to an esoteric interpretation of this rite. In this connection attention may also be drawn to passages such as ŚB. 2, 3, 2, 1–3 which mentions some internal deities or fires. In the same passage a substitution of the actual *upasthāna* is found (ŚB. 2, 3, 2, 4). For the substitution of the sacrificer see Section 7. The ideal performer is the sacrificer himself. His son and others may replace him. Moreover the priest seems to be a substitute of the sacrificer himself. On the substitution of the agnihotra of the *dīkṣita* by drinking the *vrata* milk (i.e. by offering in the *prāṇa*) see JB. 2, 38 (*Auswahl*, § 120); ŚB. 12, 3, 5, 3; GB. 1, 5, 9; SāṅkhB. 7, 3.

NOTES

[1] Keith translates "he who knows these six in the sacrificer". However, the usual term designating the sacrificer is *yajamāna* rather than *yajat*. Moreover, night and day, as well as sun and fire, do not reside within the sacrificer.

[2] Cf. TB. 2, 1, 4, 5 (translated in Section 6.15).

[3] The difference between this expiation and the following ones is that here only the fire is substituted and the hearth remains the same, whereas offering into e.g. the hands of a brahmin means a complete replacement of the sacred fire.

[4] On this identification see *Agn. and Prāṇāgn.*, ch. III, n. 14.

[5] See *Agn. and Prāṇāgn.*, ch. III, n. 16.

[6] See the reference of the preceding note on an irregularity of this passage.

[7] On the *ātmayajña* see *Agn. and Prāṇāgn.*, ch. X (p. 301 ff.).

— The subject of this section partly overlaps the preceding one. Symbolic sacrifice sometimes replaces the actual agnihotra on the basis of identifications. In the first passage translated here a (reference to a) cosmological, symbolic agnihotra is placed in the context of an appeasement of Rudra. During twelve days a special agnihotra is performed.[1] On account of the identification twelve days = year (not expressed in the KS.) the brāhmaṇa continues with a glimpse of a symbolic sacrifice in which the year and its subdivisions play a role. However, between the reference to the twelve-day agnihotra for Rudra and the symbolic sacrifice the text states (KS. 6, 7: 57.6 f.): "They kindle this Agni Vaiśvānara during a year. For him there is no share in the year nor in Vaiśvānara who has not established his fires". It seems that the twelve-day agnihotra, performed to avert the danger coming from Rudra (see n. 1), has been confused with the twelve-day agnihotra performed after the *agnyādhāna* (see JB. 1, 26–38). The composition is rather loose and based on disconnected associations. The preceding passage refers to the year, the following passage to the several stages of the fire:

KS. 6, 7: 57.7–9: The pieces of wood are the months, the large coals the seasons, the small ones the half-months, the expiring embers the nights and days.

— The MS. even explicitly states that twelve days (during which the special agnihotra for Rudra is performed) are identical with the year, the year with Agni Vaiśvānara:

MS. 1, 8, 6: 123.8–10: Him (i.e. Agni Vaiśvānara) the *āhitāgnis* (those who have established the fires) and the performers of the New- and Fullmoon Sacrifices kindle. For them the pieces of wood are the seasons,[2] the largest coals are the months, the smallest the half-months, the expiring embers the nights and days.

— Besides these temporal identifications (which after all only refer to the temporal changes in the fuel of the fire) there are also spatial and other identifications in the context of the agnihotra:

KS. 6, 6: 55.15 ff.: In his mind (i.e. mentally) Prajāpati demarcated this earth as the sacrificial bank (*vedi*) for the agnihotra sacrificer. Whatever he gives (as presents to bhikṣus or as dakṣiṇās to brahmins) there (on the earth)[3] that is given (as it were) on the sacred grass (*barhis*).[4] Even as he gives (the *dakṣiṇā*) when the cups have been set down,[5] thus he gives, whatever he gives,[6] in the middle of the sacrifice. Heaven and earth are its Sadas and Havirdhāna sheds.

Night and day are the fuel. The quarters of space are the enclosing sticks (*paridhis*); the raindrops the sprinkling waters; the plants the sacred grass;[7] the sacrificer the sacrificial post (*yūpa*).[8]

— For the continuation of this passage see Section 9, n. 1. The transition is abrupt and absurd. Evidently the only connection to be made is by an identification of the sacrificer with the victim (*paśu*). Cf. the parallel of the TB. below, in which the sun is the *yūpa* and the sacrificer the *paśu*. This may represent the original version. Perhaps the KS. or its source changed the order of the identifications and connected *yūpa* with *yajamāna*. The MS. even defends this (new?) equation with arguments.

MS. 1, 8, 7: 126.11 ff.: In his mind (i.e. in thought, mentally) Prajāpati demarcated this earth. This earth is the sacrificial bank of the agnihotra. This (earth?)[9] is the *upayāma* ladle. The plants are the sacred grass; the raindrops the sprinkling waters; the quarters of space the enclosing sticks. Whatever there is laid on,[10] that is the fuel. The sacrificer is the sacrificial post. During the ladling out he should stand. Thus he is a *yūpa* as it were, for the sake of prosperity. The agnihotra is a sacrifice which proceeds from the centre.[11] Therefore the performers of the agnihotra and the New- and Full-moon sacrifices give everything (whatever they give) on the sacred grass. For what is given in the agnihotra is given in the middle of the sacrifice.

— The parallelism between the two passages of the KS. and the MS. is complete. Another parallel is found in the TB. where the introductory sentence on Prajāpati's measuring of the earth/*vedi* is missing. The preceding context states that the calf is the introduction (*prāyaṇa*) of the agnihotra in the same way as the agnihotra is the introduction of the sacrifices. See Section 10 (n. 19) and MNU. 527. Apparently, the statement about the central position of the agnihotra for all sacrifices forms the starting-point for the present passage, where the reference to the central (*madhya*) situation of the agnihotra (as found in the Saṃhitās) is now missing:

TB. 2, 1, 5, 1–3: The earth is its Sadas shed, the space between heaven and earth the Āgnīdhra shed, heaven the Havirdhāna shed. The waters from heaven are the sprinkling waters, the plants the sacred grass, the trees the fuel, the quarters the enclosing sticks. The sun is the sacrificial post, the sacrificer the victim, the ocean the final bath (*avabhṛtha*), the year the exclamation *svagā*. Therefore everything (that is given) is given as connected with the sacred grass[12] by him who has established his fires. When he offers in the evening, he thereby makes the night fit for giving a *dakṣiṇā*. When he offers in the morning, he thereby makes the day fit for giving a *dakṣiṇā*. What he gives thereafter, that is a *dakṣiṇā*.

— It is evident that one of the elements in this passage (as well as in the two preceding ones) is the identification of the agnihotra with the other sacrifices. On the one hand sacrifice in general is placed in a symbolic (and cosmological) setting, on the other hand in this way the agnihotra becomes connected with elements belonging to the great sacrifices. The double aspect of passages like this one here is also found outside of the brāhmaṇas.[13] The central concept of all the versions in this section is that of the *dakṣiṇā*. The context of the passages varies. In the following version of the AB. an expiation for the spilling of milk seems to be the starting-point. AB. 5, 27, 10 states that in case of a spilling other milk should be acquired. In any case there should be offered, even if *śraddhā* (faith) alone is the oblation. The connection with the symbolic, cosmological sacrifice seems to be that in fact no spilling of milk can take place, if one realizes that the whole cosmos is the sacrificial place. Moreover the symbolic sacrifice has the function of an agnihotra which is not actually performed. The abstract *śraddhā* is the substitute for the concrete oblation. The expiation of AB. 5, 27 is repeated at AB. 7, 3, where, however, the sentence at the end of the paragraph which makes the connection between the expiation and the symbolic sacrifice is missing.

AB. 5, 27, 11: For him who knowing thus offers the agnihotra everything becomes connected with the sacred grass,[14] everything falls within the demarcation (of the sacrifice).[15]

AB. 5, 28, 1 ff.: Yonder sun is his sacrificial post, the earth his sacrificial bank, the plants the sacred grass, the trees the fuel, the waters the sprinkling waters, the quarters the enclosing sticks. Whatever of his becomes lost, or dies, or men drive away, all this comes to him in yonder world who knowing thus offers the agnihotra, just as what is presented on the sacred strew would come.

— Microcosmic symbolism of the agnihotra is found in the following passage in the ŚB. and the JB.

ŚB. 11, 3, 1, 1: The *agnihotrī* cow is the speech of this agnihotra; her calf is its mind. Therefore these two, mind and speech, though being one and the same, are distinct as it were. Therefore they tie up the calf and its mother with one and the same rope. Its fire is faith, its ghee truth.

JB. 1, 19: The *agnihotrī* cow is speech; her calf is the mind. They milk speech whose milk has been caused to flow by mind. They milk the mother (cow) whose milk has been caused to flow by her calf. This mind which comes first[16] is followed by speech. Therefore the mother (cow) follows the calf that walks in front. The milkpost is the heart, the rope is breath. With breath indeed speech and mind are tied up (to the heart). With a rope he ties up the calf and the mother (to the milkpost).

— In both versions a discussion on the substitutes for the oblation follows (translated in Section 5). Ultimately the internal elements mentioned in the identifications above may replace the actual elements of the rite. The difference between symbolic interpretation and substitution is often difficult to ascertain. Another microcosmic symbolism is found in the ŚāṅkhB., where the interpretation of the agnihotra as an offering of the sun into the fire and the fire into the sun has a central place.

ŚāṅkhB. 2, 8: This fire offers itself in the rising sun. Yonder sun, when it sets, offers itself in the fire at night. The night offers (itself) in the day, the day in the night. The exhalation offers (itself) in the inhalation, the inhalation in the exhalation.

— The text continues by stating that even this symbolic sacrifice (e.g. of ex- and in-halation) may suffice. Indeed the gods are satisfied even by a small portion; i.e. daily performance of the agnihotra is not required on account of this symbolism. Now the preceding passage referred to the aspect of truth.[17] The conclusion of this passage again mentions this aspect of truth in connection with the symbolism or even the substitution of the actual agnihotra.

ŚāṅkhB. 2, 8: Just as there is offered by someone who has faith as his deity, who speaks the truth (or: who is an adherent of the truth doctrine)[18] and who is an ascetic, likewise there is offered by him who, knowing thus, offers the agnihotra. Therefore knowing thus he should offer the agnihotra.

— On the offering of sun into fire and conversely see Sections 1, 11 and 13.

NOTES

[1] For a translation of this passage see 6.15.

[2] Evidently this identification is correct, whereas in the version of the KS. seasons and months have been interchanged.

[3] Apparently *tatra* refers back to *imām* (this earth). If it is not purely anaphoric, it may refer to the extra-ritual (in the same way as *adas* denotes daily life and the domain outside the ritualistic one under discussion).

[4] The earth is the *vedi*. The *barhis* is the grass strewn on the *vedi*. So everything given here on earth may be regarded as presented on the *barhis*. See also Gonda, *Savayajñas*, p. 171 and 317. ŚB. 12, 8, 2, 36 also identifies earth and *vedi* in the context of the *sautrāmaṇī* rite.

[5] Instead of *yathāsanneṣu* there should be read *yathā sanneṣu* (Oertel, *Syntax*, p. 190).

[6] Oertel, *Syntax*, p. 190 translates "He gives (the fee)". The point, however, is that any giving may be regarded as equal to the giving of a *dakṣiṇā*.

[7] Read *barhir* instead of *na hi*. See Caland, *WZKM* 23, p. 58.

[8] See also VādhS. 3, 25 translated in Section 10.

[9] The identification with *iyam* (earth) is not clear. The text may be corrupt.

[10] The text uses the verb *abhyādhā*, which is a technical term of the ritual (laying fuel on the fire). However, a more general expression is required here in order to obtain an identification with the actual ritual. Perhaps *yat kiṃ cābhyādhīyate* refers to everything which is placed on the earth.

[11] On the central position of the agnihotra among the other sacrifices see below in this passage and the version of the KS. above.

[12] Dumont remarks in a note: "If we consider the context, it is almost certain that here *barhiṣyam* 'connected with the sacrificial strew' means 'connected with the Soma-sacrifice'." However, *barhiṣyam* cannot be disconnected from the parallel versions above, in which the identification of the cosmos and the ritual in general has a central position.

[13] See e.g. MNU. 543–546, where on the one hand the sacrificer's body and life is equated with elements of the Soma sacrifices and on the other hand the identification of the agnihotra with these Soma sacrifices plays a role.

[14] For the term *barhiṣya* see n. 4 and n. 12.

[15] Keith translates "all is secured". Does *parigṛhītam* refer to the demarcation of the *vedi* (= the whole earth) by Prajāpati as described in the versions of the KS. and the MS. (*manasā ... paryagṛhṇād*)?

[16] See *JB. I, 1–65*, p. 64, n. 3.

[17] The formula accompanying the offering forms a statement of truth. See also AB. 5, 31 (Section 4, n. 21).

[18] See *Agn. and Prāṇāgn.*, ch. V (p. 240 f.).

13 *Interpretations of the agnihotra*

13.1 *The sun is offered into the fire, the fire into the sun.*

— As was stated at the end of the preceding section the offering of the sun into the fire and conversely (at the morning performance) forms a current theme in the discussion of this ritual as found in the brāhmaṇas. The aetiological myth has Prajāpati offering the sun into Agni (Section 1). The cosmic process of sunset (and sunrise) is also explained as an agnihotra; i.e. knowledge of the identity of cosmic process and ritual may substitute for the actual performance of the ritual (Section 11). In the present section the interpretation of the agnihotra as (producing) the entering of the sun into the fire and its rise from the fire is treated.[1] Impregnation and delivery are the images used to denote these actions. See KS. 6, 5 (Section 6.10, n. 3).

TB. 2, 1, 2, 9 f.: Āditya enters Agni in the evening. Therefore the fire is seen from afar by night, for the two lights are united (then). Agni rises along with and as a consequence of Āditya's rising. Therefore the smoke of the fire is seen by day.

— The text continues with a discussion of the correct form of the formula, which should mention the fire as well as the sun. See 6.10. A reference to sunset and sunrise produced by the agnihotra is found at ŚāṅkhB. 2, 2 (translated in 6.15), where, however, the fire and the offering into the fire do not play a role. Wiping off the ladle in a certain direction brings about sunset and sunrise.

ŚāṅkhB. 2, 8: This fire offers itself in the rising sun. Yonder sun, when it sets, offers itself in the fire at night.

— See Section 12 on the passage above. Even outside the agnihotra sections references to the sun's entrance in the fire are found, e.g. KS. 7, 4: 66.1; MS. 1, 5, 5: 73.11 ff. ("For these two [i.e. Indra, the sun, and Agni] are together. This one enters yonder one, when it becomes day. Therefore yonder one shines by day. That one (enters) this one [read *imam for imām*?] by night. Therefore this one shines by night"); AB. 8, 28, 9. Within the framework of other interpretations of the agnihotra this topic is mentioned several times in the ŚB. and the JB.

ŚB. 2, 3, 1, 3: When he sets, then he enters his womb, the fire, as an embryo.

ŚB. 2, 3, 1, 5: When he offers in the morning before sunrise, then he generates that (child) and it becomes a light and rises shining. But, thus is the belief[2], it would not rise, if he should not offer this oblation in it (i.e. in the fire). Therefore he should offer this oblation.

ŚB. 2, 3, 1, 36: Now they say: "In the evening he offers Sūrya into Agni, and in the morning he offers Agni into Sūrya".

— For the last passage see Section 6.10 (n. 21). This offering of the sun into the fire and conversely is also found in the esoteric discussions on the agnihotra (the *brahmodyas*). The sun and the fire are mostly identified with other entities.

ŚB. 11, 6, 2, 2: Śvetaketu Āruṇeya answered: "O great king, I offer two heats (hot oblations: *gharmau*), perpetual and overflowing with glory, into each other". "How is that?" (asked king Janaka). "The sun is one hot fluid. I offer it into the fire in the evening. The fire is a hot fluid. I offer it into[3] the sun in the morning".

— Another speaker offers light into light according to the same principle. A similar discussion is found at JB. 1, 22–25, where five brahmins are interrogated on the agnihotra by king Janaka. The first of them answers as follows:

JB. 1, 23: "As honour, O king, I offer the agnihotra. Therefore I am honour. Honour certainly there will be in my progeny in the end". To him (Āruṇi) he (Janaka) said: "What is honour, Gautama?" Pointing at the fire he said: "This is honour" and at the sun: "That is honour. So I offer that honour in this honour in the evening and this honour in that honour in the morning. These two will lead me thither where are all desirable objects. These two will ward off repeated dying for me".

— The other brahmins follow this interpretation, but take the fire and the sun as truth, brilliance, etc. Janaka, though superior in this debate, in fact does not introduce anything completely new. He also offers sun in fire and conversely, but interprets these two entities as the *gati* and the *iti* (the goal and the way towards it). Some other references to the entrance of the sun into the fire as found in the JB. are given below:

JB. 1, 8: Having thus collected it he offers it (the sun) in the evening. It passes that night in the condition of an embryo.

JB. 1, 9: When the sun sets, it offers itself in the fire. (...). When the sun rises, the fire rises after it. It offers itself in the sun.

JB. 1, 11: Nagarin Jānaśruteya used to say: "The sun here enters its lair,[4] the fire, when it sets".

NOTES

[1] See also ĀpŚS. 4, 1, 8; 4, 3, 5; 6, 5, 6.

[2] On *śaśvat* (here translated by Eggeling with "assuredly") see Minard, *Trois Énigmes* I, 589 *b*.

[3] Eggeling's translation "to him I make offering in Agni (resp. Āditya) in the evening (resp. morning)" has to be rejected. See also *JB. I, 1–65*, p. 39, n. 2.

[4] This may be preferred to the translation "womb" which does not suit the context (but has a parallel in passages such as ŚB. 2, 3, 1, 3). See also *JB. I, 1–65*, p. 42, n. 1. On *yoni* denoting the "nest" of settled, married people see Minard, *Trois Énigmes* II, 777*a*.

13.2 *Procreation and the agnihotra.*

— In fact the brāhmaṇas abound in passages which try to connect a particular ritual with fertility and procreation. Every couple in a brāhmaṇa text may be adduced to have a procreative function (the *mithuna*). However, the secondary literature claims a special relationship between agnihotra and fertility[1]. Therefore it may be useful to collect here the references to this aspect of the agnihotra in the texts themselves. The relative nature of this side of the agnihotra, however, should always be kept in mind. The frequency of this theme outside the agnihotra passages has been mentioned. Even more important may be the fact that the disappearence of the sun and its reappearance from the dark night, which forms the central theme in the speculations on the agnihotra, was described with the image of conception and delivery. This image thrusted itself upon the authors of the brāhmaṇas, who did not hesitate to use it for one of their well-known obsessions: fertility and enough food. It makes a subsidiary impression and there is no reason to speak of a fertility charm in connection with the agnihotra.

KS. 6, 5: 53.18 ff.: "Give me life; give me glory; give me offspring" (with these formulas) he sets (the milk and the kindling-stick) down in the east (i.e. near the āhavanīya). The agnihotra is a creation. If he should not set it down, the descendants would go away without returning.[2]

KS. 6, 5: 53.20 ff.: (With the formula) "In Agni is the light, the light is in Agni" he should offer the agnihotra in the evening. With a speech which has something in the interior he produces an embryo; with a speech which consists of a pair he impregnates. (With the formula) "Sūrya is the light, the light is Sūrya" (he offers) in the morning. With a speech which has something in the interior and which consists of a pair he procreates it (the embryo). (. . .) Of the two oblations there is this variation: the evening oblation is sacred to Agni, the morning oblation to Sūrya. Agni is the one who inseminates, Sūrya the one who brings forth. (. .) Agni, having poured out the sun as seed, impregnates the night. He engenders him in the morning with a speech which has something in the interior and consists of a pair. Along with and as a consequence of his being born offspring is born. He for whom the agnihotra is offered thus becomes prolific with offspring and cattle.[3]

KS. 8, 11: 94.21 f. (outside the agnihotra section): The evening oblation is sacred to Agni, the morning oblation to Sūrya. If he should offer the morning oblation with a formula mentioning Agni, he would prevent procreation beforehand. He would not do it in the regular order.[4]

KS. 6, 5: 54.9 f.: There should be offered with the right foot placed forward in the evening. He impregnates. (There should be offered) with the right foot backward in the morning. He brings forth.[5]

KS. 6, 7: 56.15 ff.: The agnihotra is a creation (by Prajāpati). This observance (of silence by Prajāpati) is a creation. He (Prajāpati) made them (the creatures) come up (or: created them) with the thought: "You are (my) production (or: coming up)". At the moment when there are bubbles as it were (on the milk), then he should look upon (the milk which "comes up", with the formula:) "You represent rising to prosperity. May I reproduce myself with offspring and cattle". The agnihotra (milk) represents coming up (or: forth), represents production. He thrives with offspring and is productive in (rearing) cattle for whom the agnihotra is offered thus. He looks upon (the milk) with a fire. The agnihotra (milk) is the female organ. The fire (or: burning grassblade) is the procreator who procreates, The agnihotra (milk) is seed.[6]

— In order to show how important the motif of fertility and creation has been in the context of the relevant agnihotra sections, the systematical arrangement of this section follows the texts rather than the related passages.

MS. 1, 8, 2: 117.17 ff.: The seed of yonder sun is offered here. Uncooked it (would be) unfit for being offered. It should be offered at the moment when it is rising. For that is cooked, sacrificially pure, a mixture (i.e. a compromise of boiling well and boiling not too much) and (as such, i.e. as every mingling or couple) procreative.[7]

MS. 1, 8, 3: 119.4 ff.: Water and milk form a couple. Out of a couple forsooth offspring and cattle are produced. This (i.e. the milk and the water which is poured on it) is a couple. On the basis of this couple the sacrificer is productive with offspring and cattle.[8]

MS. 1, 8, 4: 119.9 ff.: The agnihotra is a production of creatures. (...) He should look (at the milk with the formula) "You represent rising to prosperity. May I reproduce myself with offspring and cattle", for the sake of producing offspring and cattle.

MS. 1, 8, 5: 121.1 ff.: "Agni is the light, the light is Agni", with this speech which has something in its interior he impregnates.

With this speech, which consists of a couple, he causes a couple to procreate. (...) The evening libation is sacred to Agni. Thereby he pours out seed. That pouring of seed makes the night pregnant with an embryo. By the (oblation) sacred to Sūrya he procreates that embryo in the morning.[9] (..) But in the morning the second libation should be offered down (or: on this side of) the first one. For the birth of offspring takes place in downward direction. For the oblation sacred to Sūrya means procreation.[10]

MS. 1, 8, 6: 122.19: Manu and Manāyī procreated by (forming) a couple here (as the first people on earth). When they milk with the cooking-vessel (*sthālī*) and with the milk-pail, he is engendered through this couple.[11]

MS. 1, 8, 7: 125.9 f.: The agnihotra should be offered at nightfall and in the morning after it has become bright. (Thereby) he brings forth full-grown embryos.

MS. 1, 6, 10: 102.9 ff. (outside the agnihotra section): If he should reverse what precedes and what follows in connection with the womb,[12] he would become without offspring. (..) He offers at night with "Agni is the light, the light is Agni, hail". Thereby he places seed in the middle (or: in the interior) by means of (the two words) light. In the morning (he offers with) "Sūrya is the light, the light is Sūrya, hail". Thereby in the morning he has procreated the seed which had been placed in the interior by means of (the two words) light in the evening.

TS. 1, 5, 9, 1 (in the *agnyupasthāna* section): He offers the agnihotra (oblation). Whatever forms the property (or: self)[13] of the yajamāna, of that this (oblation) consists.[14] He pours seed in the generative organ. For Agni is the generative organ. It also burns the plants in its nearness;[15] thereupon these grow more numerous. In that he offers in the evening, thereby he pours seed. By the morning (offering) he produces it.

TB. 2, 1, 2, 7 ff.: During the night the creatures procreate. In the daytime they secure a good position. In that he offers at night, thereby he procreates. (..) Prajāpati desired: "May I produce offspring". He discovered that this agnihotra formed a couple. He offered it after the sun had risen. The one (libation he offered) with the formula, the other silently. Thereupon he reproduced himself. He for whom knowing thus they offer the agnihotra after sunrise reproduces himself.[16] (..) He says "Agni is the light". Agni indeed is the impregnator. He says (in fact) "The offspring is light". He (the priest) produces offspring for him (the sacrificer). He says (in the morning) "Sūrya is the light". In the offspring which has been produced he places seed (i.e. fertility). He says "Light is Agni". He (Agni) firmly establishes the offspring after his birth on earth.[17]

TB. 2, 1, 2, 12: He offers the second libation silently, in order to produce a pair (with the first one), for the procreation of offspring.[18]

TB. 2, 1, 4, 4: In the evening he wipes off downwards. Thereby he inseminates seed. In the morning he wipes off upwards. Thereby he produces offspring.[19]

TB. 2, 1, 5, 4 f.: He should offer the milk of two (cows) for a man who is desirous of cattle. This agnihotra forms a pair. He who knows thus is productive in offspring and cattle through couples. With the first (cow) he milks this earth, with the second yonder world. Having put (the milk of the first cow) on the fire he pours the other milk on it. By doing so he pours seed in a womb which is fertile.[20]

TB. 2, 1, 8, 3: Just as forsooth he (the sacrificer) satisfies the cow at a watering-place, just so the *agnihotrī* cow satisfies the sacrificer. He is satisfied with offspring and cattle (...), he is productive in offspring and cattle by means of couples, he for whom, knowing thus, they offer the agnihotra, as well as he who thus knows this (agnihotra).

TB. 2, 1, 9, 2: He offers with "Agni is the light, the light is Agni, hail" in the evening. Thereby he inseminates. In the morning (he offers with) "Sūrya is the light, the light is Sūrya, hail". He progenerates what has been inseminated.[21]

— It is remarkable that this fertility motif is not found in the agnihotra sections of the AB. and the ŚāṅkhB., whereas it frequently occurs in the Yajurvedic texts.

VādhS. 3, 27: The representation of all which is embraced is also formed by the agnihotra; the representation of offspring and cattle is that of embrace.[22]

VādhS. 3, 39: Somebody else said: "The firewood is a vulva, the libation is a representation of the seed. If he offers the first libation on the kindling-stick and then also the second one, then it becomes useful like seed which is emitted into a vulva and becomes offspring. If he offers the second libation aside (the stick), then it becomes lost like seed which is spent into something which is not a vulva and is spilt. Therefore now these two should be offered on the same point".[23]

ŚB. 2, 2, 4, 18: By offering the gods engendered the same procreation which is theirs now (...). He who knowing thus offers the agnihotra engenders the same procreation which they engendered then (...). Therefore the agnihotra should be offered.[24]

ŚB. 2, 3, 1, 3–5: And when he (the sun) sets, then he becomes an embryo and enters Agni (the fire) as his womb. Along with and as a consequence of his becoming an embryo all creatures become embryos. For having come to rest[25] they lie down without consciousness.[26] The reason why the night conceals (everything) here,[27] is that embryos are also concealed as it were. When he offers in the evening after sunset, he offers for the sake of him who is an embryo at that moment;[28] he acts on behalf of him (the sun) who is in the embryo state. Because he offers for the sake of him who is in the embryo state, therefore these embryos live without taking food. And when he offers in the morning before sunrise, then he brings him forth at that moment. (...).[29] Therefore he performs this offering.

ŚB. 2, 3, 1, 23: Now the second libation is made in order to produce a couple. For a pair is a couple which produces offspring.[30]

— For other couples see also ŚB. 11, 3, 2, 1 (six pairs, i.a. sacrificer and his wife). The passage translated above continues with the twofold aspect of the oblation. The second libation is connected with future, to-be-born, hope, the morrow. In this connection the text observes:

ŚB. 2, 3, 1, 29: The second (libation) is offered for the sake of progeny. He offers it silently. For that which is silently (done) is something uncertain, and something uncertain is progeny.[31]

ŚB. 2, 3, 1, 32–34: On the other hand that one (i.e. the formula) "Agni is the light, the light is Agni, hail" is a form of generation. Thereby he encloses the seed which is the light on both sides with the deity. Now seed enclosed on both sides is born. Therefore he causes it to be born by enclosing it on both sides (...).[32] And this indeed is a form of generation. Jīvala Cailaki, however, said: "Āruṇi produces only conception, not birth". He should offer with this same (formula) in the evening. And then in the morning (with the formula) "The light is Sūrya, Sūrya is the light, hail" he places the seed which is light outside by means of the deity. Now seed is born as offspring outside (the body of the mother). Thereby he reproduces it.

— The lengthy agnihotra section of the JB. does not contain more than one reference to this aspect of fertility and procreation:

JB. 1, 8: Having thus collected it he offers it in the evening. It passes that night in the condition of an embryo. Having again collected it in the same way he offers it at dawn. He causes it to be born.[33]

— Evidently this aspect of the agnihotra, which is hardly found outside the Yajurvedic texts, is secondary. Conception and delivery (as the image of sunset and sunrise) were just a motif rather than being a fundamental concept of the agnihotra, and as such it was transmitted within a number of related texts.

NOTES

[1] See e.g. Dumont, *L'Agnihotra*, p. VII: ".. qu'un des principaux objets de l'agnihotra est de perpétuer à la fois la continuité du sacrifice et la continuité de la race du sacrifiant. (...) L'agnihotra est un charme de fécondité". On the other hand Dumont regards this rite as "aussi, primitivement, un charme solaire" (p. VIII).

[2] See also Section 6.8.

[3] See also Section 6.10.

[4] This passage becomes clear only in connection with the agnihotra section (KS. 6, 5; see above), on which it is evidently based. It refers to the first offering after the *ādhāna* (see Section 14).

[5] See also Section 6.12.

[6] See also Section 6.3.

[7] See also Section 3.1. For the version of KS. 6, 7 see Section 6.3.

[8] See also Section 6.4 (n. 15).

[9] For the passage up to here see Section 6.10 (n. 8 and 9). See also 6.12, n. 3.

[10] See also Section 6.12.

[11] See also Section 5 (n. 8). The couple is produced by milking two cows (as also appears from the parallel of TB. 2, 1, 5, 4 f.; see below).

[12] This refers to the first offering after the *agnyādhāna* which does not take place in the evening (as the agnihotra should begin). The evening agnihotra means impregnation, the morning agnihotra delivery. Performing the first offering as a first (i.e. evening) agnihotra in the morning would mean a reversal of the biological process.

[13] For the identification oblation = *svam* see also JB. 1, 2 (Section 13.5, n. 10). However, MS. 1, 5, 11: 80.15 states *etad vai yajamānasya svaṃ yad agniḥ*.

[14] Keith's translation "whatever there is of the Sacrificer's own, that is (still) his" has to be rejected.

[15] Keith translates: "Then he burns at the end the plants". However, *antagata* means "being in its nearness". Sāyaṇa correctly explains that the procreative function of Agni is shown by reference to the fact that the fertility of a field burnt by Agni increases.

[16] See also Section 4 for the passage this far.

[17] See also Section 6.10 (n. 11 and 12).

[18] See also Section 6.12.

[19] See also Section 6.13.

[20] See also Section 5 (n. 4).

[21] See also Section 6.10 (n. 13).

[22] See also Section 4 (n. 28).

[23] See also Section 6.12. The passage belongs to a discussion on the meaning of the agnihotra.

[24] See also Section 3.3 (end).

[25] Eggeling translates "being coaxed" and assumes the reading *iḷitā*. For the correct reading (*ilitā*) and interpretation see Johanna Narten, *IIJ* 10 (1967/68), p. 243 f.

[26] I read *śere 'saṃjānānāḥ* instead of *śere saṃjānānāḥ*, a simple emendation by which we get rid of a translation such as "they lie down contented" (Eggeling). See also Caland, *WZKM* 26 (1912), p. 113 for conclusive arguments (the accent; the Kāṇva parallel).

[27] Eggeling: "... envelops that (sun)". However, *etat* in *tira evaitat karoti* does not refer to the sun, but is an adverb meaning "here".

[28] Again *etat*, here meaning "then".

[29] For the passage omitted here see Section 13.1.

[30] See also Section 6.10.

[31] See also Section 6.10.

[32] See 6.10, n. 20.

[33] See also 13.3 and 13.6 (n. 2).

13.3 *The agnihotra and deliverance from evil and sin.*

— The deliverance of the sun from the darkness of night, produced by the agnihotra, was not only connected with the image of procreation (delivery), but also with the release from the darkness of evil or sin.[1] So far only the morning agnihotra is entitled to play a role. In the case of fertility and procreation (the preceding section) the evening performance could be included (with the function or impregnation). In the case of deliverance from evil the evening agnihotra takes in a rather difficult position. Only by making a clear connection with sin rather than evil and by dividing the space of 24 hours into two periods in which sinful actions could be committed, was the evening performance (which is definitely not less important than the morning one) given its due place.

ŚB. 2, 3, 1, 6: Just as a snake may free itself from its skin, so does he (the sun) free himself from the evil which is the night. And just as a snake may free itself from its skin, so does he who knowing thus offers the agnihotra free himself from all evil.

JB. 1, 8: Having again collected it in the same way[2] he offers it at dawn. He causes it to be born. At its birth it (the sun) drives away all evil for him.

JB. 1, 9–10: The evil that is done in the day time, of that the sun is the cause: what is done at night, of that the fire. These two (deities) said: "If we shall (ever) be thus, we shall not be able to support the creatures. Let us be food and offer ourselves into each other". When the sun sets, it offers itself into the fire. Whatever evil the sun commits in the day time, is driven away for it by the fire at night. (...) Whatever evil the fire commits at night, is driven away for it by the sun by day. As a snake frees itself from its skin, as one pulls a rush out of its sheath, so he frees himself from all evil (sin) who knowing thus offers the agnihotra. On account of the evening oblation at night the fire drives away for him the evil that he does by day. On account of the morning oblation the sun (...). As in gold, when it has been heated, no stain, no evil at all remains, so there remains no stain, no evil at all in him who knowing thus offers the agnihotra.

— The original concept of the night being connected with evil is found in the VādhS:

VādhS. 3, 26: But those who know it say: "Darkness is evil. He should offer the evening oblation before the arrival of darkness.(...) He who knows thus becomes free from evil in this and yonder world".[3]

— The twofold (night and day) aspect in connection with good and evil is stressed by the AB., which only deals with the positive side, the good, which may be rescued by means of the *uddharaṇa* (taking fire out of the gārhapatya to the āhavanīya).

AB. 5, 26, 1 f.: Whatever good he does by day (resp. by night) he thus places in security by taking it out and transferring it to the east (i.e. to the āhavanīya).

— A different method for rescuing the good deeds and getting rid of the sinful deeds is proposed by the JB.

JB. 1, 15–16: Now they say: "The good and evil which a man does during his lifetime, what is the separation of these evil and good deeds?" (...)[4] The breaths correspond to mind, the body to speech. When he offers the first libation with speech (with a formula) and the second (reciting the formula) in thought, then he separates the evil and good deeds. (..) When he offers the first of the two evening libations (resp. morning libations) with speech, by this (libation) he rids himself of that evil which he commits by day (resp. by night). And when he offers the second (reciting the formula in thought, by this (libation) he rids himself of that evil which he commits by night (resp. by day). He keeps ridding himself of his evil deeds day by day who offers the agnihotra knowing thus.

— The central concept of the above passage is that separation of good and evil produces separation from the evil.[5] An incidental reference to being freed from evil is found in JB. 1, 28.[6]

NOTES

[1] On the Vedic conception of sin and evil and the use of the terms *pāpman* and *pāpa* see *JB. I, 1–65*, p. 39, n. 7.

[2] The passage refers to collecting the disintegrated sun at night and secondarily also (in the same way) in the morning. See also 13.6.

[3] See also Section 4 (n. 24).

[4] For the first answer to this question, which is ultimately rejected by the JB. and which has been omitted here, see *JB. I, 1–65*, p. 50.

[5] See *JB. I, 1–65*, p. 51, n. 1 on *vyāvṛtti* and *vyāvartate*.

[6] "When doing here an evil deed, (which is) dirt, he is covered over with one sixteenth part. Just as an armring (*pravṛtta*) of bad colour (*asuvarṇa*), when heated, takes on a beautiful colour, even so he comes to heaven having shifted the impurity of his evil on to his hateful rivals". For this translation which differs from the one given in *JB I, 1–65*, p. 81, see Rau, *Metalle und Metallgeräte im vedischen Indien* (Akademie Mainz 1973/8), p. 31 f. On the *pravṛtta* see Rau, o.c., p. 53 f.

13.4 *Liberation from death by the agnihotra.*

— As a parallel to the release from the darkness of night, womb and evil one might expect the liberation from death to be based on the sun's release from the nightly darkness. However, the agnihotra sections of the brāhmaṇas use different concepts in this connection. On the one hand the fire (Agni) is death, to be subdued by the oblation. See also the aetiological myth of the agnihotra (Section 1.1; especially ŚB. 2, 2, 4, 7). On the other hand the sun forms the demarcation between transitory life and eternity. Beyond the sun, situated in highest heaven, lies immortality. The same sun daily sets into the sacrificial fire. Ascending to heaven together with the rising sun means reaching this immortality and remaining beyond the sun.

AB. 5, 31, 2: If he offers before sunrise, this is like giving (something) to a man or an elephant, when the hand (or: trunk) is not stretched out. But if he offers after sunrise, this is like giving (something) to a man or an elephant after he has stretched out his hand (or: trunk). Having taken him up with that same hand (trunk) he (the rising sun) places him in heaven who knowing thus offers after sunrise.[1]

ŚB. 2, 3, 3, 7–9: He who gives out heat here is death. Because he is death, therefore the creatures on this side of him die. And those who are on the other side of him are the gods, and they are therefore also immortal. By the reins (rays) of this (sun) all the creatures are harnessed at their vital breaths.[2] Therefore also reins reach up to the *prāṇāḥ*.[2] Taking the breaths of whomsoever he wishes he rises. He dies. He who goes to yonder world without having escaped that death, him he causes to die again and again in yonder world just as in this world one does not exercise leniency for someone who is fettered but puts him to death whenever one wishes. When in the evening after sunset he offers two libations, he thereby establishes himself with these two fore-feet (or: hands) on this death. When in the morning before sunrise he offers two libations, he thereby establishes himself with these hind-feet on this death. When he rises, he rises with him. Thus he is freed from this death. This is the liberation from death in the agnihotra. He who knows this liberation from death in the agnihotra is freed from re-dying in yonder world.

ŚB. 2, 3, 3, 11–12: Day and night diminish man's store of good deeds in yonder world by their alternating flux and reflux.[3] But night and day are on this side from there.[4] So night and day do not diminish the store of his good deeds. Just as one may look down from above on the revolving wheels of the chariot while standing in the driving-box, even so does he look down from afar upon night and day. Forsooth night and day do not diminish (destroy) the good deeds of him who thus knows this liberation from night and day.

JB. 1, 11: Nagarin Jānaśruteya said: "The sun here enters its place of rest,[5] when it sets". By offering the two evening libations he establishes himself on the back of this sun. It is like getting a foothold with both feet. When now he offers these two morning libations, it lifts him up by means of these two. As an elephant rises together with the one who is sitting on the elephant-seat, even so this deity rises together with him who, knowing thus, offers (the agnihotra). This (deity) makes him go to his own world beyond which there is none higher. Whatever is beyond the sun, that is immortality. That he wins. And whatever is on this side of the sun, night and day carry this off from here,[6] just as a whirlwind may carry off.

— The parallelism between the ŚB. and the JB. is quite clear from the above. The JB. also contains a passage on being freed from that death which is Agni by subduing him with a libation.

JB. 1, 12–13: The gods were fighting with Death. Agni was Death. They said: "Come, let us try to subdue him". (. . . .)[7] They said: "Let us offer a milk libation and try to subdue him thereby". "So be it". They offered a milk libation. Thereby they subdued him. Therefore coals are the result, when they offer a milk libation (in the fire). They said: "We have subdued him by means of food. Well, let us try to subdue him once and for all". They said: "Let us offer a *soma* libation and try to subdue him thereby". "So be it". They performed a *soma* sacrifice. They offered a *soma* libation. Thereby they subdued him completely. (...) When one offers a milk libation, one subdues him (Death) thereby. And when one offers a *soma* libation, it is like finally defeating him after having once defeated him. One escapes from those two re-dyings in yonder world which are night and day.

VādhS. 3, 32: Agni is Death. If he should offer in the blazing (fire), he would offer the first libation in the mouth of Death and also the second one in the mouth of Death. Having laid the kindling-stick on that very spot where the coals are manifold as it were he should first offer a smaller quantity and then a larger one. Having suppressed Death with the first libation he mounts up to heaven with the second one.[8]

— Death, from which one tries to become released, is also night and day, as appears from the passages translated above. Especially the moment between night and day (chosen for the performance of the agnihotra) produces liberation from death.

VādhS. 3, 27: Now night and day also are death. These two do not reach that deity, the Sun. That deity rises over these two, while separating them; separating them he sets afterwards. And death does not reach him who, knowing thus, offers (the agnihotra).[9]

NOTES

[1] See also Section 4 (n. 16 and 17).

[2] The word *raśmi* is used with the double meaning of "ray of light" (of the sun) and "rein" (in the image). The verb *abhidhā* denotes the harnessing or bridling of horses. Eggeling, apparently not completely understanding this image, translates: "It is by the rays (or reins, thongs, raśmi) of that (sun) that all these creatures are attached to the vital airs (breaths or life), and therefore the rays extend down to the vital airs". The creatures are harnessed by the sun. The reins or the bridle are attached to the *prāṇāḥ*, which on the one hand denote the vital breaths, but on the other hand also the openings of the senses (mouth, etc.). These reins are the rays of light. In the typical way of reasoning of the brāhmaṇas a conclusion concerning daily life is added: Therefore reins stretch out up to the *prāṇāḥ* (= openings in the head) of the horses.

[3] Eggeling translates *pariplavamāna* by "revolving". Night and day seem to be compared to high and low tide. See also JB. 1, 5 (*JB I, 1–65*, p. 32, n. 4 and Section 4). The passing of night and day means the gradual expiration of one's credit of good deeds in yonder world. Moreover high and low tide are connected with washing away and caving in.

[4] Eggeling translates *atas* by "from him (after he has gone up to heaven)".

[5] On account of Section 13.2 one might interpret *yoni* as womb or birthplace. This translation, however, does not suit the context, where the idea of procreation does not play a role at all. The sun is an animal, an elephant on

whose back man rises to heaven in the morning. The evening had to be fitted in, though it had hardly any function in this concept. Now animals turn in and enter their lairs at night just like the sun which sets in the evening. Therefore this reference to the lair was made here.

6 On the text and its interpretation see *JB I, 1–65*, p. 43, n. 7.

7 The passage omitted here refers to butter libations and oblations in the form of a victim, which did not subdue Agni. They are Agni's favourite speciality and cause the fire to flare up.

8 See also Section 6.11 (n. 11–13).

9 See also Section 4. The same concept of night and day in connection with the right time for offering the agnihotra is found at ŚāṅkhB. 2, 9 ("Night and day are also the arms of death") and at JB. 1, 6 ("Having thus placed nourishment before the mouth of night and day he escapes from those two dyings in yonder world which are night and day").

13.5 *The agnihotra produces life (or immortality) in yonder world and in this world.*

— In the preceding section release from death was obtained by rising to heaven together with the rising sun, by subduing Death = Agni with the libation or by offering in between the two deaths of night and day. Sun, Agni and night and day were regarded as (manifestations of) death, from which the agnihotra should release the sacrificer. In the present section a more positive approach for obtaining immortality is met with. Offering a libation means producing a new life. On the one hand the identification of the āhavanīya fire with heaven plays a role; on the other hand is the water doctrine,[1] which teaches that the rain coming down from heaven ultimately is based on the smoke of the sacrificial fire, which conveys the libations (or the corpses in case of cremation). In the ŚB. version of this doctrine rebirth in the son is the result of offering agnihotra libations. This seems to represent a secondary combination of the old theory that the father is reborn in the son with the water doctrine. On the other hand, if disconnected with the individual sacrificer, this passage may be placed in the more general framework of the water doctrine which explains life on earth as due to the waters from heaven which are constantly to be fed by the oblations (especially of the agnihotra).[2]

ŚB. 11, 6, 2, 6–10 : These two libations after having been offered rise upwards. They enter the space between heaven and earth. They make the space between heaven and earth an āhavanīya fire, the wind its kindlingstick (on which there is offered), the sun-motes[3] the pure libation. They satisfy the space between heaven and earth and then rise upwards. They enter heaven. They make heaven an āhavanīya fire, the sun its kindling-stick, the moon the pure libation. They (....) satisfy heaven and then return. They enter this earth. They make this earth an āhavanīya fire, the (sacrificial) fire its kindling-stick, the plants the pure libation. (..) They enter man. They make his mouth an āhavanīya fire, the tongue its kindling-stick, food the pure libation. They satisfy man. He who knowing thus eats food, by him the agnihotra is offered (..). They enter a woman. They make her lap an āhavanīya fire, her womb the kindling-stick, — for this is called the bearer because Prajāpati bore the creatures by it — and the seed the pure libation. They satisfy the woman. He who knowing thus has sexual intercourse, by him the agnihotra is offered. The son who is born therefrom is the renascent world.[4] This is the agnihotra, Yājñavalkya. There is nothing superior to this.

— Originally the basic text of JB. 1, 17–18 had no connection with the water doctrine. Life in heaven is produced by offering in the āhavanīya (= heaven). The life thereby produced in heaven is actualised after death, when the 'soul' rises to heaven and is tested by the sun. Giving the wrong answer implies being sent back to the sphere of night and day (= death, see the preceding section). Otherwise one takes possession of the divine body procured by the agnihotra. In this text another eschatological passage (with another test of the deceased by the door-keepers of heaven) has been inserted. Here only the basic text, which is connected with the agnihotra, has been translated:

JB. 1, 17–18: Two wombs, indeed, there are. The divine womb is the one, the human womb the other. There are, indeed, also two worlds. The divine world is the one, the human world the other. (...) The āhavanīya is the divine womb, the divine world. That one, forsooth, is the divine womb, the divine world. Therefore if anyone should offer in the gārhapatya, one might think: "He does what should not be done". If he who correctly acts (by offering in the āhavanīya) offers, then he thereby emits his self in this divine womb. This self of his comes into existence in yonder sun. He who knows thus has two selves and two wombs. One self and one womb has he who does not know this. When, knowing thus, one departs from this world, the lifebreath ascends first. It announces to the gods the quantity:[5] "So much good, so much evil has been done by him". Thereupon he rises up along with the smoke (of the funeral pyre). (.....)[6] He comes to the shining one. At his arrival he (the sun) asks him: "Who art thou?" To him who announces himself by his (personal) name or by his family (name) he says: "That self of yours that has been in me,[7] that is yours (again)". After that self has been received back, the seasons run towards him from all sides, grasp him by his feet and drag him away. Night and day take possession of his world. He should announce himself to him with these words: "*Ka* (= who and at the same time = Prajāpati) am I, thou art heaven. As such I have gone to thee, the heavenly heaven". (...) To him he (the sun) says: "Who thou art, that one am I. Who I am, that one thou art. Come". He approaches that essence of good deeds. His sons enter upon his inheritance, his forefathers upon (the effects of) his good deeds. He who knows thus has two selves and two inheritances. If without knowing this one offers the agnihotra, one has only one self and one inheritance.

— The eschatological passage inserted in JB. 1, 18 and omitted here has a parallel in JB. 1, 46 (after the *pañcāgnividyā*) and JB. 1, 49–50 (after the funeral ritual). There is no explicit or direct connection with the agnihotra in these three passages, which are not translated in this publication. According to the VādhS. it is especially the first of the two libations which secures heaven:

VādhS. 3, 39: By means of the first libation let us win heaven, with the second one obtain a good position on earth with regard to offspring and cattle.[8]

VādhS. 3, 22: With this same integrated self (or: body) in the form of the year and with this agnihotra, with these utterances Prajāpati won heaven at once. He who, knowing thus, offers the agnihotra at once wins heaven with a body which is thus integrated, with the year and the agnihotra (thus integrated), with these utterances. Now those who know thus say on this point: "If someone dies after having offered at least one libation, who would have injured him if he had reached one libation. With the first libation he would have won heaven at once". He who, knowing thus, offers the agnihotra and he for whom someone, knowing thus, offers the agnihotra, wins heaven with the first libation.[9]

— On winning heaven by means of the agnihotra (in connection with *ādhāna* and cremation) see the following passage from the JB., which has a partial parallel in ŚB. 12, 5, 2, 13 (funeral ritual):

JB. 1, 2: .... Moreover the oblation is the brahmin's self.[10] This he places in his own body, in these immortal lifebreaths (= the fires). This, being placed in his own body, does not perish. Now when the mind, when the breath, sight, hearing and speech pass away, then they enter these fires. Thereupon they throw after (these lifebreaths) also this body of his in these fires (reciting) "From him thou wert born, he should be born out of thee, hail". He (arises) from this (fire) and becomes immortal in the form of an oblation, mind, breath, sight, hearing, speech, *ṛc*, *yajus*, *sāman*, *brahman* and gold. His lifebreaths become immortal. He makes an immortal body for himself here (i.e. in the *agnyādhāna* and agnihotra ritual). He who knowing thus offers the agnihotra becomes immortal.

— The following passage from the MS. lies in the same eschatological realm:

MS. 1, 8, 6: 123.18 ff.: If someone, after having given much (as *dakṣiṇās* or as *bhikṣās*) and having sacrificed much, removes (i.e. gives up, or rather has to give up) his fires, this (i.e. the fruit of his giving and sacrificing) is not lost (*na 'kṣit*) for him. The virtuous who have offered this reach (*nakṣanti*) yonder world. They are these stars (*nakṣatrāṇi*). When there is said: "Light (from heaven) has fallen down, a meteor has fallen down", then these (virtuous) are falling down. After having come and stayed (there)[11] they become associated with their own place (or position: *loka*) (on earth), when they fall down from yonder world. And he who has given much and sacrificed much and offers the agnihotra, performs the New and Fullmoon sacrifices, the Fourmonthly sacrifices and undertakes many *sattras*, for him this (store of *iṣṭāpūrta*) is inexhaustible and unlimited. The sacrifice lasts beyond the one who has sacrificed it. Therefore he should be cremated by these very two (sacrificial) fires. Thereby he rises after his own (merit of stored up) sacrificial rites.

— The text continues with some details on the use of the fires for the cremation to be compared to JB. 1, 49. Note that Oertel's translation (*Syntax of Cases*, p. 310) has to be corrected. On winning heaven see also the following passage from the JB., which in some respects seems to belong to the preceding section (sun-into-fire, fire-into-sun), but on the other hand rather belongs to the present one, since the sun itself forms the sphere of immortality. The context is that of a *brahmodya*:

JB. 1, 23: Pointing at the fire he (Āruṇi) said: "This is honour" and at the sun: "That is honour. So I offer that honour in this honour in the evening and this honour in that honour at dawn. These two will lead me thither where are all things one may desire. These two will ward off repeated dying for me".

— The other brahmins replacing honour by something else state the same. The superior kṣatriya Janaka identifies the sun with the *gati* (goal) and the fire with the *iti* (means for coming there). He may rightly say: "These two will ward off repeated dying", for sun is immortality.

NOTES

[1] See *Agn. and Prāṇāgn.*, ch. VI.

[2] On this passage see the reference in n. 1. It has to be observed that here the theory of five successive fires is explicitly connected with the agnihotra, whereas a similar *pañcāgnividyā* is found in the BĀU. and the ChU. without any clear relation to this ritual. In JB. 1, 45 the only connection between the water doctrine of the *pañcāgnividyā* and the fire ritual is its occurrence in the agnihotra section of this brāhmaṇa. Moreover there are some fundamental differences between the ŚB. and the other mentioned passages. In the ŚB. the starting-point of the fertilizing stream of fluid does not lie in heaven, but with the agnihotra sacrificer. Instead of agnihotra libations the corpses burnt at the cremation play a role in the water doctrine of the Upaniṣads and the JB. In the ŚB. the son as the product of the fifth sacrifice (the coitus-agnihotra) is called the *loka pratyutthāyin*. The passage of the JB. ends (1, 46 first paragraph) with a sixth sacrifice in the form of the cremation. Its product is called the *loka punarutthāyai*. The transformation is evident.

[3] On *marīci* meaning sunmote see Minard, *Trois Énigmes* II, 97 *a*.

[4] The *loka pratyutthāyin* (see n. 2). The context of this passage is formed by a discussion between king Janaka and three brahmins. Janaka states that even the best of them, Yājñavalkya, does not know the rising, the destination, the resting-place, the satisfaction, the return and the renascent world of the two libations. Yājñavalkya approaches Janaka as a pupil, and learns about the rising and the renascent world in the passage translated here.

[5] Read *sa heyattāṃ devebhya* (*JB I, 1–65*, p. 57, n. 12).

[6] The passage omitted here is the insertion mentioned in the introductory remarks.

[7] This refers to the self produced in the sun by offering in the āhavanīya, the divine womb. See the beginning of this passage.

[8] These words are spoken by Āruṇi in the context of a discussion on the right interpretation of the agnihotra.

[9] See also Section 6.5 (end). The integration of Prajāpati's self mentioned in this passage is produced by the fourfold ladling out.

[10] Cf. 13. 2, n. 13.

[11] See Oertel, *Syntax of Cases*, p. 299 f., whose translation I have not followed here.

13.6 *Reintegration of the dispersed sun by the performance of the agnihotra.*

— Just as in Section 13.3 the twofold (evening and morning) aspect of the agnihotra produces a problem. While in 13.3 the evening performance did not fit in with the interpretation, here the morning performance does not suit it. If the setting and disintegrating sun is reintegrated by the evening agnihotra, it can hardly be reintegrated again at dawn. Perhaps, however, this interpretation originally applied only to the morning performance, which should collect the scattered sun and make it rise again. The passage as it stands would imply that all the actions including the milking and the cleansing of the vessels should take place after sunset, which appears doubtful. The version of the JB. combines the reintegration of the sun with the other interpretations of the agnihotra as found in 13.1–3.

JB. 1, 7–8: Yonder sun goes off sixfold when it sets. "It has gone off" the ancient knowers of the traditional legends used to say, but now (one says): "it has gone down". When it sets, it enters the brahmin with faith, cattle with milk, the fire with glow, the plants with sap, the waters with juice, the trees with pith. When the brahmin cleanses the vessels used in the agnihotra ritual and when he is occupied with them he thereby collects in this (agnihotra libation)[1] the faith with which it has entered him. And when they milk the milk (used for the agnihotra) he thereby collects in this (oblation) the milk with which it has entered the cows. And when he pokes the charcoals he thereby collects in this (oblation) the glow with which it has entered the fire. And when he illuminates (the milk) with a (burning) grassblade he thereby collects in this (oblation) the sap with which it has entered the plants. And when he pours water on (the milk) he thereby collects in this (oblation) the juice with which it has entered the waters. And when he lays a kindling-stick on the fire he thereby collects in this (oblation) the pith with which it has entered the trees. Having thus collected it (in the agnihotra oblation) he offers it in the evening. (...)[2] Having again collected it in the same way he offers it at dawn. (...)[2] Moreover it (the sun) thinks: "This one certainly collects me properly. Well, let him reach old age sound in life and limb, unbroken". And it also thinks: "This one certainly knows me properly. Well, let me enter him". It enters him who knows thus. It is the sole hero who shines here, it is Indra, it is Prajāpati. To him therefore is offered by the one who, knowing thus, offers the agnihotra.

VādhS. 3, 24: The sun sets in seven entities: in the fire, the earth, the cattle, the waters, the plants, the trees and the brahmin. Now they say: "How does he collect it from these?" When he pushes the coals (out of the gārhapatya, in order to heat the milk on it) (... thereby he collects it from the fire ......),[3] thereby he collects it from the earth. When they milk the cow, thereby he collects it from the cattle. When he pours water on (the hot milk), thereby he collects it from the waters. When he illuminates (the milk) with (burning) plants, thereby he collects it from the plants. When he lays two kindling-sticks on (the āhavanīya fire), thereby he collects it from the trees. And when the brahmin offers, thereby he collects it from the brahman class. In this way now he collects it from these. These represent seven large quantities.[4] Fire is a large quantity (i.e. stands for all the fires); the earth is a large quantity (itself); cattle is a large quantity (... etc.). Every night and morning he wins the world of seven sacrificers of large quantities (i.e. institutors of sacrifices in which many cows are slaughtered or presented as *dakṣiṇās*) who, knowing thus, offers the agnihotra and for whom someone, knowing thus, offers the agnihotra.[5]

NOTES

[1] For this correction of Caland's and my own translation (as given in *JB I, 1–65*) see Ingeborg Ickler's review in *OLZ* 1976 (?).

[2] For these two omitted passagessee Sections 13.2–3.

[3] The text of the ms. has a gap here.

[4] Caland doubts whether *badva* "hier die gewöhnliche Bedeutung einer gewissen grossen Zahl hat". Evidently, some sort of large amount or quantity should be denoted here. The singulars (e.g. brāhmaṇa) stand for the totality of the group (i.c. brahman). In this way an enormous increase of the agnihotra oblation and its import is achieved. The whole earth, the whole class of brahmins, all the fires contribute to this agnihotra.

[5] In a way this passage belongs to the section on the identification of the agnihotra with the more impressive (Soma) sacrifices (Section 10).

13.7 *The agnihotra avoids being eaten in return and other reversals in yonder world (story of Bhṛgu).*

— A complete rendering of the Bhṛgu story as found in the ŚB. and the JB. need not be given here. For the version of the JB. and references to the many translations of this passage see *JB. I, 1–65*, p. 99. Bhṛgu visits yonder world and sees some horrible visions. People cut others into pieces and eat them as they have been cut or eaten in this world (as trees or plants). Having returned to earth he learns from his father (Varuṇa) the explanation of the visions and the corresponding expiations by means of the agnihotra:

JB. 1, 43–44: "Yes", he said; "those who in this world offer[1] the agnihotra without knowing thus and cut trees and lay them on the fire, those the trees, having taken human form, eat in their turn in yonder world". "What is the expiation for this?" "That he lays here (i.e. in the agnihotra ritual) a kindling-stick on the fire, that is its expiation. By that (expiation) it is avoided". (...) "Yes", he said; "those who in this world offer the agnihotra without knowing thus and cook for themselves animals which cry out are eaten by these animals in their turn in yonder world after they have taken human form". (..) "That he offers here the first oblation with speech (i.e. with a formula recited aloud), that is its expiation". (..) "Yes", he said; "those who offer the agnihotra in this world without knowing thus and cook themselves rice and barley, which inaudibly utter sounds,[2] are eaten by rice and barley in return in yonder world after they have taken human form". (..) "That he offers here the second libation (reciting the formula) in thought, that is its expiation". (..) "Yes", he said; "they (i.e. two women guarding a large property) were Faith and Non-Faith. If any in this world offer the agnihotra without knowing thus and sacrifice without faith, then it (i.e. this sacrifice) goes to Non-Faith; if (they sacrifice) with faith, it (goes) to Faith". (..) "That he eats here twice with his finger, that is its expiation". "Yes", he said; "if any in this world offer the agnihotra without knowing thus and shed (or: press out) the blood of a brahmin, then it (the blood) becomes that stream filled with blood; and the black naked man with a club who guarded it, he is Wrath. This (blood) indeed is his food". (...) "That he eats here with the ladle, that is its expiation. By that (expiation) it is avoided. And the water that he tosses upwards to the north after having washed the spoon, that is the stream filled with ghee. Out of this (stream) golden men draw up all things one may desire with golden cups". (...) "Yes", he said; "these,[3] forsooth, were my worlds". "By what are they to be won?" "By fivefoldly taking this (milk out of the pot) and lifting (it) out (into the *sruc*)". He (i.e. the son, Bhṛgu) said: "There is indeed nowhere outside the agnihotra an opportunity for the conquest of a world (in heaven). (So) today (will be) my fastday preceding the establishment of the sacred fires". Thus they arranged it for him. He who, knowing thus, offers the agnihotra, is not eaten in yonder world by the trees after they have taken human form, nor by the animals, nor by rice or barley. And his meritorious works and sacrifices do not go to Faith and Non-Faith. He wards off the stream filled with blood. He obtains the stream filled with ghee.

ŚB. 11, 6, 1, 8–12: He (i.e. Varuṇa) said: "The men you saw in the eastern region being divided into pieces by (other) men who were hewing off their limbs one by one saying "This (piece) is yours, this is mine", those were the trees. When he takes a kindling-stick from the trees and lays it on (the āhavanīya fire), he thereby subdues (or: obtains) the trees and wins the world of the trees. And the men you saw in the southern region being divided into pieces by (other) men who were cutting off their limbs one by one saying "This is yours, this mine", those were the cattle. When he offers milk, he thereby subdues the cattle and wins the world of the cattle. And the men you saw in the western region who while being silent[4] were eaten by silent men, those were the plants. When he illuminates (the milk) with a (burning) straw, he subdues the plants and wins the world of the plants. And the men you saw in the northern region who while crying aloud were eaten by crying men, those were the waters. When he pours water to (the hot milk of the agnihotra), he subdues the waters and wins the world of the waters. And the two women you saw, one being beautiful and the other too beautiful, the beautiful one is Belief. When he offers the first libation, he subdues Belief and overcomes Belief. The too beautiful one is Unbelief. When he offers the second libation, he subdues Unbelief and overcomes Unbelief. And the man who was standing between them, the black one with yellow eyes and with a staff in his hand, he was Wrath. When he pours water into the spoon and pours it out, he thereby subdues Wrath and overcomes Wrath. He who, knowing thus, offers the agnihotra thereby overcomes everything and subdues everything.

— Bhṛgu is convinced, and decides to establish his fires in order to perform the daily agnihotra. Note that JUB. 4, 5, 3 identifies the sun at the time of agnihotra with Bhṛgu.

NOTES

[1] I read *juhvato* instead of *ajuhvato*. See *JB I, 1–65*, p. 106, n. 15.

[2] I read *vyāharantam* and *vyāharataḥ*. See o.c., p. 107, n. 18.

[3] I.e. the worlds described in the passage omitted here filled with rivers of lotuses and crowds of Apsaras.

[4] For a criticism of Eggeling's translation "sitting still" see o.c., p. 107, n. 18.

13.8 *The daily food taken twice a day forms the remains of the agnihotra sacrifice.*

— The connection between the daily meals and the daily agnihotras is an obvious one and consequently it was not left unobserved. The *prāṇāgnihotra bhojanavidhi* had one of its starting-points in this parallelism. The food taken after the agnihotra performance was regarded as its *dakṣiṇā* by some texts.[1] In the present section the agnihotra is almost considered to be the justification for the meal.

TB. 2, 1, 5, 3–4: As many gods as ate unoffered (food) became lost. (Then) having cut off this agnihotra from the total (food)[2] they offered it. Therefore they say: "The gods saw (i.e. conceived) the agnihotra as the expiation for (faults committed in) the houses".[3]

What he (the priest) offers in the evening, that is for the eating of (the rest of) the oblation at night, in order that the sacrificer does not become lost. What he offers in the morning, that is for the eating of (the rest of) the oblation during the day, in order that the sacrificer does not become lost. What he eats after that (offering), that has been offered (i.e. that forms a rest of the oblatory material).

ŚB. 2, 3, 1, 11–12: When he offers in the evening after sunset, (he does so thinking:) "I must offer to the gods of this life-producing fluid,[4] on which we subsist though it belongs to them". What he afterwards eats as his evening meal, he eats as the rest of the offering of which the *bali* oblations have been cut off as portions to be offered. For he who offers the agnihotra eats (only) the rest of the offering.

NOTES

[1] See VādhS. 3, 34 (Section 10; cf. also ṢaḍvB. 4, 1, 15–16 in the same section).

[2] Dumont's interpretation (".. after they had made a division of the whole of it (i.e., after they had divided it into the Evening-Agnihotra and the Morning-Agnihotra)") is definitely untenable.

[3] Dumont: "the restoration of their houses". Cf. MNU. 527.

[4] For the preceding context (ŚB. 2, 3, 1, 10) see Section 5. On the syntax of the dependent clause see Whitney, *AJPh* 3 (1882), p. 396 (criticizing Eggeling's translation and remarking that the accent of *upajīvāmas* implies a dependent clause).

13.9 *Offering the two daily agnihotras means giving men to gods as dakṣiṇās and conversely.*

— In Section 10 several symbolical *dakṣiṇās* of the agnihotra have been mentioned. See also Section 12 in which every giving is connected with the agnihotra and regarded as a *dakṣiṇā*. In the present section the situation is somewhat different. The alternating aspect of the two daily performances (i.a. connected with the entrance of the sun into the fire and conversely, as well as with inhalation and exhalation) takes in a central position here. The context (see Section 12) has the same relation with the *dakṣiṇās*.

AB. 5, 28, 3–6: He alternately leads both groups, gods and men, as dakṣiṇās, and all whatever there is here. By the evening oblation he leads men as *dakṣiṇās* to the gods and also all whatever there is here. Having been lead as *dakṣiṇās* for the gods they lie down in a relaxed sleep and at home as it were. By the morning oblation he leads the gods as *dakṣiṇās* to men, and also all whatever there is here.[1] Having discovered (them), as it were, they (i.e. men)[2] leap up (saying): "I will do that" and "I will go there". The world which a man wins by giving all this is as great a world as he wins who, knowing thus, offers the agnihotra.[3]

NOTES

[1] Human beings awakening at sunrise together with the performance of the agnihotra experience the confrontation with everything here in this world as being presented with a *dakṣiṇā*. Daylight and the vision of all which is happening is a gift.

[2] Keith seems to take the gods as the subjects of this sentence. However, the leaping up and the planning of what one is going to do evidently refer to human beings rather than to the gods.

[3] Again the rather simple, daily agnihotra provides as much profit as some much more expensive rites. See also MS. 1, 8, 6: 124.11 ff.: "When he offers in the evening, he thereby obtains thousand cows of plenty, when in the morning (again) thousand ones".

13.10 *The agnihotra provides food.*

— The agnihotra sections of the brāhmaṇas abound with references to obtaining offspring and cattle in connection with this rite. The other obsession of the Vedic Indians, food, hardly seems to have any relation to the agnihotra as far as its obtainment is concerned. Indeed food and the two daily meals definitely belong together with the two performances. However, the agnihotra does not produce food; at least not directly. In connection with the water doctrine the libations returning from heaven in the form of rain further the fertility on earth and produce a rich vegetation. In this section one instance of the obtainment of food by a sacrificer "who knowing thus performs the agnihotra" is found. It is purely incidental.

ŚB. 2, 3, 2, 14–15: He should try to effect one of these (stages of the fire) for a year,[1] whether he offers himself or some one else offers for him. If he should offer now in this way, now in another, this would be like digging for water or some other food and stopping in the midst of it. But if he offers completely (going up to the end, not stopping in the midst),[2] this would be like digging for water or some other food and quickly striking upon it. These libations, forsooth, are spades (for the digging up) of the food. He does strike upon this food, if, knowing thus, he offers the agnihotra.

NOTES

[1] Eggeling translates: "Let him endeavour to adhere to some one of these (gods or fires) for a year". The desiderative *upertsati* of *upārdh* should be

rendered more accurately. The point is that one of the several stages of the fire (which correspond to several deities) should be produced. The adherence lies in *eka* rather than in *upertsati*.

[2] The terminology from the digging (stopping in the midst: *sāmi*) is shifted to the offering itself. I doubt whether *sārdham* can mean "uniformly" (Eggeling). It denotes "together with the complement, with the other half", i.e. the opposite of *sāmi*.

13.11 *The agnihotra is a vajra.*

TB. 2, 1, 5, 11: Aruṇa, the son of Upaveśa, used to say: "In the agnihotra I throw a thunderbolt (*vajra*)[1] at my rivals in the evening and in the morning. Therefore my rivals are inferior to me". One ladles out four times, offers twice; the kindling-stick is seventh. Seven verses has the Śakvarī (stanza). The thunderbolt has the same nature as the Śakvarī ('the powerful'). Therefore every night and morning the sacrificer throws a thunderbolt at his rival in the agnihotra (ritual). He prospers himself; his rival becomes lost.[2]

NOTES

[1] On the *vajra* see Minard, *Trois Énigmes* II, 868. For other symbolical *vajras* (i.e. in the ritualistic sphere) see Gonda, *Savayajñas*, p. 261 (who also refers to rivals to be attacked with *vajras*). Now see also Tapan Kumar Das Gupta, *Der Vajra. Eine vedische Waffe*, Wiesbaden 1975.

[2] For this type of identification based on numbers see also TB. 2, 1, 3, 9 (see Section 6.5) and ŚāṅkhB. 2, 3 (Section 6.17, n. 10–12).

— The establishment of the fires (*agnyādhāna*) represents the (ritual) birth of the *āhitāgni*, the agnihotra his life,[1] and his cremation the establishment of a new life in heaven. There is a clear parallelism between *agnyādhāna*[2] and cremation.

ŚB. 2, 2, 4, 8: When he (i.e. the agnihotrin) dies and they place him on the fire (of the funeral pyre consisting of his own fires),[3] then he is born from the fire. And the fire burns only his body. Just as he is born from his father and mother, so he is born from the fire. But he who does not offer the agnihotra does not come into existence (in yonder world), thus they say.[4] Therefore the agnihotra should be offered.

— The preceding passage contains the aetiological myth of the agnihotra. By offering (the agnihotra) Prajāpati freed himself from Death (= Agni).

ŚB. 2, 3, 3, 3–6: When he establishes the two fires (i.e. gārhapatya and āhavanīya), he generates him (Agni). Having generated him he maintains him. Just as he generates and maintains him in this world, even so he (Agni) generates and maintains him in yonder world. Therefore one should not remove him (the fire) in between, for then he (apparently) becomes fed up with him.[5] Just as he (the sacrificer) prematurely becomes fed up with him in this world, even so does he (Agni) prematurely become fed up with him in yonder world. Therefore one should not remove him (the fire) prematurely. When he dies and when they place him on the (funeral) fire, then he is generated from the fire. He (Agni) who is the son now becomes his father.[6] Therefore there has been stated with reference to this by the ṛṣi in a verse (ṚS. 1, 89, 9) "O gods, there are hundred autumns (i.e. years) available in which you have instituted the becoming old and decrepit of our bodies and in which sons become fathers. Do not destroy our lifetime in the midst of its course", for he (Agni) who is the son now becomes again the father. And therefore it is that he should establish the two fires.

— The preceding passage (ŚB. 2, 3, 3, 1–2) gives the aetiological myth of the *agnyādhāna* (Agni having been created by Prajāpati tries to consume everything and is ultimately taken up and reproduced by man).[7] The following passage continues with the death motif.[8] The most evident connection between ritual birth (*agnyādhāna*), rebirth in heaven (through the cremation) and the life of a ritualist (the agnihotra performed from *agnyādhāna* up to cremation) is found in the JB.

JB. 1, 1–2: In that here they churn out the fires, thereby they produce the sacrificer's lifebreaths. (...)[9] He produces for himself these five lifebreaths. Having threefoldly divided them (as the three sacred fires) and having made them divine powers[10] he keeps offering in them (for the rest of his life). (..)

— After having shown that the fires in which are offered represent the sacrificer's life(breaths), the text continues by stating that the oblations consequently have the function of food. The fires and the sacrificer's *prāṇāḥ* are nourished and maintained through the agnihotra.

(..) He offers life and in (the) life (breath) there is offered. It is therefore food which he offers in the lifebreath (when he offers the agnihotra). (...) When now the mind, when the breath, sight, hearing and speech pass away, then they enter these fires. Thereupon they throw after (these lifebreaths) also this body of his in these fires (reciting) "From him thou wert born, he should be born out of thee, hail". He (arises) from this (fire) and becomes immortal in the form of an oblation, of mind, breath, sight, hearing, speech, *ṛc*, *yajus*, *sāman*, *brahman* and gold. His lifebreaths become immortal. He makes an immortal body for himself here (i.e. in the agnyādhāna and agnihotra ritual). He becomes immortal who knowing thus offers the agnihotra.[11]

— The VādhS. includes these speculations in the *agnyādhāna* section.

VādhS. 3, 4:[12] Having thus established him (Agni) here (in the *agnyādhāna* ritual) he should take care of him (by kindling and feeding)[13] until his (own) death.[14] He should maintain him as long as is the duration of man's lifetime here. As long as is Agni's lifetime in yonder world, Agni maintains him in yonder world. Therefore, after having established him here, he should take care of him until his death. (...) When, knowing thus an *āhitāgni* departs from this world, and when they place him whose time had come[15] on the fire, Agni produces him for yonder world. He maintains him who has thus been generated, as long as is Agni's lifetime in yonder world. (..) This son becomes a father. It has been said (in the verse ṚV. 1, 89, 9) "O gods, there are hundred autumns ..."[16] Just as here in this world man behaves towards the fires, even so the fires behave towards him in yonder world.

— The parallelism with ŚB. 2, 3, 3, 3–6 is evident; borrowing from that text (rather than the other way round) is probable. In its *agnyādhāna* section the VādhS. also has another passage in which the cremation plays a role. The situation, however, is completely different. The essential point of this passage (missed by Caland, who remarks: "Der Gedankengang ist nicht deutlich") is that the first offering in the established fires does not belong to the regular couples of evening and morning agnihotras. The *pūrṇāhuti* offered at the end of the *agnyādhāna* is not identical with the first agnihotra performance, since this ritual starts with an evening agnihotra. How should this offering in the newly established fire be considered? As a morning performance with the corresponding morning formula? As an evening performance with the corresponding evening formula? TB. 1, 1, 6, 9 decides that there should be offered in the new fire without using one of the two formulas, i.e. silently.[17] This isolated *agnyādhāna-agnihotra*, however, should have a counterpart just as the ordinary agnihotra with its evening and morning performances. The cremation forms the counterpart.

VādhS. 3, 11: Now they say (or ask):[18] "The agnihotra libation which is offered directly after the fires have been established[19] is that a morning libation or an evening libation?" "Or is there perhaps also the existence of a counterpart of this libation?"[20] When, knowing thus, an *āhitāgni* departs from this world and when they place him whose time had come on the fire, then this (offering of the corpse) is the counterpart of this (*agnyādhāna-agnihotra*) libation. For this (cremation) is, so to say, neither a morning libation nor an evening libation.[21] For a man dies either before or after (an agnihotra performance).[22]

NOTES

1 See *Agn. and Prāṇāgn.*, ch. III. The agnihotra is considered to be *jarāmarya* or *jarāmūrīya* (probably "ending with old age", i.e. "lifelong") by JB. 1, 51 and ŚB. 12, 4, 1, 1 in the context of the expiations. MNU. 547 calls the agnihotra *jarāmarya* in the context of a symbolical sacrifice (identified with the agnihotra) which is represented by life itself.

2 On this point see *Agn. and Prāṇāgn.*, ch. III.

3 The cremation and the funeral ritual in general is often connected with the agnihotra (e.g. by the ŚB.). JB. 1, 46–49 (in the agnihotra section) also deals with the funeral. On the cremation by means of the own sacred fires see JB. 1, 49, as well as MS. 1, 8, 6: 124. 5–9 (in the agnihotra section!!).

4 On this translation of *śaśvat* see Minard, *Trois Énigmes* I, 589 *b*.

5 Eggeling is wrong in translating "for too soon it languishes for him". For *glā* with dative see Delbrück, *Altind. Synt.*, p. 142 ("er empfindet zu früh Widerwillen gegen ihn", probably taking the agnihotrin as the correct subject instead of Agni).

6 This reversal of the positions of son and father also becomes evident in some of the mantras recited in the funeral ritual. See *JB. I, 1–65*, p. 128 ff.

For the connection with similar mantras in the *agnyādhāna* ritual see o.c., p. 129.

[7] See Section 1.1.

[8] See Section 13.4.

[9] The elaborate description of the production of the lifebreaths through the process of churning fire is omitted here.

[10] On *prāṇāḥ* (lifebreaths, vital powers, senses) being called *devāḥ* (sense-functions) see *JB. I, 1–65*, p. 22, n. 12.

[11] JB. 1, 47 (in the passage on the funeral ritual which has been incorporated in the agnihotra section) agrees with this passage at the end. The mantras in both passages refer to the reversal of the roles of *āhitāgni* and Agni (father and son). See also the funeral ritual of ŚB. 12, 5, 2, 13 and 15 which forms a parallel for both passages.

[12] Caland does not translate this "schwierigen Passus, dessen Überlieferung vielleicht fehlerhaft ist". The comparison with parallel passages, as made in this publication, throws new light on this passage.

[13] For my interpretation of *agniṃ kṛ-* cf. the compound *agnikārya*.

[14] For *mṛtyuvantam* (Caland: "mit dem Tode versehen") see *JB. I, 1–65*, p. 229, n. 21.

[15] A free rendering of *diṣṭam ita-* "der zu seinem Schicksal gekommen ist" (Caland, who refers to *diṣṭagamana* in Hir. pitṛmedhasūtra). See also VādhS. 3, 11 (below; *diṣṭam itam*), ChU. 5, 9, 2 (*diṣṭam itam* instead of *ito;* see Oertel, *KZ* 68, p. 58–61) and *diṣṭabhāva, diṣṭānta* and *diṣṭā gatis* (mentioned by M.-W.'s dictionary).

[16] See above (ŚB. 2, 3, 3, 3–6).

[17] For this particular agnihotra see also KS. 8, 11 (he should offer with a full ladle, to Prajāpati, in thought, i.e. silently) and MS. 1, 6, 10: 102.10 (the actual agnihotra is delayed till the evening; instead some oblations are poured out). On these passages see also Section 13.2.

[18] The turn of phrase *tad āhur* belongs to the sphere of the *brahmodyas* and mostly introduces a question (theoretically once put forward in a debate, and actually answered in the text). Caland did not assume the existence of questions here.

[19] Caland: "welche in den nacheinander gegründeten Feuern geopfert wird". However, *anvag* should not be taken with *āhiteṣu*. Moreover it is doubtful whether the *āhuti* is offered in more than one fire; moreover, Caland's translation of *anvag* is doubtful. I interpret *āhiteṣv agniṣu* as an loc. abs. and take *anvag* with *hūyate* as meaning "directly afterwards" (i.e. after the fires have been established).

[20] Caland, not assuming a question, translates: "Sie ist aber auch das Gleichgewicht dieser Spende", without explaining what is "Sie" or "diese Spende".

[21] Since the cremation is neither an evening nor a morning agnihotra, it may correspond to the Agnyādhāna-agnihotra which likewise does not belong to one of the two categories.

[22] Probably this means that the death of the agnihotrin means the end of the regular agnihotra. If he dies at night after the evening performance, he dies before one set of two agnihotras has been accomplished. If he dies in the daytime, the situation is even more simple, since the cremation cannot take in the place of the evening performance (without a following morning performance), nor can it function as a morning performance (which has already been carried out).

15 *The agnihotra performed after the agnyādhāna (during twelve days)*

— On the so-called agnihotra performed directly after (or at the end of) the *agnyādhāna* see the end of the preceding section. The first twelve days of the agnihotra form a special period. JB. 1, 26–36 deals extensively with the symbolism of these twelve days. Its translation is omitted here. For the transference of this agnihotra of twelve days from brahman by way of Prajāpati, the gods and the ṛṣis to man, see Section 1.4 (JB. 1, 37). JB. 1, 38 states that the oblatory material should be milk, coagulated milk, and clarified butter and water, each of these to be used during three days. The four periods of three days are identified with the great sacrifices. See Section 10. The text then continues with a ritualistic description of these twelve days:

JB. 1, 38: The sacrificer himself, wearing new clothes, should offer the agnihotra in fires that are permanently maintained, not leaving home. Having sacrificed with *soma* or with a sacrificial victim during the thirteenth night he should dismiss (those fires; i.e. he should no longer permanently maintain all three fires), as one would dismiss (i.e. send off) people after having supplied them with provision (for the journey). The primeval mortals offered this agnihotra during twelve days. Because of it for them (i.e. for the mortals who have lived since that time) the cow yields milk, the ox draws, the horse is bridled,[1] the mule serves (man), the elephant is harnessed and draws.

Part of this passage occurs with some small differences as a quotation from the Śāṭyāyani Br. in ĀpŚS. 5, 23, 3. No other brāhmaṇas refer to this twelve-day agnihotra in their agnihotra sections. It is obvious that the period of twelve days is a shortening or representation of the year. Originally a period of one year with special regulations seems to have been observed.[2] An expiatory agnihotra of twelve days (used to avert Rudra's wrath) is identified with the year by MS. 1, 8, 6: 123.7 ff.

NOTES

[1] Read *ādhānapratihito* for *ādadhānaḥ prahito*.

[2] See MS. 1, 6, 11: 103.11 ff.

— Since the interrelationship of the several versions of this subject has been extensively treated elsewhere (*JB. I, 1–65*, p. 66 ff.), a different approach can be chosen here. First it may be useful to give a translation of the oldest passage.

MS. 1, 8, 10: (The agnihotra milk) is sacred to Rudra[1] when it is still in the cow, to Vāyu[2] when the calf has been admitted to the cow, to the Aśvins[3] when it is being milked, to Soma[4] when it has been milked, to Varuṇa[5] when it has been placed on the fire, to Mitra[6] when there is a film on its surface, to the Maruts[7] when it has bubbles, to Pūṣan[8] when it rises (to the brim), to Sarasvatī[9] when it flows over, to Viṣṇu[10] when water is being poured on it, to Heaven (*svarga*)[11] when it has been removed from the (gārhapatya) fire, to Tvaṣṭṛ when it is being ladled out, to Dhātṛ when it has been ladled out, to Viśvakarman when it has been taken up, to Savitṛ[12] when it starts being brought forward (to the āhavanīya), to Heaven and Earth[13] when it is being taken forward, to Indra and Agni[14] when it has been set down near (the āhavanīya), to Prajāpati[15] when it reaches the kindling-stick (on which the offering takes place), to the All-gods (or: all the gods)[16] when it has been offered.

— The version of the AB., which differs on some points, has made a context to this *vaiśvadeva*.

AB. 5, 26, 5–8: He who knows the agnihotra as sacred to all gods, sixteenfold and rooted in cattle is successful through the agnihotra sacred to all gods, sixteenfold and rooted in cattle. It is sacred to Rudra when it is in the cow (. . . . .).[17] This is the agnihotra which is sacred to all gods, sixteenfold and rooted in cattle. He who knows thus is successful through the agnihotra which is sacred to all gods, sixteenfold and rooted in cattle.

— The *vaiśvadeva* of TB. 2, 1, 7, which is not sixteenfold, but seventeenfold, and which lacks a particular context, in several respects agrees with the AB. The relation between the two brāhmaṇas is often difficult to establish. These texts do not form a unity and therefore every section (i.c. the agnihotra section), sometimes even each single passage must be compared. As a whole the agnihotra section of the TB. seems to be older, but not without exceptions.[18] In the present case its *vaiśvadeva* may have been based on, or influenced by, the AB. The passage of the AB. appears to be based directly on the MS. Note the use of *gavi sat* (for *gavi*), *upā-*

vasṛṣṭam (for *upasṛṣṭam*) and *śarogṛhītam* (for *śaras*). On the other hand the AB. correctly places *śarogṛītam* ("with a film on its surface") in ninth position (like the TB.) instead of in sixth (like the MS.). On some points both versions seem to be based directly on the MS. (i.e. the one version agrees with the MS. where the other differs). However, the agreements between the TB. and the AB. are remarkable in cases where the MS. differs. The anteriority of the AB. may also appear from the following comparison: MS. *mārutam bindumat* (in 7th position) has a partial parallel in AB. *mārutaṃ viṣyandamānam* (in 7th position). AB. has taken the seventh item of the series of deities and connected it with another stage of the milk. In the next (8th) couple AB. now connects *bindumat* with *vaiśvadevam*. The TB., which does not read *bindumat* like the AB. and the MS., but *bhindavaḥ*, here seems to have borrowed from the AB. (*vaiśvadevam bindumat*) and reads *vaiśvadevāḥ bhindavaḥ*. The development MS. – AB. – TB. is obvious here. Besides this *vaiśvadeva* of TB. 2, 1, 7 (which need not be translated here since it only mentions seventeen dedications of the milk),[19] the same brāhmaṇa has another *vaiśvadeva* in 2, 1, 8, 2 f., which is ninefold and placed in the context of a passage on milking the agnihotra cow. Obviously the occurrence side by side of two *vaiśvadevas* points to later addition. If our analysis has been correct, the first passage has been inserted and is partly based on the AB. The second passage agrees with the MS. in several respects, but also with the first passage.

TB. 2, 1, 8, 2 f.: This (agnihotra milk) is sacred to Vāyu when the calf has been admitted to the cow,[20] to the Aśvins when it is being milked, to Mitra[21] when it has been milked, to Aryaman when it is being removed from the fire, to Tvaṣṭṛ when it is being ladled out, to Bṛhaspati when it has been ladled out, to Savitṛ when the priest sets out to the āhavanīya with the milk, to Heaven and Earth when it is being taken (to the āhavanīya), to Indra and Agni when it has been set down near (the āhavanīya). He who offers the agnihotra offers to all these deities.

— The first reaction of the Taittirīyas to the AB. was the insertion of the first *vaiśvadeva*, in which the original version of the TB. (as translated above) was adapted to the version of the AB. Another reaction to the sixteenfold agnihotra of the AB. is found in an *anvākhyāna* of VādhS. 3, 37, which explicitly refers to a seventeenfold agnihotra. Its *vaiśvadeva* is completely identical with the TB. The context[22] connects this seventeenfold agnihotra with the seventeenfold *vājapeya* (which has seventeen *stotras*). The passage of the VādhS. seems to have been adopted by JB. 1, 21, which is secondary in omitting the explanation of the seventeenfold character of the *vājapeyā*[23] and in mixing this passage up with another on the stumbling-block (*sthāṇu*) of the agnihotra. For the seventeenfold *vaiśvadeva* of the JB. see the reconstruction of *JB. I, 1–65*, p. 68.[24] The critical ed. has 13 items, ms. *ya* 15 items. A remoter parallel is found in the

ŚB. Śauceya Prācīnayogya interrogates Uddālaka Āruṇi on the agnihotra (11, 5, 3, 1–4). Uddālaka's answer does not only refer to the *vaiśvadeva* of the milk, as treated in this section, but also to the general *vaiśvadeva* of the agnihotra rite.[25]

ŚB. 11, 5, 3, 5–6: He (Uddālaka) said: "My agnihotra cow is Iḍā, Manu's daughter; my calf is sacred to Vāyu; the (cow) is likewise (sacred to Vāyu) when the calf has been admitted to her; their meeting is the Virāj; when being milked (the milk) is sacred to the Aśvins; when it has been milked to the All-gods; to Vāyu when it is being taken (to the gārhapatya); to Agni when it has been placed on the fire; to Indra and Agni[26] when it is being illuminated; to Varuṇa when water has been poured upon it; to Vāyu when it is being taken from the fire; to Heaven and Earth when it has been removed from the fire; to the Aśvins when it is being ladled out; to the All-gods when it has been ladled out; to Mahādeva when it has been lifted up; to Vāyu when it is being taken (to the āhavanīya); to Viṣṇu when it has been held down.

— This *vaiśvadeva* of the ŚB. obviously does not belong to the line of development MS.–TB.–AB.–TB.–VādhS.–JB. It should be noted that the corresponding sūtra (KŚS. 25, 2, 3) does not follow the ŚB. There are some agreements between the ŚB. and the other texts. The version of the GB., which has the same context, differs in some points.

GB. 1, 3, 12: He (Uddālaka) said: "When in my cow Iḍā it is sacred to Rudra; to Manu when she has been summoned (to be milked); to Vāyu when the calf has been admitted to her; to Virāj when the calf is being lead away;[27] to the world (or this world, the earth: *jagat*)[28] when the calf has been lead away; to the Aśvins when it is being milked; to Soma when it has been milked; to Bṛhaspati when one sets out with the milk (for the gārhapatya); to Heaven and Earth when it is being taken (to the gārhapatya);[29] to Agni when it is being placed on (the gārhapatya); to Vaiśvānara when it has been placed on (the fire); to Viṣṇu when it is being illuminated; to the Maruts when it has been illuminated; to Pūṣan when it rises; to Varuṇa[30] when it has overflown; to Sarasvatī[30] when water has been poured on; to Tvaṣṭṛ when it is being removed (from the fire); to Dhātṛ when it has been removed; to the All-gods[31] when it is being ladled out; to Savitṛ[31] when it has been ladled out; to Bṛhaspati[31] when the priest has set out with the milk (for the āhavanīya); to Heaven and Earth when it is being taken (to the āhavanīya);[29] to Indra when it is being placed near (the fire); to Bala when it has been placed near (the fire). The kindling-stick is sacred to Agni (...), the second libation to Prajāpati; therefore it is fuller.

NOTES

[1] Rudra is often connected with cattle in the brāhmaṇas, mostly in an unfavourable respect (because he produces contagious diseases).

[2] Cf. ŚB. 12, 4, 1, 11, where the calf is the wind which makes the cow of heaven yield milk (rain).

[3] The Aśvins are also connected with spending fluid (mostly called honey).

[4] The product milk is frequently called *soma* in symbolical contexts.

[5] The milk in the *agnihotrasthālī*, which is placed on, or rather near, the gārhapatya (= earth), represents the ocean (= Varuṇa). See, however, also n. 6.

[6] Mitra and Varuṇa represent two different aspects of the milk. The fresh milk put on the gārhapatya belongs to Varuṇa, the boiled milk to Mitra. See Gonda, *The Vedic God Mitra* (Leiden 1972), p. 25 and 35 and *Dual Deities* (Amsterdam 1974), p. 194.

[7] The bubbles or drops are the raindrops produced by the Maruts. In other versions they denote the plurality of the gods as represented by the Viśve Devas.

[8] Whatever the correct etymology of Pūṣan may be, he is often connected with with *puṣyati* "to thrive, increase" in Vedic texts. Pūṣan is mentioned in a formula recited when the calf which should make the milk swell, is led to the cow (see e.g. ĀpŚS. 6, 3, 10). Here the milk in the *agnihotrasthālī* swells up (i.e. rises).

[9] Sarasvatī, the "flowing" deity.

[10] This identification at first sight does not make much sense. Moreover, *pratinīyamānam* has no parallel in the other versions, which omit the addition of water. The 10th item of the series of stages is *pratiṣṭhāpyamānam* in the reconstructed version of the JB. So one might be induced to replace *pratinīyamānam* by *pratinidhīyamānam* or to interpret *nī* as lead rather than as pour. The identification of this drawing from the fire in three moves with Viṣṇu (of the three steps) looks convincing. However, the verb used to denote the pouring of water is *pratyānī* (BŚS. 3, 5, 3) or even *pratinī* (in the corresponding sūtra MŚS. 1, 6, 1, 18). So *pratinīyamānam* should be retained and refer to the pouring of water. The connection with Viṣṇu may be based on the soothing action of the water. Viṣṇu gives *śānti*.

[11] The milk leaves the earth (= gārhapatya) and is bound for heaven (= āhavanīya).

[12] The beginning of an action is often made on the instigation (*prasava*) of Savitṛ.

[13] The space between the two fires is the space between heaven and earth.

[14] Indra and Agni are the two deities of the agnihotra (connected with the two daily performances). For Indra in the function of Sūrya cf. 4, n. 2; 6.15, n. 14.

[15] See Section 6.9 for Prajāpati's relation with the kindling-stick.

[16] On the one hand the separate category of the Viśve Devas is often mentioned at the end of an enumeration, on the other hand *vaiśvadevam* may also refer to all the gods mentioned before. On the encompassing function of the final and often additional element (especially in connection with the Viśve Devas) see *JB. I, 1–65*, p. 87 ff.

[17] The AB. differs from the MS. in making the overflowing milk sacred to the Maruts and in connecting the Viśve Devas, instead of the Maruts, with the bubbles. The position of the Maruts in the series of deities remains the same, viz. 7th. There are some more differences.

[18] See the discussion on the right time for the performance of the agnihotra, *JB. I, 1–65*, p. 29 f., where the situation is comparable. The original, older passage of the TB. is augmented by an insertion which obviously is based on the AB.

[19] Of the 19 stages of the milk in the MS., 11 are found in the TB. without important changes. Of the other six four have a parallel in the AB.

[20] The context refers to this action. This may have been the cause of its being mentioned first and of the omission of the first stage (*raudraṃ gavi*).

[21] This dedication has no parallel. Moreover the fresh milk is not sacred to Mitra according to other texts (see n. 6). Is the text corrupt?

[22] See Section 10 (n. 46).

[23] See Section 10 (end).

[24] The differences between the JB. and the VādhS. (= TB.) are: "sacred to Agni and Soma" instead of "sacred to Soma" (when it has been milked); "sacred to the Maruts" instead of "sacred to the All-gods" (when there are bubbles; — here the JB. agrees with the MS.); "sacred to Viṣṇu" instead of "sacred to Dhātṛ" (while being taken from the fire; — the parallelism of the actions is not complete; moreover the tenth item of the MS. is also connected with Viṣṇu); "sacred to the All-gods" instead of "sacred to Bṛhaspati" (after it has been ladled out; cf. ŚB. below). Evidently the version of the JB. has been influenced by the MS.

[25] See Section 6.15.

[26] See Gonda, *Dual Deities*, p. 295.

[27] Thus, I translate (not without doubts) *vatsam unnīyamānam*. See M.-W.'s dictionary: "to lead away (e.g. calf from its mother)". All the other items refer to stages of the milk. A locative is used do denote a particular situation of the cow (*raudraṃ gavi*). The accusative *vatsam unnīyamānam* is odd. An absolute acc. or an acc. of extension of time may be assumed here. See 6.1, n. 8. Or should *unnīyamānam* refer to the milk which is rising towards (acc.) the calf on account of its presence and its sucking?

[28] If the last mentioned interpretation of n. 27 should be correct, the calf would represent the earth. Cf. JB. 1, 39 which refers to heaven and earth in connection with the cow and the calf which has been led to her.

[29] This late brāhmaṇa contains several additions to the transmitted *vaiśva-deva* of the other texts and of its source, the ŚB. Heaven and earth should be connected with the course between gārhapatya (earth) and āhavanīya (heaven), not with movements towards the gārhapatya. Cf. MS. (Section 16, n. 13).

[30] Some items have been transposed. Varuṇa belongs to the water which is added, Sarasvatī to the overflowing milk. See the versions of the MS. and the ŚB.

[31] Again a transposition. The milk (and the priest) setting out for the āhavanīya is sacred to Savitṛ (see n. 12). When it has been ladled out it is sacred to the All-gods (cf. ŚB. "having been milked" and "having been ladled out" = *vaiśvadeva*), who represent totality, instead of Savitṛ.

— Since the concept of *tarpaṇa* plays a role in the daily *gṛhya* ritual, the occurrence of the root *tṛp* and its derivations in agnihotra contexts should not be left unnoticed. All kinds of powers are satisfied, gratified or pleased in the so-called *vaiśvadeva* of the agnihotra (see Section 6.15). There, however, the root *prī* is used (in JB. 1, 41 together with *tṛp*). In the following passages the satisfaction of all kinds of powers is explicitly expressed by *tṛp*.

TB. 2, 1, 5, 10: The gods who come in the evening and those who come in the morning come to the house of the performer of the agnihotra. If he should not satisfy them, they would keep aloof from his offspring and his cattle. If he should satisfy them, they, being satisfied, would satisfy him with offspring and cattle. In the evening he touches at the same time (both ladles), saying: "With the gods who come in the evening"; in the morning saying: "With the gods who come in the morning". (Thereby) he satisfies the gods who come in the evening as well as those who come in the morning. They, being satisfied, satisfy him with offspring and cattle.[1]

TB. 2, 1, 8, 3: Just as he satisfies (refreshes) the cow upon descent into a river (*tīrtha*), even so the cow of the agnihotra satisfies the sacrificer. He is satisfied with offspring and cattle, he knows heaven, he sees (i.e. lives to see) his son and his grandson, he is productive in offspring and cattle by pairs, he, for whom, knowing thus, they offer the agnihotra, as well as he who thus knows this (agnihotra).[2]

— The particular knowledge of the implications of the agnihotra can only refer to the *vaiśvadeva* of the milk, which has been treated in the preceding passage. Apparently all these gods have been satisfied and will satisfy the sacrificer in their turn. The AB. version of this *vaiśvadeva* also mentions prosperity (especially in connection with cattle) as the result of this agnihotra.

JB. 1, 41: Then he wipes off (the ladle). When he wipes it off the first time, he thereby gratifies the Gandharvas and the Apsarases. To him the Gandharvas and Apsarases say: "Thy faith must not disappear. Become satisfied with all one may wish. Reach the world of heaven". (...)[3] When he eats twice by means of his finger, when he eats the first time, the *prāṇa* and *apāna* thereby are satisfied. To him (...)[3]

ŚB. 11, 6, 2, 6–10: These two libations after having been offered rise upwards. They enter the space between heaven and earth. They make the space between heaven and earth an āhavanīya fire, the wind its kindling-stick, the sun-motes the pure libation. They satisfy the space between heaven and earth and rise upwards then. They enter heaven (...). They satisfy heaven and then return. They enter this earth (...). They satisfy this earth and then rise upwards. They enter man (..). They satisfy man. He who, knowing thus, eats food, by him the agnihotra is offered (..). They enter a woman (..). They satisfy the woman. He who, knowing thus, has sexual intercourse, by him the agnihotra is offered.[4]

— See also the beginning of ŚāṅkhB. 2, 7 (Section 1.3) for *tṛpti* in connection with the agnihotra. On the successive *tṛptis* produced by the *prāṇāgnihotra bhojanavidhi* see below (cf. ŚB. 11, 6, 2, 6–10 above on eating food by way of agnihotra):

GB. 1, 3, 14: If someone, knowing thus,[5] eats and drinks, thereby his speech becomes satisfied. When speech has become satisfied, fire (Agni) becomes satisfied. When fire (Agni) has become satisfied, the earth becomes satisfied. When the earth has become satisfied, all beings which are connected with the earth, become satisfied. (...).[6] If someone, knowing thus, eats and drinks, then his right hand here is the *juhū* ladle, his left hand the *upabhṛt* ladle, his throat the *dhruvā*, food the oblation, his breaths (*prāṇāḥ;* or: vital powers) the fires. There is always sacrificed, always offered; food and drink are always given in the form of the agnihotra by him who knows thus and who, knowing thus, offers the agnihotra.[7]

VādhS. 3, 21: Prajāpati thus offered this agnihotra. By that he became successful, by that he satisfied all beings (..). Going to heaven he transferred it to his sons, the gods. The gods offered it, they thereby satisfied all beings (...). Going to heaven the seers transferred it to their sons, the brahmins. The brahmins thus partake of this agnihotra. He who, knowing thus, offers the agnihotra, becomes successful, satisfies all beings, attains all he can attain, and wins the world of heaven.

— The few passages in which *tṛp* plays a role in the context of the agnihotra all point to a general, cosmic satisfaction which includes all beings. It is one of the secondary aspects of this rite which seem to connect it with the *gṛhya* ritual.

NOTES

1 See Section 6.5 (n. 16).

2 See Section 6.1.

[3] Repetitions have been omitted. The text also states that the *udāna* and *apāna* are satisfied. However, the *samāna*, *vyāna* and the embryos are propitiated (*prī*).

[4] See Section 13.5.

[5] The preceding context refers to an esoteric expiation for the extinction of all fires as taught by Uddālaka Āruṇi (cf. ŚB. 11, 5, 3, 8–13). If all fires become extinguished and no wind is blowing, one should offer the oblation into oneself, i.e. eat it.

[6] The rest of this classification has been omitted. The other *prāṇāḥ* satisfied here are *prāṇa*, *cakṣuḥ*, *manas* and *śrotram*. A similar identification with cosmic elements is found there. See also GB. 1, 2, 22 for an identical (but shortened) *tarpaṇa*.

[7] This *prāṇāgnihotra* passage has a parallel in ChU. 5, 19 ff. and ŚāṅkhĀ. 10. See *Agn.* and *Prāṇāgn.*, ch. IX.

— The agnihotra plays an important part in the esoteric discussions, the *brahmodyas*, in which in addition to the brahmins the kṣatriyas also participated. It is, however, to be noted that the oldest agnihotra sections hardly contain any reference to these discussions. KS. (6, 6), MS. (1, 8, 7) and TB. (2, 1, 9) (as well as GB. 1, 3, 15) only mention an internal discussion among the Praiyamedhas on the agnihotra. The typical context of contest is missing. Since this passage in the GB. is preceded by some sort of *brahmodya* (the interrogation of Uddālaka followed by an exposition on the *prāṇāgnihotra*) and followed by some questions and answers on the exclamation *svāhā* in the typical style of the *brahmodyas*, one may assume that the passage on the Praiyamedhas[1] originally represented such a *brahmodya*. Another passage in which the context of the debate is missing is the *pañcāgnividyā* of JB. 1, 45–46. The parallels of the ChU. and the BĀU. place this doctrine in the context of the defeat of a young brahmin in an interrogation by a kṣatriya. Perhaps even these parallels do not represent real *brahmodyas* (verbal contests). On the other hand one should bear in mind that several levels of *brahmodyas* may have existed. Every inquiring into the nature of ritualistic and cosmic problems seems to have been denoted by the term *brahmodya*, as may appear from the technical term *brahmavādin*. These "scholars" are always introduced in the text when a question is raised (or an objection to a particular approach is made). The TB. e.g. has several references to *brahmavādins*, i.e. to the existence of *brahmodyas*. However, there is no denying that the real *brahmodyas* (discussions with aggressive aspects in which often some issue is at stake) are found only in late brāhmaṇas such as the ŚB., JB. and GB. This should warn us against drawing hasty conclusions as to the original nature of these verbal contests.[2] Some translations of the frameworks of these discussions are given below.

ŚB. 11, 5, 3, 1 ff.; Śauceya Prācīnayogya came to Uddālaka Āruṇi for a discussion thinking "I want to know the agnihotra". He said: "Gautama, what is thy agnihotra cow, what the calf? (..) What is (the milk) when being milked? (...)[3] Why, having offered, dost thou shake (the ladle)? (....)".[4] He (Uddālaka) said: "My agnihotra cow is Iḍā, Manu's daughter, my calf is sacred to Vāyu (...). When being milked (the milk) is sacred to the Aśvins (...).[3] When, having offered, I shake (the ladle), this is for Vāyu (...).[4] "This (knowledge), dear sir, belongs to both of us in common" he (Śauceya) said. Thus instructed Śauceya said: "I will ask thee a question, sir". "Ask, Prācīnayogya" he answered. He said: "If .....".[5] "Indeed, I did not know this" he (Śauceya) said. Śauceya, thus instructed, said: "Here are logs of fuel and kindling-sticks.[6] I must approach thee, sir, (as a pupil)". He said: "If thou hadst not spoken thus, thy head would have fallen off. Come, approach me (as a pupil)". "So be it" he said. He initiated him with the *upanayana* ritual and told him that utterance which conquers sorrow: Truth. Therefore one should speak truth.

— A close parallel of this passage is found in the later GB., which seems to have borrowed and enlarged on it.

GB. 1, 3, 11–14: Prācīnayogya came (to Uddālaka saying) "I want to ask thee about the agnihotra, Gautama". "Ask, Prācīnayogya". "Sacred to what deity (is the agnihotra milk while being) in the cow called Iḍā[7] (....)[3] Sacred to what deity does he thrice lift upwards the ladle after having offered? (.....)".[4] He said: "It is sacred to Rudra while being in the cow Iḍā (....)[3] When, having offered, I lifted the ladle thrice upwards, I thereby gratified the Rudras. (...)".[4] "This is so as thou, my dear, hast said. But let me ask you (once more) a question". "Ask, Prācīnayogya". "If ...".[5] "This is so as thou, dear Sir, hast said. I want to approach thee as thy pupil". "If thou hadst not spoken thus, thy head would have fallen off". "Well, I will teach thee in order that it will not fall off for thee".[8] "If someone, knowing thus, eats and drinks, his speech thereby becomes satisfied. (...)".[9]

— The obviously secondary version of the GB. makes an addition to the original passage (see n. 9); moreover the beginning of the passage, in which the name of Uddālaka has been omitted, seems to have been brought into connection with a preceding *brahmodya* in which Uddālaka was involved. In the ŚB. the two *brahmodyas*, which have no relation at all (the subject being different and Uddālaka being defeated in the first), are clearly separated by other passages. In the GB. as usual everything goes wrong. After an interrogation by Svaidāyana (GB. 1, 3, 6–8) Uddālaka gives gold to him in order to avoid a public debate.[10] Parallel to the version of the ŚB. Svaidāyana dissuades his fellow-brahmins from a debate. In the ŚB. thereupon Uddālaka comes to Svaidāyana in order to receive instruction on the questions asked by him (Svaidāyana) before. In the version of the GB. Svaidāyana's fellow-brahmins come to Uddālaka as his pupils and want to receive instruction on the questions (what questions???) asked by him before. So Uddālaka instead of Svaidāyana gives an exposition of these ritualistic problems in GB. 1, 3, 9–10. Linking up with this passage in GB. 1, 3, 11 Prācīnayogya comes to him (i.e. obviously to Uddālaka of the preceding section; therefore no explicit mentioning of his name was required) and addresses him as Gautama in a question on the agnihotra. There can be no doubt on the secondary character of the composition of this brāhmaṇa. A similar close parallel is found between passages of the JB. and the ŚB. (and to some extent the VādhS.) dealing with a discussion between Janaka and Yājñavalkya. Here the relation between the texts is less perspicuous, though arguments may be adduced[11] to prove that the version of the JB. is less original.

ŚB. 11, 3, 1, 1 ff.: Regarding this[12] Janaka, king of Videha, asked Yājñavalkya: "Do you know the agnihotra, Yājñavalkya?" "I know it, great king". "What is it?" "Milk". "If there were no milk, with what would you offer?" (...)[13] He said: "Then (i.e. if even water and other substitutes would be missing) there would be nothing here, and still this would be offered, viz. truth into faith". "You know the agnihotra, Yājñavalkya. I give you a hundred cows" he said. Concerning this there are also these verses:[14] (......)

JB. 1, 19: Now as to this[12] Janaka, king of Videha, asked Yājñavalkya: "Do you know the agnihotra (oblation), Yājñavalkya?" "I know" he said. "What is it?". "Milk". "If there would be no milk, whereby would you perform the offering?" (...)[13] He said: "Then, indeed, there would be nothing at all here, and yet there would be offered here, viz. truth into faith". To him he spoke: "You know the agnihotra, Yājñavalkya. Honour to you. A thousand (cows) we give to you, Sir". Then he recited to him (the verse):[14] "(...)". (This means: ...) Vājasaneya said: "(...)". By saying that he meant (...).

— Apparently the JB., borrowing this passage from the Vājasaneyins of the ŚB., has tried to improve the composition by including the verses and responding verses in the discussion between Janaka and Yājñavalkya. This operation does not look quite successful. After the boon of hundred or thousand cows the debate has no continuation. A secondary parallel is found in the VādhS.

VādhS. 3, 40: Janaka, the king of Videha, asked Vājasaneya: "If, O priest, there would be no milk, with what would you offer the agnihotra?" (....)[13] "You think that you are too clever (....).[15] But (even if everything would be missing here) there is offered as it were". "That, dear Sir, I must try to know".[16] He (said): "Then thus come nearer to me". He came nearer. To him he said: "Yonder sun, O great king, is offered (into the fire)[17] in the evening, (the fire)[17] into the sun in the morning".

— The passage ends with a vocabulary ("come nearer") which reminds us of the esoteric talk between Yājñavalkya and Ārtabhāga. The contents of Yājñavalkya's words, however, are rather meagre and bring nothing new. The *anvākhyāna* of the VādhS. tries to confirm the position of its brāhmaṇa in these esoteric discussions by adducing an old and rather too well-known doctrine which once was put forward by TB. 2, 1, 6, 5. The secondary adaptation is evident. A less obvious connection between the ŚB. and the JB. is found in the following two passages which do not represent two versions, but rather two vague parallels.

ŚB. 11, 6, 2, 1 ff.: Janaka, the king of Videha, once came together with some brahmins who were driving about,[18] Śvetaketu the son of (Uddālaka) Āruṇi, Somaśuṣma Sātyayajñin and Yājñavalkya. He said to them: "How does each of you perform the agnihotra?". Śvetaketu, the son of Āruṇi, said: "I offer into each other two heats .."[19] (..) Then Yājñavalkya said: "When I take out the fire, then I present (offer)[20] the agnihotra. When the sun sets, all the gods follow him. When they see this fire taken out by me, they turn back (towards it). Having cleansed the vessels (used for the agnihotra) and having them placed ready, and having the agnihotra cow milked, I satisfy them, seeing them while they see me". "Yājñavalkya, your investigation most closely approximates the (true nature of the) agnihotra. I give you a hundred cows" he said; "but even you do not know (or: refer in your investigation to) the rising, the destination,[21] the resting-place, the satisfaction, the return and the renascent world of these two (libations)". Having spoken thus he mounted his chariot and drove off.[22] They said: "This rājanya[23] has outwitted us in the debate. Come on, let us challenge him to a debate". Yājñavalkya said: "We are brahmins and he belongs to the *rājanyas.*[23] If we should defeat him, whom would we say to have defeated? But if he should defeat us, they would say of us that one of the *rājanyas* had defeated brahmins. Do not take this (plan) seriously". They approved of this (suggestion) of his. But Yājñavalkya mounted his chariot and drove away after (the *rājanya*). He overtook him. He (Janaka) said "(Is it) to know the agnihotra, Yājñavalkya?" "The agnihotra indeed, great king". "These two libations after having been offered rise upwards (...)[24] The son who is born therefrom is the renascent world. This is the agnihotra, Yājñavalkya. There is nothing superior to this". Thus he spoke. Yājñavalkya gave him a free choice. He said: "O Yājñavalkya, let there be for me an unrestrained freedom of questioning you". Since that time Janaka was a brahmin.

— Janaka represents the more progressive point of view (as in the preceding *brahmodya* of this section both Janaka and Yājñavalkya). Mental agnihotras, *prāṇāgnihotras* and *pañcāgnividyās* form the new topics. The traditional metaritualism of the brahmins does not go beyond the well-known alternation sun-into-fire, fire-into-sun, and identifies sun as well as fire with traditionally favourite objects as glory and light. Now it is remarkable that in the following debate from the JB. the same old views are put forward by the brahmins, but Janaka hardly surpasses them at first sight. On closer examination, however, it turns out that only the way of presenting the material is traditional; the ideas put forward by Janaka are different. Most of the brahmins identify sun and fire with the same high aim. The most evolved point of view is mentioned by the last brahmin (cf. Yājñavalkya in the ŚB.), Vaiyāghrapadya, who connects the sun with the *arka* and the fire with the *aśvamedha*. Janaka starts also from the sun-into-fire and fire-into-sun concept, adopts the differentiation introduced by Vaiyāghrapadya, but makes a more important identification. By equating the sun with the *gati* (the goal of the sacrifice: immortality) and the fire with the *iti* ("the way towards this goal"?) he makes the agnihotra a means of deliverance. Very impressive and new, however, is Janaka's view not at all. Several passages in Section 13.4 contain the same ideas in a different form.

JB. 1, 22–25: Āruṇi, Vājasaneya, Barku, Vārṣṇa, Priya Jānaśruteya and Buḍila Āśvatarāśvi Vaiyāghrapadya, these were five great brahmins. They (once) said: "Janaka, that king of Videha, is well-instructed on the subject of the agnihotra. He considers himself superior to us in disputation. Come, we shall make him discuss the agnihotra". They came there. They said to a pupil (who received them): "Announce us". He announced them. For them after they had been announced (to the king), he (the king) prepared separate seats, (vessels of) water, *madhuparka* drinks, abodes (to stay overnight), (i.e.) the five obeisances separately to each of the five. Then he went to have a meeting with them, having shaved the hair of his head and beard, having cut his nails and anointed his eyes and body, carrying a staff and wearing sandals. He said to them: "O brahmins, how is it that you have invited us for a debate?" "You are superior to us in the debate". Then he took the initiative and asked them: "Brahmins, how do you offer the agnihotra?" "You outwit us indeed in the debate", they said, "since you have taken the initiative and questioned us who are more than one. Gautama, answer (first)". He said: (...).[25] "Well-offered! I must gratify you, gentlemen", thus he (Janaka) praised. (...) "Well-offered!", having thus praised, he said: "Assuredly, to him who might tell me what are the goal (of the sacrifice; or of life in general) and the means for coming there in the agnihotra, I should like to give a boon". They said: "We have not studied the goal and the means for coming there in the agnihotra.

You must tell us the goal and the means for coming there in the agnihotra. We separately give you five boons". Pointing at the fire he said: "This is the means for coming there (or: the way: *iti*)" and at the sun: "That is the goal. So I offer that goal in this means for coming there in the evening and this means for coming there in that goal at dawn". (..) "Well-offered!", having thus praised they said: "Choose the boons we have granted". He said: "This is my choice: Let me give you separately (i.e. each of you) thousand (cows) and five hundred horses". These were the reflections on the agnihotra, these were the aims. These very aims he obtains who knows thus and for whom (a priest) knowing thus performs the agnihotra.

— Finally there is a passage in the VādhS. which is not a formal *brahmodya* in the sense of a contest in which reputation or boons form the stake. The discussion takes place between Uddālaka and two famous pupils, Yājñavalkya and Kauṣītaki. On the one hand the discussion makes a rather artificial impression. The *guru* questions his pupils who might be supposed to have obtained their information from him himself. On the other hand one may assume that studentship (*brahmacarya*) did not always imply a unique period from *upanayana* up to *samāvartana*, to be concluded on reaching a certain age. The really famous debaters travelled about and were students at several places.

VādhS. 3, 39: With (Uddālaka) Āruṇi some old-time scholars[26] were living as students, viz. Kauṣītaki, Vājasaneya (and others).[27] Āruṇi (once) asked them during a rest taken in the daytime: "How does the one (of you) interpret (lit.: know) the agnihotra, how the other, how a third?". The one said: "The kindling-stick is a mouth, the oblation represents the food. (...)"[28] But Āruṇi said: "Thus you consider it, but we consider: Let us win heaven with the first libation and find a firm footing in offspring and cattle in this world with the second libation". The old-time scholars ranged oneself on the side of Āruṇi,[29] for he included in his interpretation (lit.: knew) both worlds, this and yonder one.[30]

NOTES

1 See Section 6.14.

2 See author, *IIJ* 16, p. 90, n. 17.

3 For the complete *vaiśvadeva* of the milk see Section 16.

4 For the *vaiśvadeva* of the actions performed after the offering (occurring separately from the other *vaiśvadeva* in the older texts) see 6.15.

5 Prācīnayogya's questions refer to expiations for the extinction of the fires. Since the expiations are left out of account in this publication, these

questions and the answers have not been translated here. It should be noted, however, that these expiations have a rather esoteric character. They teach the identification of fires and *prāṇāḥ* and are important for the prāṇāgnihotra. See *Agn. and Prāṇāgn.*, ch. III.

[6] The usual attributes of the pupil who wants to be initiated by a guru.

[7] Miss Gaastra, *Das Gopatha Brāhmaṇa*, p. 38 erroneously assumes a word *gavīḍa*.

[8] Again one of the secondary, nonsensical traits of this GB. The teaching does not prevent the loss of his head (what would happen to all other uninitiated brahmins?); it is the admission that the other debater has a superior knowledge and the confirmation of this admission by wanting to become his pupil which saves him.

[9] For the passage omitted here see Section 17 (n. 5). It is definitely a later addition by the GB. See *Agn. and Prāṇāgn.*, ch. III (p. 224) for arguments.

[10] See author, *IIJ* 16, p. 88.

[11] See *JB. I, 1–65*, p. 62.

[12] The interrogation is preceded by some equations (cow, calf etc. are identified with vital powers in man) in both versions. In the JB. some essential equations are missing. The introductory symbolism as well as the conclusion of the interrogation refer to a mental substitute of the agnihotra (as usual introduced as an expiation).

[13] For the passage left untranslated here see Section 5.

[14] The verses, which originally did not belong to the discussion, have been placed after this debate, because they also refer to symbolic or mental performances of the agnihotra. The *pravāsa* of the agnihotrin (left out of account in this publication) forms the subject.

[15] Janaka almost went to far in his questioning, a point which irritates Yājñavalkya in other debates (BĀU. 3, 6; 3, 9, 24 f.). The VādhS. introduces *sat* and *asat* as the substitutes for the oblation; quite odd and only used to make Janaka's question "If there were no *sat* and *asat* . . ." more extreme. Without *sat* and *asat* no cosmos can exist. The version of the VādhS. is obviously secondary, as appears from this cosmogonic motif (cf. ṚV. 10, 129, 1), which is out of place here. There is a gap in the text. So much is clear that Yājñavalkya seems to have declared that the situation of *na sat, nāsat* was found before this cosmos came into existence.

[16] Perhaps instead of *vividiṣāṇīti* there should be read *vividiṣāmīti* (cf. ŚB. 11, 5, 3, 1).

[17] There is a gap in the text, which causes no problems, since the doctrine is well-known.

[18] See author, "Vedic *dhāvayati*", *IIJ* 16, p. 88 f.

[19] Eggeling's translation has to be rejected (see 13.1, n. 3), because the usual theory is that the sun enters the fire or is offered into it. See 13.1 for a partial translation of what has been omitted here.

[20] Eggeling translates ". . I thereby raise". The meaning of *udyam* probably is "to hold up, present, offer". The time of the *uddharaṇa* and of the offering are different. According to the ŚB. (and perhaps also Yājñavalkya) there should be offered after sunset, but the *uddharaṇa* should take place before sunset (ŚB. 2, 3, 1, 7). Taking out the fire before sunset means presenting the agnihotra to the gods before they disappear with the setting sun. In fact Yājñavalkya's ideas agree with ŚB. 2, 3, 1, 7, where the gods come as guests to one's house and disappear if the fire has not been taken out in time. See Section 4 (n. 46 ff.). Yājñavalkya's interpretation hardly brings anything new, and, moreover, does not refer to the central concept of the agnihotra.

[21] On *gati* see Minard, *Trois Énigmes* II, 172 *a*.

[22] See author, *IIJ* 16, p. 89. n. 13.

[23] According to M.-W.'s dictionary *rājanyabandhu* should mean "the friend or connection of a prince (generally used in contempt)", an analysis of the compound which has to be rejected. See, however, also the meaning attributed to *kṣatrabandhu* "'a mere Kshatriya', i.e. a Kshatriya by birth but not by his actions (a term of abuse)". Probably the pejorative aspect was originally absent. The compound denotes someone who belongs to the group of the rājanyas or kṣatriyas. The explicit reference to the class to which someone belongs may have produced the pejorative connotation which in fact belongs to the agonistic context rather than being inherent in the term itself. Janaka is not a bad or mean kṣatriya — this view would not be upheld even by these brahmins —, but the fact that he is a kṣatriya would have to disqualify him. The pejorative aspect seems to be present also in the compounds *dvijabandhu* and *mātṛbandhū* ("an unnatural mother"; i.e. someone who has to be counted among the category of the mothers without actually, i.e. biologically, being a mother).

[24] See Section 13.5 for a complete translation of Janaka's doctrine of the five fires.

[25] See Section 13.1 for a translation of Gautama's (i.e. Uddālaka's or Āruṇi's) views. The interpretations of the other brahmins come almost to the same.

[26] The expression *pūrve śrotriyāḥ* would seem to point to a comparatively late date for this sūtra, which mostly is regarded as belonging to the brāhmaṇa period (see e.g. Renou, *Écoles vediques*, p. 179: ".. ou plutôt le Vādhūla est en tous points similaire à un Br."). One may doubt whether even late brāhmaṇas such as the ŚB. would refer to Yājñavalkya as a *pūrva*.

[27] Caland remarks that *yat* (translated by "wie", i.e. "such as") is grammatically odd. Mostly it denotes "namely". The difficulty lies with the plurality of the *śrotriyāḥ* who give their opinions and the two names mentioned here.

[28] For the views of the pupils on the way of offering the libation on the kindling-stick see Section 6.12.

[29] Caland: "Die Konstruktion des Schlusssatzes, wo *āruṇino* aus *āruṇinā u* kontrahiert zu sein scheint, ist schwierig; meine Übersetzung ist nur ein Versuch". His translation runs: "Da fielen die Gelehrten der früheren Zeit dem Āruṇi, der zuletzt geredet hatte, bei". Indeed, the contents of this sentence should be that the others decide to agree with Āruṇi. I take *āruṇo* as a genitive with *jaghanyena* ("behind"). Either *jaghanyena* is corrupt for *jaghanena*, or it has the same meaning as *jaghanye* or *jaghanyam*. The genitive *pūrveṣām* has the force of an instrumental with the verbal adjective *pratikrāntam*. The expression may refer to an ancient way of voting, i.e. to take one's stand behind someone, to range oneself or line up with someone.

[30] The pupils had stated that the second libation should be poured on top of the first libation, at least not beside the kindling-stick. Āruṇi takes the same view, but uses a superior argumentation. Caland observes that the sūtra (not to be confused with the *anvākhyāna*) prescribes: *uttara uttarām āhutiṃ juhoti*, "wo *uttare* mit *uttarārdhe* gleichzusetzen ist". Of course the pupils know that the second libation should not hit upon the first one (the *sthāṇu* problem). If now they reject offering beside the kindling-stick, it is obvious that they offer beyond (*atihāya* as some sūtras state) the first libation, since a backward movement is out of the question in the ritual. On the ritual the brahmins agree here. On account of his metaritualism Āruṇi is quoted here honoris causa (*asya praśaṃsārtham* as the commentary on the sūtra states; see *AO* 4, p. 4).

APPENDIX

The agnihotra and the gṛhya ritual

Yājñavalkya already noticed the *gṛhya* aspects of the *śrauta agnihotra*.[1] The rite also has a counterpart in the *gṛhya* ritual and the authors of the *gṛhya sūtras* do not fail to refer to the *śrauta* texts for details which both rituals have in common.[2] He who has set up his *gṛhya* fire[3] is identified with the *āhitāgni*.[4] The daily evening and morning libations are regarded as *agnihotras*.[5] This correspondence was not left unnoticed in secondary literature.[6] However, it may be useful to collect the relevant facts in order to have a better insight into this question of relationship.

It seems to be rather useless to speculate on the original character of the fire ritual, whether one fire was used or more (as in the systematized *śrauta agnihotra*). It is beyond doubt that the *agnihotra* in one or other form should be old.[7] The fire ritual as described in the *gṛhya sūtras* is definitely later than its *śrauta* counterpart (on which it may have been modelled in some respects) though it may continue an old tradition.

The relation between the non-*śrauta* evening and morning ceremonies and the *agnihotra*, however, is more complex than might be assumed at first sight. It is not merely a question of elaborately offering in a sacred fire (the *āhavanīya*) compared to a simpler libation in the *gṛhya* fire. All kind of ancillary rituals belonging to the *agnihotra* as well as to the Hindu daily ceremonies make the exact connection obscure. Several daily rites[8] (i.a. the *prāṇāgnihotra bhojanavidhi*, left out of account here because of its extensive treatment elsewhere) have been regarded as continuations of the agnihotra. The direct *gṛhya* counterpart no doubt is the daily *homa* in the *aupāsana* fire every night and morning (*sāyaṃprātar*). A confusing factor is formed by the existence of other daily offerings which according to some texts are also offered *sāyaṃprātar*,[9] viz. the *vaiśvadeva* and the *devayajña* among the "five great sacrifices" (*pañcamahāyajñas*). To put it quite plainly at the very outset: the *sāyaṃprātarhoma* is different from the *vaiśvadeva*, and the latter is identical with the *devayajña*.

The so-called *pañca mahāyajñāḥ* in fact represent a systematization based on texts[10] rather than being (originally at least) a fixed reality. Indeed, honouring gods, other beings, ancestors, guests and the sacred script was a daily duty. There was, however, no established fivefold ritual. The texts do not agree on the *pitṛyajña*. Is it the *tarpaṇa* belonging to the early *saṃdhyā* and *snāna* ritual? Or does it refer to a *baliharaṇa* performed after the *devayajña*? Both *tarpaṇa* and *baliharaṇa* include in their worship gods and *bhūtas* beside the *pitṛs*. The position of the *brahmayajña* (recitation or study of sacred texts) is not fixed either. The coherent (and very short) *pañcamahāyajñas* as described by Raṅgachari, *The Sri Vaishnava Brahmans* (Madras 1931), p. 92–93 are an obviously late systematization. If according to some texts the *devayajña* means the offering in the fire to the gods, this does not imply that the *sāyaṃpratārhoma* may serve as the *devayajña*. It is the *vaiśvadeva* which, having a more general connection with the gods, fulfils this function. Kane, *Hist. of Dh.* II, 1, p. 699 seems to be wrong in connecting ŚGS. 1, 5 (*huta* = *agnihotra*) with the *mahāyajñas*. Ram Gopal, *India of Vedic Kalpasūtras* (Delhi 1959), p. 388 f. includes both the *vaiśvadeva* and the *aupāsanahoma* among the *devayajñas* without differentiating the time and the implication of the performance.

By extension (?) the *vaiśvadeva* seems to denote the *devayajña* as well as the *bhūtayajña* and the *pitṛyajña*.[11] In so far as it refers only to the offering into the fire, a clear distinction has to be made with the *sāyaṃprātarhoma*, the direct representative of the agnihotra. First it should be noted that both rituals (explicitly mentioned under their own name or not) are found in different passages in the *gṛhya* sūtras.[12] Comparing these data one at once discovers several distinguishing marks. The time of the (agnihotra) *sāyaṃprātarhoma* corresponds to the (varying) regulations of the *śrauta* texts. As a rule the moments of sunset and sunrise form the starting-points.[13] The *vaiśvadeva*, however, which is likewise performed twice a day (i.e. in the morning and in the evening), is offered at different moments, since it is correlated to the two daily meals.[14] This means that the morning *vaiśvadeva* is performed at noon rather than at sunrise. The evening *vaiśvadeva* may diverge less from the time of the agnihotra performance. The same shift of time may be seen in connection with the continuation of the agnihotra in the *prāṇāgnihotra bhojanavidhi*.

Since the *vaiśvadeva* belongs to the two daily meals and its oblatory material is formed by the food,[15] the oblation forms another distinguishing mark. The *sāyamprātarhoma* is performed with rice or barley, though other material is allowed.[16] The food of which the *vaiśvadeva* is the fore-offering (i.e. the daily *bhojana* represents the rest of the oblation) may be given to all kinds of animals and even to Caṇḍālas.[17] This would be out of the question with the (*gṛhya*) agnihotra.

The fire into which the *aupāsana homa* is offered is the sacred *gṛhya* fire, whereas the *vaiśvadeva* may even be offered into a *laukika* fire.[18]

The deities of the *sāyamprātarhoma* also occur in the *śrauta* agnihotra. The formulas run: *agnaye svāhā* (first libation in the evening), *prajāpataye svāhā* (according to some texts recited in thought or silently); *sūryāyā svāhā* (in the morning), *prajāpataye svāhā*.[19] In the *vaiśvadeva* several gods are invoked (in the dative with *svāhā*). The texts do not completely agree, but the following deities occur in most versions: Agni, Soma, Dhanvantari, Viśve Devāḥ, Prajāpati and (Agni) Sviṣṭakṛt. Further Dyāvā-Pṛthivī, Anumati, Sarve Devāḥ, a.o. are mentioned by some texts. So there can be no doubt about the difference between the two rituals.

Turning again to the *sāyamprātarhoma*, which seems to be more sacred than the *vaiśvadeva* and which represents the *gṛhya* version of the agnihotra, one may draw attention to the following agreements with the *śrauta* rite. The dedications to the deities have been mentioned above. The second libation, which in the *śrauta* version also belonged to Prajāpati, here is either accompanied by the formula *prajāpataye svāhā*, or is silently offered (as in the agnihotra). The second libation is larger according to some texts.[20] The ritual seems to be definitely simpler than in the agnihotra. Indeed a *samidh* is placed on the fire before the offering.[21] According to some texts the preparatory actions are the same as in the agnihotra. The offering, however, is performed with the hand instead of a sacrificial ladle, if at least the usual oblations of rice or barley are made. Some texts show a closer agreement with the *śrauta* rite. If the material of the agnihotra is used, the usual actions of this rite seem to take place as well.[22] Parallel to the *uddharaṇa* of the fire from the *gārhapatya* to the *āhavanīya* taking place before sunset and sunrise according to ŚB., the single fire should be kindled before sunrise and sunset.[23] Just as in the agnihotra the evening performance is regarded as the first; i.e. the *gṛhya* agnihotra should start with an evening offering[24] after the *gṛhya* version of the *agnyādhāna*.

Here we touch upon the problem of the difference between the sacred fires and their being set up and the single *gṛhya* fire which has a different *ādhāna*. In secondary literature statements sometimes are made about the parallelism between the *śrauta ādhāna* and its *gṛhya* counterpart. The fundamental difference, however, is that no fixed *ādhāna* ceremony is prescribed by the *gṛhya* sūtras. The parallelism with the *agnyādhāna* is sometimes realized; even *punarādhānas* are mentioned. However, the establishment of the *gṛhya* fire has a different background. Every independent person should have his own fire. He should not wait till he has reached a certain age or a particular amount of wealth. On the one hand this restriction limits the period within which the fire has to be established. On the other hand no uniform *ādhāna* is found, since opinions on the moment of becoming independent may differ. In this respect the most important caesura is the marriage. Several texts prescribe the use of the marriage fire for the daily offerings; i.e. the kindling of the fire used at the marriage ceremony forms the *ādhāna*. ĀśvGPariś. (ed. Aithal) 13 even observes that he who does not retain his marriage fire for this use and still considers himself to be a householder should not take food, since he cooks in vain. The implication of course is that one should eat only the remains of the oblation offered in this fire (the *aupāsanahoma*).[25]

The end of the period of studentship (which in practice does not make a great chronological difference) may also be used for the establishment of an own fire. The *snātaka*, who still has to marry in order to become a *gṛhastha*, becomes an independent person at the *samāvartana*. He takes his own fire from the guru's fire on which he has laid the *samidh* for the last time.[26]

When the head of the family dies, the eldest son takes over his position and establishes his own fire.[27] In fact the *gṛhya* fire is not only the fire which has a personal bond with the adult, settled, male human being, it is the fire of the hearth of the family as well.

When the inheritance is divided, i.e. probably in case of a partition of the joint family, fires may also be set up (by the adult males).

These are the four possibilities mentioned in the *gṛhya* sūtras.[28] These four refer to the moment of setting up the fire. The nature of the fire and the ceremony on the one hand depend on the circumstances, on the other hand are connected with definite aims. The position of the *snātaka* leaves no room for options. He just takes fire from his guru and a real *ādhāna* ceremony does not seem to be performed. When the head of the family dies, his fire should be extinguished[29] and a new fire has to be set up by his successor. In this case he may take fire from the house of rich or respected people,[30] but he may also produce fire with the two *araṇis* by churning. An official *ādhāna* ceremony after the model of the *śrauta ādhāna* is then possible.[31] The marriage fire does not seem to be connected with *ādhāna* ceremonies. However, even those who take their fire from the guru's fire or retain the marriage fire are not completely excluded from *ādhāna* ceremonies, since the texts prescribe *punarādhānas* (in fact perhaps taking over the position of the real *ādhānas*) for the extinction of the fire or the omission of offering in it for twelve days or more.[32].

Parallel to the *pūrṇāhuti* at the end of the *agnyādhāna*[33] which does not coincide with the first (i.e. evening) agnihotra, a special offering has to be made in the *gṛhya* ritual.[34] By doing so the evening is reserved for the first real *aupāsanahoma*, just as the agnihotra starts with the evening performance.[35] The parallelism with the *śrauta agnyādhāna* shows that the *aupāsanahoma* offered in the newly established fire is the real representative of the agnihotra.

Having clearly distinguished the *sāyamprātarhoma* from the *vaiśvadeva (devayajña)* we may now try to find traces of the agnihotra in the *vaiśvadeva* as well. The agnihotra lives on in several ceremonies. The *sāyamprātarhoma* continues (or rather runs parallel to) the offering in the fire. It is concerned with the same deities and remains connected with the same time of the day for the performance. I.e. the original basic concept of the sunset-sunrise rituals recurs in the *aupāsanahoma*. It is also possible that the *gṛhya* version of the agnihotra — which is performed with one fire, without a priest, and from the point after which one is considered to have become an adult, i.e. generally from the time of marriage — is hardly less original than the *śrauta* form — which is performed with more fires, with a priest sometimes replacing rather than assisting the *yajamāna*, and starts with the *ādhāna*, which does not coincide with marriage. The *prāṇāgnihotra* continues one aspect of the agnihotra, viz. the identity of fires and *prāṇāḥ* proclaimed by some brāhmaṇas. Other aspects of the agnihotra may be present in other daily ceremonies.

The *vaiśvadeva* especially seems to be linked up with the agnihotra on account of the speculations about the meal as the remains of the daily agnihotra.[36] This forms the basic agreement and the basic function of the *vaiśvadeva* as well. It is, of course, difficult to ascertain the meaning of a *gṛhya* rite like the *vaiśvadeva* for lack of exegetical evidence provided by the brāhmaṇas. The name *vaiśvadeva* is rather meaningless. It just seems to denote that a plurality of deities is concerned.[37] There may be no specific relation with the separate group of the Viśve Devas, which indeed does occur in the formulas of this sacrifice. The aim of a *vaiśvadeva* (with the Viśve Devas originally in final position?) probably is for completeness and for the avoidance of any harmful exclusion. In the *gṛhya* context the *vaiśvadeva* seems to represent just sacrifice to the gods. It is a fire ritual, which implies that in all versions Agni is the first deity mentioned in the formulas. Other typically sacrificial deities like (Agni) Sviṣṭakṛt and Prajāpati are also found in all texts. The Viśve Devas on the one hand cannot be missing in a group as the *vaiśvadeva* series; on the other hand it may be borne in mind that the Viśve Devas (or in general all the deities) have a special relation with the meal and hospitality. They are the guests coming at night and leaving in the morning in the context of agnihotra speculations.[38]

This brings us to the problem of a possible relationship with the agnihotra, which also has a *vaiśvadeva* (or even two).[39] However, the agreement is rather superficial. The deities of the agnihotra have a clear function (by doing this or that he honours this or that deity; the milk in this or that stage is sacred to this or that deity), which is missing in the *gṛhya* rite. Moreover there is no correspondence with regard to the names of the deities. E.g. Dhanvantari,[40] occurring in all the versions of the *vaiśvadeva*, is not found in the context of the agnihotra. The *gṛhya* sūtras have a *vaiśvadeva* sacrifice, the brāhmaṇas interpret part of the agnihotra as a *vaiśvadeva*. The *vaiśvadeva* of the agnihotra might have been produced due to influence of the *gṛhya* rite (the reverse seems to be excluded) but for its early occurrence in the brāhmaṇas. Probably the only agreement is the desire to include as many other deities as possible in the Agni-offering.

It may be noted that some texts replace Agni, the first deity of the *vaiśvadeva*, by Sūrya in the morning,[41] or mention the deities of the agnihotra (i.e. Agni and Sūrya, probably alternating; Prajāpati also occurs in all versions) in first position.[42] Some agreement with the daily fire ritual was realized at least by some texts.[43] Strictly speaking the agnihotra (or its counterpart in the *gṛhya*, the *aupāsanahoma*), regarded as the sacrifice before the meal, would seem to make the *vaiśvadeva* superfluous, especially at night when agnihotra or *aupāsanahoma* (or perhaps even both) as well as *vaiśvadeva* precede the *bhojana* within a short time. One cannot help thinking that at least the evening *vaiśvadeva* (to Agni, Soma, Prajāpati, Sviṣṭakṛt a.o.) and the evening *aupāsanahoma* (to Agni and Prajāpati) partly overlap. The morning *vaiśvadeva* (at noon) formed a far better substitute for the agnihotra as a foreoffering for the *bhojana*. The Hinduistic daily rites take place thrice rather than twice a day, as appears from the *saṃdhyās*. Some aspects of the agnihotra recur in the ceremonies of daybreak and sunset, others in the midday *saṃdhyā* at noon, viz. the *vaiśvadeva* and the *prāṇāgnihotra bhojanavidhi*.

The morning ritual with agnihotra aspects is not only found in the *aupāsanahoma*. It has been observed elsewhere that the *saṃdhyā* ceremonies continue the Vedic agnihotra[44]. The *tarpaṇa* is interesting in this connection. In Section 17 a survey has been made of all kinds of *tarpaṇa* passages in the context of the agnihotra. In fact several other passages in which the root *prī* instead of *tṛp* was used might be drawn into the comparison. The *vaiśvadeva* in which all kinds of actions are explained as gratifications of all kinds of powers better compares to the *tarpaṇa* than to the *vaiśvadeva* sacrifice (at least as far as its *devayajña* offering in the fire is concerned). The principle is the same: inclusion of everyone and everything in the worship. Especially the concept of completeness is important. It is not only the fear of omitting someone or the concept of *avayajana* ("abschicken") which plays a role. In some brāhmaṇa passages on the *tarpaṇa* in the agnihotra ultimately (by way of identifications) the whole cosmos becomes satiated.[45] The *tarpaṇa* at daybreak (which does not refer to the *pitṛs* only) and the *baliharaṇa* after the *vaiśvadeva devayajña* (a *baliharaṇa* for *bhūtas* and *pitṛs*, but also for some gods) have the same function as the *vaiśvadeva tarpaṇa* and in general the gratification of all kinds of powers at the end of the agnihotra.

The scenario of the daily duties of the ancient, orthodox Hindu, in which the Vedic ceremonies are retained and no non-*śrauta* (i.e. *gṛhya* or later Hinduistic) rituals are excluded or shortened, shows several duplications of actions and aims. The duplication of actions (i.c. offering in the fire three times twice a day: *agnihotra*, *aupāsanahoma*, *vaiśvadeva*) is obvious. The duplication of aims is less evident. The collection of interpretations of the agnihotra presented in this publication has some parallels in the ritual of the *āhnikāni*. Apart from the correspondences noticed above one may draw attention to the following (sometimes rather incidental) agreements.

The daily *brahmayajña* being regarded as a regular sacrifice (it is one of the *mahāyajñas*) requires a *dakṣiṇā*. ĀśvGS. 3, 4, 5 states that what is given after the *brahmayajña* forms the *dakṣiṇā*. See also TĀ. 2, 13. Cf. the situation of the agnihotra as described in Section 12 (TB. 2, 1, 5, 3).

The *mahāyajñas* seem to produce an expiation for "injury or death to sentient beings".[46] Cf. the story of Bhṛgu, Section 13.7.

The *saṃdhyā* ritual also removes sin or evil (*aghamarṣaṇa*) in connection with the worship of the sun. This reminds us of an interpretation of the agnihotra (Section 13.3). Indeed there are three *saṃdhyās* and two agnihotras, but the midday *saṃdhyā* gives the impression of being secondary in this connection.[47] Manu 2, 102 states that the morning *saṃdhyā* removes the sin of the night and the evening *saṃdhyā* the sin of the day, which corresponds remarkably to the agnihotra interpretations.

The same alternation of sun and fire which plays a role in the agnihotra is found in the *saṃdhyās*. According to VaiSmS. 1, 3 one sips water with the mantra "May Sun and Wrath guard me" (TĀ. 10, 25) in the morning, with "May Fire and Wrath guard me" (TĀ. 10, 24) in the evening. Note that the sūtra starts with the morning ritual in its description of the *āhnikāni*, whereas the order of the mantras in the TĀ. agrees with the agnihotra.

The central part of the *brahmayajña* (see Rangachari, o.c., p. 75) consists of *oṃ bhūr bhuvas suvaḥ, satyaṃ tapaḥ śraddhāyāṃ juhomi*. Cf. the esoteric interpretation of the agnihotra in Section 5 (truth offered in faith). For the combination of *satya, tapas* and *śraddhā* see ŚāṅkhB. 2, 8 (end of Section 12). See also the *deva-pitṛ-yāna* passages of ChU. 5, 10, 1 (*ye ceme 'raṇye śraddhā tapa ity upāsate*) and BĀU. 6, 2, 15 (*ye cāmī araṇye śraddhāṃ satyam upāsate*). The *brahmayajña* should be performed outside the village[48] (i.e. *āraṇye*) and represents a symbolical sacrifice according to ŚB. 11, 5, 6, 3–8. There may be a connection with the symbolism of the agnihotra.

Some mantras of the *āhnikāni* have parallels in the agnihotra. According to Rangachari, o.c., p. 74 f. (see also Kane, o.c., p. 704) the *brahmayajña* starts with *vidyud asi* .. and ends with *vṛṣṭir asi* .. just as the agnihotra (and other rites). The *āghāra* described by

VaiSmS. 1, 12 (a prototype of *gṛhya* sacrifice involving the oblation of melted butter rather than being an *āhnika*) has several correspondences, e.g. the mantras "Burnt away is the Rakṣas ..", "The welfare making ones are you..", etc. The mantra "The rising ones are you.." has lost its original function, since there is no rising milk. "Here did Viṣṇu stride" seems to accompany the removal of the butter from the coals (*udvāsana*), which takes place in three stages in the agnihotra and therefore was connected with Viṣṇu (*vaiṣṇavaṃ pratiṣṭhāpyamānam*; see the *vaiśvadeva* of Section 16). When the butter is put on the fire, the mantra "Sagara are you" is recited. In view of the identification of Varuṇa and ocean one may compare *vāruṇam adhiśritam* (Section 16).

So concluding one may state that the *śrauta* agnihotra, the most performed Vedic sacrifice, has left traces in several (daily) rituals. Its mantras, actions or implications play a role in the *sāyaṃprātarhoma (aupāsanahoma)*, the *prāṇāgnihotra (bhojanavidhi)*, the *vaiśvadeva (devayajña)*, the *saṃdhyā* rites and (probably) in *gṛhya* libation sacrifices in general. The *agnihotra* came to denote the sacred fire in later Sanskrit and (perhaps) in Pali. It is hard to say whether early *āhnikāni* may have existed which might have influenced the esoteric interpretations of the agnihotra in the brāhmaṇas.

NOTES

[1] See ŚB. 2, 3, 1, 21: the agnihotra is a *pākayajña* rather than a (*śrauta*) *haviryajña*, because part of the oblation is not offered, but eaten by the performer. On the correct meaning of *pāka* in this compound see Pierre Rolland, *Un rituel domestique vedique. Le Vārāhagṛhyasūtra* (Aix-en-Provence 1971), p. 20 and 149. On the use of the term see e.g. ĀpGS. 1, 2, 9 and PārGS. 1, 1, 17. GB. 1, 5, 23 already mentions the *sāyaṃprātarhomau* (i.e. the *gṛhya* counterparts of the agnihotra) among the *pākayajñas*.

[2] ŚGS. 1, 3, 17 ("The sprinkling with water is done as indicated (in the śrauta sūtra)"); ŚGS. 1, 3, 9 ("But the time (for offering) is fixed, because an expiation has been prescribed for him who has neglected the time at the agnihotra"); ŚGS. 1, 1, 12 (= ĀśvGS. 1, 9, 4) ("The time for kindling it and for offering in it has been explained by (the rules established for) the agnihotra"); ĀgnGS. 1, 6, 3 ("'Having first offered a smaller amount he offers more as the second libation' thus says the brāhmaṇa (on the agnihotra)"); ĀpGS. 1, 2, 9–11 (referring to the treatment of the agnihotra in the brāhmaṇas).

[3] Several terms are used to denote the single fire used in the *gṛhya* ritual corresponding to the *āhavanīya* among the *śrauta* fires: *aupāsana, aupāsanika, aupasada, aupanāyanika, vaivāhika, āvasathya, śālāgni, gṛhya, smārta*. The origin of this fire is also manifold, as appears from the names.

[4] BhārGS. 3, 18 (= ĀgnGS. 2, 7, 9) ("Now we shall discuss (those expiations) which are regarded as the *gṛhya* expiations. The others should be the sacred (*vaitānika*) ones. 'On account of the deity who is mentioned (in both

rituals) and the results (of both sacrifices) as mentioned in the sacred tradition the same deities as found in the agnihotra play a role in the ritual performed in the *aupāsana* fire, the same obligations as there are for the *āhitāgni* apply here, the same world (in heaven) as for the *āhitāgni* is (reserved) for him who offers in the *aupāsana*' thus says Śāṭyāyani Brāhmaṇa"); HirGS. 1, 26, 3 ("On account of his worship devoted to this (fire the sacrificer) is considered as an Āhitāgni (i.e. as one who has set up the Śrauta fires)", tr. Oldenberg; cf. also ĀgnGS. 2, 7, 2).

[5] Bhāradvāja Pariśeṣa sūtra 188 identifies the *gṛhya* fire with the *agnihotra* fire. Laghvāśvalāyana Smṛti 1, 50 gives prescriptions on the exact time for the fire ritual and remarks that the *āhitāgni* and the *ekāgni* should perform the rite *svasvoktavidhinā;* i.e. there are differences, but they are only relative. ĀpDhS. 1, 4, 14, 1 mentions the agnihotra as one of the daily duties after one has become settled and married. Obviously this does not refer to the *śrauta* agnihotra, since the *agnyādhāna* does not coincide with the marriage, whereas the establishment of the gṛhya fire is often regarded as the kindling of the marriage fire.

[6] See e.g. Oldenberg, *SBE* XXX, p. XXVII and Kane, *Hist. of Dh.* II, 1, p. 678.

[7] Oldenberg, *Religion des Veda*, p. 438 n. 1: "Dass dieser morgendliche und abendliche Ritus schon auf die ṛgvedische Zeit zurückgeht, wird durch Stellen wie Ṛv. IV, 2, 8, VII, 1, 6 wahrscheinlich gemacht". The AV. explicitly mentions the agnihotra several times. The sunrise ritual seems to be old, as may appear from the fact that according to Weber (*Ind. Stud.* IX, p. 292) the proper time for sacrifice was just before sunrise in the Avesta. See also Gonda, *Dual Deities* (Amsterdam 1974), p. 134 referring to evidence for the agnihotra in the ṚV.

[8] Gonda, *Viṣṇuism and Śivaism*, p. 74 remarks that the Hindu *saṃdhyā* rites have replaced the Vedic agnihotra. If *saṃdhyā* denotes the total ritual of sunrise and sunset rather than the specific *saṃdhyāvandana*, this may be correct.

[9] See Hillebrandt, *Ritual-Litteratur*, p. 74: "Nur Āśv. schreibt die Opfer a-c (i.e. the *deva-*, *bhūta-* and *pitṛyajñas*) so in unmittelbarem Zusammenhang mit den *sāyaṃprātarhomau* vor, dass (1, 2, 2) eine deutliche Scheidung zwischen beiden nicht erkennbar ist und sich nur aus den andern Sūtren ergiebt". It may be observed here that *sāyaṃprātar* denotes twice a day in a very general sense. The two daily *bhojanas* are taken *sāyaṃprātar*, but the morning *bhojana* (chronologically coinciding with *prāṇāgnihotra* and *vaiśvadeva*) is not breakfast taken at sunrise. It rather takes place at noon.

[10] ŚB. 11, 5, 6, 1 mentions them after a description of great *sattras* and tries to show that these daily, simple rites are also *mahāyajñas* or *mahāsattras* (see Oldenberg, *SBE* XXX, p. XX). A similar glorification is often to be seen in connection with the daily agnihotra. Compare especially ŚB. 12, 4, 1, 1 calling the agnihotra a *dīrghasattra* after having dealt with *dīrghasattras* in the preceding passage. ŚB. 11, 3, 3, 2 regards the *brahmacārya* as a *dīrghasattra*. This typical brāhmaṇa approach of the simple (*gṛhya*) ritual has been gratefully adopted by the sūtras, expecially by ĀśvGS. 3, 1, which "undertakes, quite in the way of the Brāhmaṇa texts, to explain their meaning" (Oldenberg, o.c., p. XX). The authority of the brāhmaṇa caused its coining of a new term to be accepted universally. The *manuṣyayajña* e.g. is no daily ritual at all. Hospitality indeed is a duty which may be fulfilled daily or even twice a day if the occasion arises. Several days, however, may pass without a *manuṣyayajña*.

[11] See Stenzler's note on ĀśvGS. 1, 2, 1 and Rolland, o.c., p. 179 on VārGS. 17. "Some medieval works like the Smṛtyarthasāra (..) state that the vaiśvadeva really comprises the three daily sacrifices" (Kane, *Hist. of Dh.* II, 2, p. 744). The lack of unity is due to the theoretical character of the *pañca mahāyajñas*. If the *pitṛyajña* is regarded as the *tarpaṇa* with water in the early morning, there is no reason to make the *vaiśvadeva* refer to three *yajñas*. If, however, the complex of ritual actions immediately preceding the *bhojana* is considered to include *deva-*, *bhūta-* and *pitṛyajñas*, the *vaiśvadeva* may be said to cover all the three *yajñas*, being an *āhuti* followed by a *baliharaṇa*.

[12] For the *sāyaṃprātarhoma* see ŚGS. 1, 3, 14–17; ĀśvGS. 1, 9, 1–7; PārGS. 1, 9, 1–4; KhādGS. 1, 5, 7–17; GGS. 1, 3, 1–15; HirGS. 1, 7, 23, 8–9; ĀpGS. 3, 7, 19–22; BhārGS. 1, 18; 3, 3; BGS. 2, 6, 17–21; VaiGS. 3, 6; ĀgnGS. 1, 6, 3; MGS. 2, 3, 1–2; JGS. 1, 23; KauśS. 72, 27–28; 73, 2. For the *vaiśvadeva (devayajña)* see ŚGS. 2, 14, 1–4; ĀśvGS. 1, 2, 1–3; PārGS. 2, 9, 2; KhādGS. 1, 5, 20; GGS. 1, 4, 3–4; HirGS. 1, 2, 7, 21–23; ĀpGS. 3, 7, 26; BhārGS. 3, 12; BGS. 2, 8, 1–9; VaiGS. 3, 7; 6, 17; ĀgnGS. 1, 7, 2; MGS. 2, 12, 1–3; VārGS. 17, 1–4; KāṭhGS. 54, 1; JGS. 1, 23; KauśS. 73, 16. It is remarkable that so many sūtras mention both sacrifices. All of them deal with these daily rites separately. Only JGS. 1, 23 takes them together (but keeps them apart). Some sūtras deal elaborately with the *vaiśvadeva ;* others just mention it (e.g. ĀpGS. "The deities of the Vaiśvadeva are the Viśve Devas"; Is this translation given by Oldenberg correct? — Cf. KāṭhGS. 47, 11 *yajeta ... vaiśvadevīṃ bahudevateṣu*).

[13] In Hinduistic times the *prātarhoma* tends to be delayed due to the extensive *saṃdhyā* ceremonies, but there is warned against too long *saṃdhyās* in order to keep the *prātarhoma* within the prescribed limits of time. VaiSmS. 6, 15 states that the *homa* should take place after *snāna*, *saṃdhyā* and *brahmayajña*, i.e. definitely after sunrise, but *uditahomins* are found even in the brāhmaṇas. Other sūtras prescribe an earlier *homa*, e.g. PārGS. 1, 9, 2 (after sunset and before sunrise). GGS. 1, 1, 27–28 makes a distinction between the kindling (before sunset and sunrise) and the offering (after sunset, after or before sunrise). ĀśvGS. 1, 9, 4 refers to the agnihotra for the right time. If both the *śrauta* and the *gṛhya* agnihotra are performed, the *gṛhya homa* may precede or follow the other (Kane, *Hist. of Dh.* II, 2, p. 1000).

[14] The time of the *vaiśvadeva* is the fifth part of the day (Kane, o.c., p. 744). The *vaiśvadeva* in its widest sense (i.e. including the *baliharaṇa*) is the ritual preceding the meal. Therefore VaiSmS. 3, 7 states: *vaiśvadevakāle prāptam atithiṃ śaktyā tarpayed* "If at the time of the Vaiśvadeva-offering a guest arrives, he should satiate him according to his ability" (tr. Caland). VaiSmS. 6, 17 explicitly states that there should be offered (at the time of the meal) even if one should omit a meal (*gṛhastho yat pakvaṃ bhuñjīta pakvena tena bhokṣyann abhokṣyan vāpi .. vaiśvadevaṃ juhuyāt*). The sūtras (e.g. PārGS. 2, 9, 1 ff.) take the *vaiśvadeva* with the *mahāyajñas* preceding the *bhojana*. The situation with the Śrī Vaiṣṇavas as described by Rangachari, *Sri Vaishnava Brahmans*, p. 92, with a separate *vaiśvadeva* and an immediately following *pañcamahāyajña*, is obviously secondary. The *Somaśambhupaddhati* (ed. Hélène Brunner-Lachaux, Pondichéry 1963), IV, 38 mentions a fire offering to Agni, Soma, Agni-Soma and Agni Sviṣṭakṛt, i.e. some sort of *vaiśvadeva*, which strangely enough is performed with ghee in the early morning. For the regular midday *vaiśvadeva* see IX, 5 (to Agni, Soma, Sūrya, Bṛhaspati, Prajāpati, Sarve Devāḥ, Viśve Devāḥ, Agni Sviṣṭakṛt).

[15] JGS. speaks of the *sāyaṃprātaraśana* (cf. BGS.: *yadaśanīya*). VaiSmS. 6, 17 refers to *yat pakvaṃ bhuñjīta*. The material of VārGS. 17, 3 is *haviṣyaṃ*

siddham ("substance oblatoire cuite", tr. Rolland; see also Dresden's note on MGS. 2, 12, 1 *vaiśvadevasya siddhasya*). Instead of this food one may, however, even offer just a kindling-stick (see TĀ. 2, 10) or water (Kane, *Hist. of Dh.* II, 2, p. 744). The same freedom of substitution is found in connection with the *sāyaṃprātarhoma* and the agnihotra (especially in esoteric expiations).

[16] GGS. 1, 3, 6 mentions oblations "prepared or raw". Curds, milk or rice-gruel of course should not be offered with the hand (GGS. 1, 3, 8). If the sacrificer does not obtain fit oblatory material before the moment of the next offering, he may use fruits, leaves, herbs or even water (GGS. 1, 9, 16–17). VaiSmS. 6, 15 prescribes rice or the substance used for the agnihotra. The difference is offering with the hand or with a ladle.

[17] See e.g. ĀpDhS. 2, 9, 5.

[18] VaiSmS. 6, 17 *aupāsanāgnau laukikāgnau vā;* BGS. 2, 8, 2 *aupāsane pacane vā.* See also Kane, *Hist. of Dh.* II, 2, p. 741 referring to Śātātapa. The *Smṛtyarthasāra*, p. 47 states: *snātako brahmacārī vā pṛthakpākī vaiśvadevaṃ kuryāt strī bālaś ca kārayet.* This implies that the establishment of an own sacred (*gṛhya*) fire was not required for the *vaiśvadeva*, which primarily functions as the presentation of part of the meal. The *aupāsana* has a personal relationship with the one who has set it up, which is confirmed by the daily agnihotra or *aupāsanahoma*. The *vaiśvadeva* sacrifice, which mostly seems to be offered in this *aupāsana* fire, does not have this connection. Offering something of every meal is essential. If somebody takes his meal separately, he has to perform a separate, own *vaiśvadeva*, even if he has not established a sacred (*gṛhya*) fire. On the other hand if somebody has his own fire, but eats together with the rest of the family, he does not perform a separate *vaiśvadeva*. See Kane, *Hist. of Dh.* II, 2, p. 714: "All the members of a joint undivided family are to perform separately saṃdhyā, brahmayajña and agnihotra (if they have consecrated the śrauta and gṛhya fires), but devapūjā and vaiśvadeva will be only one for the whole family".

[19] ĀpGS. 3, 7, 19–21, however, seems to have formulas to Agni (resp. Sūrya) and Agni Sviṣṭakṛt. Cf. ŚB. 2, 3, 1, 23 regarding the second libation to Sviṣṭakṛt.

[20] ĀgnGS. 1, 6, 3 explicitly states this. Other sūtras which make the *aupāsanahoma* an exact counterpart of the agnihotra undoubtedly imply it. According to Rangachari, o.c., p. 81 this second libation should not touch the first. Cf. Section 6.12 (on the *sthāṇu*).

[21] See e.g. ŚGS. 1, 3, 16; GGS. 1, 3, 1 ff.

[22] GGS. 1, 3, 1 ff. has an extensive description of the rite and even mentions the *sruva* to be used if e.g. milk forms the oblation.

[23] See GGS. 1, 1, 27–28 (see also n. 13) and cf. ŚB. 2, 3, 1, 7 ff. See also KauśS. 73, 1 *purodayād astamayāc ca pāvakaṃ prabodhayed gṛhiṇī.*

[24] See e.g. GGS. 1, 1, 23.

[25] It is remarkable that in this respect the *vaiśvadeva* is more essential than the *sāyaṃprātarhoma.*

[26] According to some texts, e.g. Karmapradīpa 1, 6, 13, this only applies to *snātakas* who are engaged. Thus there is not much difference between the *aupanāyanika* and the *vaivāhika* fire.

[27] This may refer to the situation of a joint family in which only one sacred fire is used. On the other hand the use of more fires within the joint family is not excluded. See n. 18 (end). On problems connected with the marriage and consequent *ādhāna* of younger brothers before the eldest has married see Karmapradīpa 1, 6, 1 ff. According to MGS. 2, 1, 1 the (eldest, apparently

still unmarried) son should regard the house-fire (of the father, which he sets up anew) as the marriage-fire (i.e. the usual *aupāsana* fire) when the father has died.

[28] ŚGS. 1, 1, 2–5 deals with all the four possibilities; some texts mention some of them. ĀśvGPariś. 12 (ed. Aithal) even refers to the fire or *araṇis* of the *jātakarma* ceremony (see also ĀśvGPariś. 5). BGS. 2, 6, 17 starts from the *upanayana: yasminn agnau upanayati, tasmin brahmacaryaṃ, tasmin vratacaryaṃ, tasmin samāvartanaṃ, tasmin pāṇigrahaṇaṃ, tasmin gṛhyāni karmāṇi kriyante.*

[29] See Caland, *Bestattungsgebräuche*, p. 113 ff. and MGS. 2, 1, 1 ff.

[30] See e.g. GGS. 1, 1, 15–19.

[31] For the *gṛhya ādhāna* see PārGS. 1, 2, 1–13, which agrees with the *śrauta* rite on several points (see also Oldenberg's introduction, *SBE* XXIX, p. 265 ff.). In spite of PārGS. 1, 2, 4 "All ceremonies are performed as at the cooking of the cātuṣprāśya food" (tr. Oldenberg) — i.e. all the ceremonies were to agree with the *śrauta agnyādhāna* — I seriously doubt whether in all the occasions mentioned for the "establishing" of the fire such extensive ceremonies took place. For a description of the *ādhāna* after the death of the head of the family see e.g. KāṭhGS. 46.

[32] For a *punarādhāna* see e.g. HirGS. 1, 7, 26, 6 ff.

[33] See Section 14, n. 17. The *pūrṇāhuti* is also offered at the end of the *agnicayana* (see e.g. BŚS. 10, 52: 55.6 ff.).

[34] ŚGS. 1, 2, 11 prescribes a full oblation (in the morning) with a verse sacred to Viṣṇu or silently. The silent libation (silent in order to avoid the formulas of the agnihotra or the *aupāsanahoma*, because this offering in the morning cannot be the first agnihotra) has a close parallel in the *śrauta* version. Apparently Viṣṇu takes over the position of Prajāpati in this text. PārGS. 1, 11, 1 states that in the fourth night of the marriage ceremony (i.e. at home) the husband establishes the fire in the morning. He offers (1, 11, 3) "To Prajāpati, svāhā". This offering forms the counterpart of the *pūrṇāhuti* of the official *ādhāna*. Apte, *Social and Religious Life in the Gṛhya Sūtras*, p. 211 is wrong in regarding "the oblations of fried grain etc. prescribed for the wedding" as the substitutes of the *pūrṇāhuti*. BhārGS. 3, 2 and KāṭhGS. 46, 9 deal with a *pūrṇāhuti* at the end of the establishment of the *gṛhya* fire. The formula *sapta te agne samidhaḥ* .. recited on this occasion is also found in the *śrauta ādhāna* and the *agnicayana* (see e.g. TS. 5, 7, 4, 1–2 and 1, 5, 3, 2 f.). VaiSmS. 1, 19 prescribes it for the *pūrṇāhuti* and applies it (6, 16) for a *pūrṇāhuti* concluding the *punarādhāna*. VaiSmS. 6, 14 mentions (in the context of the marriage ritual of the fourth day) a mess of boiled rice destined for Agni or a *vaiśvadeva*. This replaces the *pūrṇāhuti* of the *ādhāna* ritual. It is remarkable that the vaiśvadeva is mentioned. Caland (in a note on his translation) is rather surprised that this should be done according to "some ritualists". However, only the rice mess is generally accepted (see e.g. MGS. 1, 14, 11; sacred to Prajāpati!!). The *vaiśvadeva* is not found in the parallels. The *aupāsana (prātar) homa* is avoided and replaced by the less sacred *vaiśvadeva*.

[35] See also the preceding note. The first offering in the fire always is a morning libation, but it never belongs to the *sāyaṃprātarhomau*. The difficulty of the passage ŚGS. 1, 2, 9–11 (on which see Oldenberg's note in *SBE* XXIX) turns on the problem that the first offering after the *ādhāna* takes place in the morning, that one establishes the fire for a *sāyaṃprātar* ritual and that consequently the first offering should take place in the evening (see also KhādGS. 1, 5, 6). In the marriage fire kindled in the fourth night the first

oblation is offered in the morning. Therefore it should not be an official *aupāsanahoma*. GGS. 1, 1. 22–23 regards the putting of a *samidh* on the guru's fire as a morning oblation. The first real *aupāsanahoma* is an evening oblation. The ritual starts *sāyam* and has a counterpart *prātar*. The putting of a *samidh* on the fire functions as the *pūrṇāhuti* of the *ādhāna* ritual (which is not officially performed by the *snātaka* who takes his fire from the guru).

[36] See Section 13.8, and also 5.2.

[37] See the end of n. 12.

[38] See 18, n. 20. Hārīta, quoted by *Gṛhastharatnākara*, p. 291, states that all gods (*sarvā devatāḥ*) enter one's house in the form of a visiting brahmin. If one does not honour the brahmin, the *prāṇadevatāḥ* leave this bad host. So brahmin = *sarvā devatāḥ* (or: Viśve Devas); Viśve Devas = rays of light = *prāṇāḥ* (cf. ŚB. 2, 3, 3, 7–9; Section 13.4).

[39] See Sections 6.15 and 16.

[40] Dhanvantari (i.a. the divine physician) may have a special connection with food, even if Gray's interpretation of this deity (*JAOS* 42, p. 329) is rather hypothetical (cloud-god; connection with rain and fertility).

[41] See Kane, *Hist. of Dh.* II, 2, p. 742.

[42] See ĀśvGS. 1, 2, 2.

[43] See VārGS. 17 prescribing that the preparations before the sacrifice should be carried out "as for the agnihotra" (*agnihotravat*). VaiSmS. 3, 7 has formulas to the Agnihotra, Vaiśvadevayajña, Brahmayajña, Devayajña, etc.

[44] See n. 8.

[45] See Section 17, especially GB. 1, 3, 14. See also Rangachari, o.c., p. 59: "He performs the tarpaṇam believing that devatas, ṛshis and pitṛs have in them the aṃśam of God. That is to say he should believe that the Spirit of God is in all these". This refers especially to *tarpaṇas* as found in GB. 1, 3, 14. For the typical function of the *tarpaṇa* as the conclusion of the sacrifice (in the agnihotra context: the *vaiśvaḍeva* passages in which the root *prī* is often used instead of *tṛp*) see also VaiSmS. 1, 20 (where *tṛp* does not occur, but a parallel to the agnihotra *vaiśvadeva* is found).

[46] Kane, *Hist. of Dh.* II, 1, p. 698 (see also 699).

[47] In general the midday *saṃdhyā* seems to be secondary as appears from the fact that VaiSmS. 9, 13 (i.e. in the dharma sūtra) has an appendix on 1, 3 (in the gṛhya sūtra) dealing with the rite at midday.

[48] See Kane, o.c., p. 701.

BIBLIOGRAPHY

Agn. and *Prāṇāgn.*, see Bodewitz

BODEWITZ, H. W., *Jaiminīya Brāhmaṇa I, 1–65. Translation and Commentary. With a Study: Agnihotra and Prāṇāgnihotra. OR-T* XVII. 1973.

BUITENEN, J. A. B. VAN, *The Pravargya. An Ancient Indian Iconic Ritual Described and Annotated.* Poona 1968.

CALAND, W., *Das Jaiminīya-Brāhmaṇa in Auswahl.* Amsterdam 1919.

——, *Die altindischen Todten- und Bestattungsgebräuche.* Amsterdam 1896.

DELBRÜCK, B., *Altindische Syntax.* Halle 1888.

DUMONT, P.-E., *L'Agnihotra. Description de l'agnihotra dans le rituel védique d'après les Śrautasūtras.* Baltimore 1939.

GONDA, J., *The Savayajñas (Kauśikasūtra 60–68. Translation, Introduction, Commentary).* Amsterdam 1965.

——, *The dual deities in the religion of the Veda.* Amsterdam 1974.

Gṛhastharatnākara. A Treatise on Smṛti by Caṇḍeśvara Ṭhakkura. Bibl. Ind. 249. 1928.

HEESTERMAN, J. C., *The Ancient Indian Royal Consecration.* The Hague 1957.

HILLEBRANDT, A., *Ritual-Literatur.* Strassburg 1897.

HOENS, D. J., *Śānti. A Contribution to Ancient Indian Religious Terminology.* The Hague 1951.

HORSCH, P., *Die Vedische Gāthā- und Śloka-Literatur.* Bern 1966.

JB. I, 1–65, see Bodewitz.

KANE, P. V., *History of Dharmaśāstra* II. Poona 1941.

KEITH, A. B., *Rigveda Brahmanas: The Aitareya and Kauṣītaki brāhmaṇas of the Rigveda translated from the original Sanskrit. HOS* 25. 1920.

LÉVI, S., *La doctrine du sacrifice dans les Brāhmaṇas.* Paris 1898.

Mélanges d'Indianisme à la mémoire de Louis Renou. Paris 1968.

MINARD, A., *Trois Énigmes sur les Cent Chemins. Recherches sur le Śatapatha-Brāhmaṇa. I–II.* Paris 1949–1956.

OERTEL, H., *The Syntax of Cases in the Narrative and Descriptive Prose of the Brāhmaṇas.* Heidelberg 1926.

OLDENBERG, H., *Die Religion des Veda.* Berlin 1923[3].

RAU, W., *Staat und Gesellschaft im alten Indien nach den Brāhmaṇa-Texten dargestellt.* Wiesbaden 1957.

RENOU, L., *Vocabulaire du Rituel Védique.* Paris 1954.

——, *Les écoles Védiques et la formation du Veda.* Paris 1947.

RANGACHARI, DIWAN BAHADUR K., "The Śrī Vaishnava Brahmans", *Bull. Madras Govt. Mus.*, N.S., General Section II, 2. 1931.

Smṛticandrikā by Devaṇṇabhaṭṭa. II Āhnikakāṇḍa. Mysore 1914.

Smṛtyarthasāra. Ānandāśramasaṃskṛtagranthāvali 70. 1912.

SPEYER, J. S., *Vedische und Sanskrit-Syntax.* Strassburg 1896.

Śrautakośa. Ed. C. G. Kashikar, R. N. Dandekar a.o. I: *Sanskrit Section; English Section* 1–2. Poona 1958–63.

WACKERNAGEL, J. (A. Debrunner; L. Renou), *Altindische Grammatik* I–III. Göttingen 1896–1957.

GENERAL INDEX

On account of the systematic arrangement of the translated passages and because of the extensiveness of the table of contents an index of all kinds of terms denoting aspects of the agnihotra is superfluous. In fact this should be a general index. On the other hand several Sanskrit words have been included, mostly technical, ritualistic terms from the appendix.

INDEX OF SANSKRIT TERMS

INDEX OF SANSKRIT TEXT-PLACES